Nationalism
and
Gender

JAPANESE SOCIETY SERIES

General Editor: Yoshio Sugimoto

Lives of Young Koreans in Japan
Yasunori Fukuoka

Globalization and Social Change in Contemporary Japan
J.S. Eades Tom Gill Harumi Befu

Coming Out in Japan: The Story of Satoru and Ryuta
Satoru Ito and Ryuta Yanase

Japan and Its Others:
Globalization, Difference and the Critique of Modernity
John Clammer

Hegemony of Homogeneity:
An Anthropological Analysis of *Nihonjinron*
Harumi Befu

Foreign Migrants in Contemporary Japan
Hiroshi Komai

A Social History of Science and Technology in
Contempory Japan, Volume 1
Shigeru Nakayama

Farewell to Nippon: Japanese Lifestyle Migrants in Australia
Machiko Sato

The Peripheral Centre:
Essays on Japanese History and Civilization
Johann P. Arnason

A Genealogy of 'Japanese' Self-images
Eiji Oguma

Class Structure in Contemporary Japan
Kenji Hashimoto

An Ecological View of History
Tadao Umesao

Nationalism and Gender
Chizuko Ueno

Native Anthropology
Takami Kuwayama

Nationalism
and
Gender

Chizuko Ueno

Translated by
Beverley Yamamoto

Trans Pacific Press
Melbourne

This English edition first published in 2004 by
Trans Pacific Press, PO Box 120, Rosanna, Melbourne, Victoria 3084, Australia
Telephone: +61 3 9459 3021 Fax: +61 3 9457 5923
Email: info@transpacificpress.com
Web: http://www.transpacificpress.com

Copyright © Trans Pacific Press 2004

Designed and set by digital environs Melbourne.
enquiries@digitalenvirons.com

Distributors

Australia
Bushbooks
PO Box 1958, Gosford, NSW 2250
Telephone: (02) 4323-3274
Fax: (02) 4323-3223
Email: bushbook@ozemail.com.au

USA and Canada
International Specialized Book
Services (ISBS)
920 NE 58th Avenue, Suite 300
Portland, Oregon 97213-3786
USA
Telephone: (800) 944-6190
Fax: (503) 280-8832
Email: orders@isbs.com
Web: http://www.isbs.com

Japan
Kyoto University Press
Kyodai Kaikan
15-9 Yoshida Kawara-cho
Sakyo-ku, Kyoto 606-8305
Telephone: (075) 761-6182
Fax: (075) 761-6190
Email: sales@kyoto-up.gr.jp
Web: http://www.kyoto-up.gr.jp

UK and Europe
Asian Studies Book Services
3554 TT Utrecht
The Netherlands
Telephone: +31 (30) 289 1240
Fax: +31 (30) 289 1249
Email: info@asianstudiesbooks.com
Web: http://www.asianstudiesbooks.com

ISBN 1-8768-4353-5 (Hardback)
ISBN 1-8768-4359-4 (Paperback)

National Library of Australia Cataloging in Publication Data

Ueno, Chizuko, 1948–.

    Nationalism and gender.
    ISBN 1 876843 53 5 (pbk.).
    ISBN 1 876843 59 4.

    1. Comfort women – Asia. 2. World War, 1939–1945 –
    Atrocities. 3. Service, Compulsory non-military – Asia. 4.
    Soldiers – Japan – Sexual behavior. 5. Japan – History –
    1926–1945. I. Title.

940.54/05/095

Contents

Translator's Introduction

Even from the overly close perspective of the early 21st century, it is clear that the final decade of the 20th century, a century frequently described as the bloodiest in history, was a period of heady political change that brought with it massive political, economic and ideological shifts and re-alliances. The reunification of Germany in 1989 and the collapse of the Soviet Union, which followed almost immediately after, heralded the beginning of the post-Cold War era. The symbolic ending of the Cold War era was also marked by the uncontested handover of Hong Kong to China and the extension of NATO membership to former Warsaw Pact nations (Hein and Selden, 2000:14). Just as the end of the Second World War brought in its wake new geo-political alliances that totally re-shaped the post-war international map, so too the collapse of communism and a world that had been organised around two ideologically opposed superpowers opened the way for new political, economic and security alliances to be forged across old Cold War lines. It also created a world order gravitating around a single superpower, the United States.

Post-Cold War Politics and Historical Memory

The 1990s was, then, a period of adjustment to a new geo-political reality and also a waking up to the possibilities of this new post-Cold War era. It created the right conditions for the rise of democracy movements in much of Eastern Europe, and also in Taiwan and South Korea. These democracy movements in turn spurred feminist activism tied in with the international women's movement, particularly in Taiwan and South Korea. As we will see, the rise of a strong women's movement in South Korea and a lesser extent Taiwan, was to be a significant factor in events that would rip open an emotional and ideological hole in the fabric of Japanese society and expose areas that those on the political right, at least, had thought had been successfully covered over and lost to the deeper recesses of history.

Yet, unless one is a meticulous housekeeper, any moving of furniture immediately exposes to view dirt and forgotten spots and blemishes that had been covered over when these items had been in their former location. So too, this shifting of former Cold War alliances laid bare unresolved conflicts that had been covered over by the power structures that had been erected in the immediate post-World War II era. Of interest here, is the way in which unresolved issues of history surfaced with force, creating tensions both within and between nations in large areas of Eastern Europe and Asia. In the words of Hein and Selden:

> Historical memory of World War II suddenly gained new potency. Suppressed but not forgotten, old conflicts born of colonialism and war took on new urgency. This was particularly pertinent for the former Axis powers, which then had to bring to all future international negotiations not only the long neglected baggage they had accumulated during World War II but also that of the Cold War. As Germany and Japan moved from decades of political subordination to the United States (or in the case of East Germany, to the Soviet Union), they also lost the protection they had enjoyed from accepting full responsibility for their wartime acts. Grievances once swept under the rug by expensive American brooms in the name of anti-communist unity, (or by less expensive brooms in the name of Communist unity) were exposed to public view once again (Hein and Selden, 2000:15).

For Japan, the 1990s witnessed the bitterest battle yet, both within its borders and across borders with neighbouring Asian countries, over the issues of war responsibility and the politics of national narratives of history. These two issues spurned more academic and popular writing on the subject in Japan during this period than at any other time since the end of World War II, or what more accurately should be referred to as the Asia-Pacific war[1]. In *Nationalism and Gender*, Ueno Chizuko steps right into the middle of this discursive battle over how the Asia-Pacific war, a discredited war, should be remembered and adjudicated. In so doing, she not only explores the issues of war memory and war responsibility, but also questions the nature of the historical narrative itself and its guardianship largely by men of privilege and power both in the academy and government.

The Comfort Women Issue and the Politics of Memory

The most highly contested and bitterly fought over issue within this debate over war responsibility and memory has been that of the euphemistically named military comfort women (*jūgun ianfu*). These women, more accurately re-named military sexual slaves by survivors, their support groups and United Nations special rapporteurs Radhika Coomaraswamy (1996) and Gay J. McDougall (1998), were systematically recruited, generally by force, deception or under conditions of debt slavery, during the period 1937 to 1945 and forced under slave-like conditions to serve the sexual 'needs' of the Japanese military during the Asia Pacific war (see Yoshimi, 2000, 29; Coomaraswamy, 1996). Conditions in fact were brutal, degrading and unhealthy with women often forced to serve several tens of soldiers every day. Many did not survive their ordeal, while many others were silenced for close to five decades by patriarchal norms that attempt to shame the victims rather than the perpetrators of sexual abuse and rape. The terrible physical and psychological injuries they sustained from this period – including sexual transmitted infections, secondary infertility, pelvic inflammatory infection, Post-Traumatic Stress Disorder – went undiagnosed, untreated and unnoticed as a direct result of the silence that was imposed upon the survivors. It is estimated that during the period 1937 to 1945 between 50,000 and 200,000 women were forced into military sexual slavery. Among the victims, Korean women were the most numerous, followed by women from China, Southeast Asia and Japan (Yoshimi, 2000:30).

The long and damaging silence of the former comfort women was finally and decisively broken in December 1991 when Kim Hak-sun and two other Korean survivors, who came forward under aliases, filed a suit at the Tokyo District Court seeking an apology and compensation from the Japanese government. It was this bold step by three survivors that unleashed an extremely bitter debate around the issue of war memory and responsibility, one that has yet to find a resolution even today. Yet the fact of the comfort women was not itself unknown. As historian Yoshimi Yoshiaki,[2] another central player in the dispute points out, the comfort women issue had been raised on a number of occasions prior to the 1991 lawsuit. The issue of Korean comfort women was raised in a novel written by Tamura Taijirō entitled *Shunpuden* (A prostitute's story), published in 1947 and later made into a movie. In 1973, Senda Kakō published a series of two books under the title *Jūgun ianfu* (Military comfort women) where he investigated the actual conditions of the comfort women (Yoshimi, 1995:33). There also exist numerous diaries and personal letters of ex-soldiers who had written in a completely unashamed and largely untroubled manner about their relationships with comfort women.

Despite an awareness of the existence of comfort women, 'social concern about its gravity was never widespread' (Yoshimi, 1995:33). Indeed, although the Allied Forces were fully aware of the comfort women system at the end of the war, they had even repatriated some of the survivors, those responsible for its design and execution were not brought to trial at the International Military Tribunal for the Far East (Tokyo Trials). The exception here, which is of itself extremely telling, is the Batavia Trial[3] in which Dutch comfort women who had not formerly been prostitutes were offered some kind of justice. Thirteen officers were tried and 11 sentenced for their crimes, but that was the full extent of the justice that was handed down. The fact that Asian comfort women and Dutch women who had formerly worked as prostitutes were never considered as legitimate targets for even this kind of limited justice by the Allied Forces makes clear the interaction of racism and sexism (with its attendant double sexual standard) in the treatment of survivors. As John Dower makes clear, the trials were 'fundamentally a white man's tribunal' (Dower, 1999:469), with little awareness of its own racist and sexist assumptions. It would take another 45 years before the oppressive double lenses of patriarchy and nationalism would be shattered, allowing for the dissemination of a different view of the comfort women system and its survivors; one seen through the lenses of feminism and a more gender-sensitive human rights perspective.

In *Nationalism and Gender,* Ueno Chizuko applies the lenses of feminist theory and social constructionism to consider not only the comfort women issue per se, but also the various interpretations that have been applied to it. But before moving on to a more substantive introduction to its content, I would like to weave another thread into the historical tapestry that provides the backdrop to the comfort women issue emerging as a bitterly contested issue in the 1990s. By this 'other thread' I am referring to the incredible achievements of the international women's movement in the 1990s particularly in raising to the top of the human right's agenda the issue of violence against women.

Violence Against Women

As is discussed in *Nationalism and Gender*, the early 1990s witnessed a paradigm shift that created the right conditions for the comfort women system to be seen as a violation of the survivors' human rights and, hand-in-hand with this, a Crime against Humanity.[4] This paradigm shift saw the shame associated with rape and sexual abuse move from the shoulders of the victims to the shoulders of the perpetrators. This in turn created the right conditions for the survivors to come forward. To understand this shift we need to look back at the steady progress made by feminist activists in the last two decades of 20th century in redefining human rights in a way that included rather than excluded women.

The United Nations Decade for Women (1975–1985) represented both the culmination of feminist activists' calls for the full integration of women in society and for gender equality, and the beginning of a new and more prominent place for the international women's rights movement in the world. As Arvonne Fraser notes: 'During the decade there was an explosive growth in the number, style and content of women's organizations' (Fraser, 2001). By the Third World Conference on Women held in Nairobi, Kenya in 1985, the new international women's movement was incredibly diverse, but there was also growing 'solidarity among women in recognizing discrimination even across lines of intense political disparities' (Fraser, 2001:53). Of interest to us here is the emergence of violence against women as an issue at a Non-Government Organisation (NGO) Forum at the conference. The achievement of daily discussions, which drew links between 'violence in the home, violence in society, and violence between nations', was two long paragraphs written into the Forward Looking Strategies that came out of the conference (Fraser, 2001:55). Looking back on this from the early 21st century, where the issue of violence against women is now extremely prominent, it is perhaps difficult to appreciate just how radical it was for an issue that previously fell outside the parameters of human rights theory and activism to be placed on the agenda. Yet this was only the beginning, as women were now networking across national borders on the issue of violence against women and drawing international attention. Once the ball was rolling, it was hard to stop the momentum with discussion and activism focusing on violence against women in all areas of society, leading ultimately to the redefining of what was meant by the word *human* in human rights. As Fraser notes:

> It was the violence against women issue, especially domestic violence, that finally drew international attention to the idea that women's rights are human rights. The issue transcended race, class, and cultures and united women worldwide in a common cause. It dramatically illustrated women's subordinate position as no other issue had (Fraser, 2001:56).

At the 1993 World Conference on Human Rights held in Vienna, women's rights as human rights emerged dramatically as the number one issue on the agenda. The tide had turned, and government and NGO delegates were at last paying lip service at least to the idea that violence against women was an important human rights issue. The Vienna Declaration and the Programme of Action specifically declared that 'the human rights of women and the girl-child are inalienable and indivisible part of human rights' (cited Fraser, 2001:57), radically expanding the concept of human rights itself. It also became clear that it was going to be impossible to deal with the issue of violence against women without a merging of the 'public' and 'private' spheres in human rights theory and practice.

The United Nations Fourth World Conference on Women held in Beijing in 1995 (generally referred to as the Beijing Conference) further strengthened the gains that had been made at the Vienna Convention. From then on the issue seemed to take on a life of its own as women networked and campaigned for safety and security in their lives and that of their communities. Links began to be made between different forms of violence. In the words of Sally Engle Merry, violence against women:

> grew from a focus on rape and battering in intimate relationships to rape and gender violence enacted by states in warfare, torture, and imprisonment as well as during interethnic violence. Trafficking of sex workers, the AIDS pandemic, and particular social practices that have an impact on women such as female genital cutting have been defined as instances of violence against women (Merry, 2001:83).

By drawing links between different forms of violence it became clear that women's vulnerability to violence stemmed in a large part from their subordinate position in society and from social and cultural definitions of masculinity and femininity. This in turn located many cultural practices as standing in complete opposition the right of women to protection from violence (Merry, 2001:91). Few would expect such a radical paradigm shift to be taken lightly by the, often male, gatekeepers of such cultures, and a predictable backlash ensued.

Ironically, it was at the Beijing Women's Conference that feminist activists from Korea and Japan suddenly found themselves unable to transcend national boarders on one issue of violence against women; namely the comfort women issue. The Korean women's movement, theorizing from the perspective of women who had been subjected to colonisation under Japanese rule, understood the comfort-women issue primarily as a national rather than a gender one. There was undisguised, raw anger from Korean delegates when one Japanese feminist, namely Ueno Chizuko, suggested to participants at an NGO forum on the comfort women that it was going to be important for feminism to transcend nationalism if progress on the issue was to be made. Just as Black feminist in the United States have told their white sisters in no uncertain in terms that they do not have the luxury of ignoring the issue of race in their lives, so too Korean women berated Ueno for not recognising that for women in Asia who had been the wrong end of colonialism and imperialism, nationalism was not something that could be left out of the debate.

Yet, regardless of what was said at the NGO forum, there was networking and co-operation across traditional lines of national enmity on the comfort women issue. Even before the Beijing Conference, Korean and Japanese women's groups were working together in the early stages of organising the Women's International War Crimes Tribunal 2000 on Japan's Military Sexual Slavery, which took place in Tokyo from December 8th to 12th 2000. This was a People's Tribunal that was set up to judge the responsibility of the late Emperor Hirohito and high-ranking officials within the wartime Japanese government for military sexual slavery and rape as Crimes against Humanity. The Tribunal was a very successful and high profile attempt to make up for the failure of the Occupation Forces to prosecute those responsible for the comfort women system during the Tokyo Trials, and the continuing inaction of the Japanese state in this area over the past 55 years. Four inter-nationally renowned judges presided over the proceedings and 75 survivors from nine different countries and regions testified. At the heart of the organisation process was the Violence Against Women and War Network (VAWW-Net Japan) working closely with the Korean Council for Women Drafted for Military Sexual Slavery by Japan[5] (hereafter, Korean Council). Clearly in this instance support groups were able to transcend national borders and the confines of colonial history. Nevertheless, there can be no denying that nationalist rather than gender issues have dogged much of the debate on the comfort women issue on both sides.

The Korean Women's Movement and the Comfort Women Issue

The Korean Council has served as a central hub for women's activism in Korea around the comfort women issue from the beginning. In May 1990, Korean Women's Groups issued a joint statement timed to coincide with then Prime Minister Roh Te-Woo's visit to Japan demanding an apology and compensation from the Japanese government over the *Teishintai* (volunteer corps) issue. It should be noted that, although the term *Teishintai* (*Chŏngshindae* in Korean) refers to Korean men and women who were forcibly mobilised by the Japanese wartime regime, as this forced labour also included many women serving at military comfort stations, in the minds of most Koreans it has become a euphemism for the comfort women (Kovener in Yŏnghi, 1998).

It was also the Korean Council that painstakingly recorded the testimony of former comfort women and paved the way for Kim Hak-sun and two other Korean survivors to come forward and demand an apology and compensation. The backdrop to the formation of the Korean Council as a support group of former comfort women are the successes of the international women's movement and its impact on the fledgling Korean women's movement.

As noted above, by the mid-1980s the voice of the international women's movement was not only being heard, but also being taken seriously. The 1980s and 1990s saw an incredible shift in human rights politics and the way in which violence against women was understood. The energy and vision of the international women's movement spurred on the Korean women's movement. The movement, which has close ties with the social reform movement, expanded greatly after democratisation in 1987. As Yamashita Yeong-ae has pointed out, the growing strength of the women's movement and women's studies led directly to the comfort women issue surfacing in Korea and then later in Japan.

Since the end of the 1980s, the expansion of the women's movement under the civilian regime has been striking. Women's studies has progressed both in quality and quantity, and slowly but surely women's issues and the position of the women's movement has begun to change. After the establishment of the Korean Sexual Violence Relief Centre in January 1991, studies of rape, sexual harassment, prostitution, and other issues of sexual violence emerged and Korean scholars began to pay attention to gender issues. One link in the chain of events occurred when students in the faculty of women's studies asked women's organizations to bring public attention the comfort women issue (Yamashita, 1998:60).

Despite the gender perspective among students of women's studies, the comfort women issue generally was understood as a national one in the 1990s. It was another unresolved issue in the past relationship between Japan and Korean; colonizer and colonised. This goes a long way to explaining why a nationalist card was played when women's activists finally took the comfort women issue to the public and the government, despite an awareness that the long silence surrounding the comfort women issue was in large part due to the fact that it was 'a women's issue in a male-centred society' (Yamashita, 1998:60). The dominant nationalist perspective that the comfort women system was a crime committed against the Korean nation rather than the individual survivors specifically served to cloud the issue when it did emerge in the public domain. Yamashita Yeong-ae has daringly pointed out the anti-feminist consequences of constructing the comfort women issue in terms of an unresolved dispute between colonizer and colonised – Japan and Korea – rather than in terms of a gender analysis which recognises that women from other nations, including Japan, were also subjected to confinement and sexual abuse as a result of the comfort woman system (Yamashita, 1998).

The gender insensitive approach of the Korean women's movement in building its case for the former comfort women, particularly in the early days, is something that Ueno Chizuko underscores in *Nationalism and Gender*, partly by drawing on the work of Yamashita. In particular she notes the inadvertent utilization of discrimination against prostitutes and a sexual double standard by Korean women's activists in attempt to gain widespread sympathy for their cause.

The Response in Japan to the Comfort Women Issue

The comfort women issue barely generated any interest in Japan until Kim Hak-sun and the two Korean survivors came forward and gave testimony in 1991. The initial demand by Korean women's groups for apology and compensation in May 1990 hardly created a stir at the time. The government's initial response was to ignore the issue, but finally it offered the following statement at a House of Councillors Budget Committee meeting on 6 June 1990:

> In regard to comfort women...it appears that the persons thus treated were led around by civilian operators following the military forces. We consider it impossible for us to investigate and make a definitive statement as regards to the actual conditions pertaining to this practice (*Dai 118 kai kokkai sangiin yosan iinkai kaigiroku*, cited and translated in Yoshimi, 1995:34).

The government could be quite confident in its position, as it is certainly no state secret that the military government systematically destroyed official documentation in the closing days of the Asia–Pacific War. This act of a defeated government appears to have included the routine destruction of nearly all data concerned with the comfort stations and comfort women (Yoshimi, 1995:34). Moreover, the government could also be confident that there would be few who would question that official documentation was necessary to *prove* what went on, despite living proof in the form of the testimony of former comfort women, an army doctor and the few soldiers who have been willing to come forward. Indeed, much of the debate since Kim Hak-sun and the two other former comfort women filed suit in 1991 has been over standards of proof, with few challenging the privileging of official documentary sources. While those on the side of the survivors and their supporters have fought for oral testimony to be accepted as proof, even here there has been a tendency to bow to the higher *authority* of written documentation. Or at least, this is the argument of Ueno Chizuko in *Nationalism and Gender*.

This debate over standards of proof has focused overwhelmingly on the method of recruitment. Those on the right, including members of the government, argued that there was no proof (read official documentation) that the military, and as a result the wartime government, were directly involved in recruiting or running the comfort stations. When Yoshimi Yoshiaki dug up documents from the Japanese Self-Defence Agency offering evidence 'attesting to the fact that' the military had 'planned, constructed and operated comfort stations' (O'Brien in Yoshimi, 1995:7), the Japanese government was forced to admit involvement and issue an apology to the survivors. Despite this, Yoshimi's evidence was not taken as conclusive by everybody involved, with those on the right bitterly opposed to any suggestion of liability or criminality on the part of the government. Some have even taken to threats of violence and/or actual violence in attempts to stop the public broadcast of anything that may present the comfort women as anything other than 'lowly' prostitutes (see Takahashi, 2001). They have used similar tactics to try and stop the publication of textbooks containing a brief mention of the comfort women (McCormack, 2000:64–65).

Of particular note are the influential group calling themselves the Liberal View of History Group (Jiyūshugi shikan kenkyūkai), a name that would appear to be a deliberate bid to mislead as their agenda is far from liberal (*jiyūshugi*) in the conventional usage of the word. The Liberal History Group, in order to serve their own nationalist agenda, have attempted to focus the debate myopically on the issue of recruitment. There argument is that the comfort women were prostitutes who had gone to the comfort stations of their own free will. They have challenged the former comfort women and their supporters, including historians like Yoshimi, to offer proof in the form of official documentation that there was *systematic* forced recruitment of the comfort women, knowing full well that such proof would be almost impossible to come by. According to Ueno, rather than challenge the terms of the debate, those on the side of the comfort women have attempted to fight by the rules of the Liberal View of History Group and, as a result, orthodox positivist history. When the method of recruitment should have been secondary to the slave-like conditions under which the women were forced to serve the sexual 'needs' of the Japanese military (after all, even if a marriage is entered into voluntarily it does not nullify the crimes of marital rape, confinement and abuse), it was this that became the focus of attention. Could systematic forced recruitment be proved or not? Ultimately, even Yoshimi

Yoshiaki, cornered in a live television debate, had to admit that such 'proof' was not available[6] (Ueno, 1999:155). The background to this focus on methods of recruitment conceals what Ueno refers to as 'discrimination against prostitutes'. The hidden 'logic' is as follows: If recruitment was forced then the women could justifiably be referred to as sexual slaves and indeed a Crime against Humanity had occurred. However, if the women went voluntarily with the recruiters they could justifiably be regarded as prostitutes and, as such, given a patriarchal logic that places prostitutes way beyond the category *human,* Crimes against Humanity cannot be said to have occurred.

Nationalism and Gender

Nationalism and Gender can be regarded as the product of Ueno's scholarly frustration with a debate that has tended to confine itself within the limited parameters of positivist history and a patriarchal double standard that places women who have sex for money beyond the pale when it comes to protection and justice within the criminal law and human rights systems. Ueno has a reputation for the sharpness of her theorizing and the fearless way that she takes on those who she feels are reinforcing oppressive thought and power structures. Indeed, such is her notoriety for fearless confrontation that one male-write wrote a 'tortured, self-searching' book entitled *Who's Afraid of Ueno Chizuko?*, which made the best seller lists in the early 1990s (Sand, 1999:121). Another bestseller that used her name was written by TV personality Haruka Yoko and entitled *Tōdai de Ueno Chizuko ni kenka o manabu* (Learning how to argue from Ueno Chizuko at Tokyo University). At a packed lecture that Ueno gave at the Kitakyushu City Women's Centre MOVE[7], where additional rooms with satellite links had to be set up to take the crowds that overflowed from the 500-seater lecture theatre, Ueno joked that she was sure the high turn out was due to Haruka Yoko's bestseller and not her own books, which she modestly said do not sell nearly as well. However, Ueno's books do sell and her name is without a doubt an incredible crowd puller.

In addition to public notoriety, Ueno is also a prolific and highly respected writer within the Japanese academic community and has gained a solid reputation as a feminist scholar internationally. Ueno has held the post of Professor in the Department of Sociology at Tokyo University since 1994, and was promoted to the post of Head of Department earlier this year. Sand suggests her appointment as professor at Japan's most prestigious university is the ultimate mark of her acceptance by a male-dominated, conservative Japanese academy (Sand, 1999:120). Nevertheless, I would suggest that it shows less an acceptance and more the overwhelming respect she has generated as a result of her work even among those who do not share her political or theoretical perspective. Despite her elevation to the higher echelons of the academic hierarchy, Ueno continues to play the role of *enfant terrible* in her attempts to challenge and dismantle the male-dominated, conservative aspects of Japanese academia and society.

Ueno's popularity within Japan is attributed to 'a combination of the high quality of her research, her choice of controversial research topics, her ability to write in an accessible prose style, and her frequent use of provocative images' (Buckley, 1997:272). *Nationalism and Gender* is perhaps not one of her most accessible pieces of writing as it assumes an understanding of Japanese history in general and women's history in particular. Yet, there can be little doubt that it is an extremely important piece of work, that it is provocative, interesting and relevant to current issues not only in Japan but to feminist theory generally, and well worth any effort involved in reading it.

The Japanese edition of *Nationalism and Gender* (Nashonarizumu to jendā) was first published in 1998 by Seidosha. Since then it has seen 13 re-prints and sold over 21,500 copies. It was translated into Korean in 1999 and this edition has sold several thousand copies. Both the original Japanese and Korean editions have received good reviews in the media and generally provoked a positive response from popular audiences. However, in Japan *Nationalism and Gender* has also provoked some negative criticism from a few women's activists, which is understandable as they themselves are targets of Ueno's cutting analysis. As touched upon above, Ueno accuses comfort women support groups of reinforcing a sexual double standard that serves to draw a line between *good women* (virgins and mothers) and *bad women* (prostitutes) by insisting on the *purity* of the Korean comfort women at the time they are were abducted. She argues that in a bid to gain widespread support for the cause the support groups have fallen into the trap of creating the *model victim*, where the crime is the violation of a pure woman's honour. As Ueno is aware, one of the many achievements of the international women's movement in the 1990s was to make clear that rape is not an issue of honour, but of gendered sexual violence. Women's activists in turn, and somewhat unfairly, have criticised Ueno for ignoring the issues of racism and nationalism. In a similar vein, Yoshimi Yoshiaki, Suzuki Yūko and other historians dedicated to unearthing the truth of the comfort women system have also reacted angrily to Ueno's depiction of them as 'conscientious historians' who despite their hard work have rather ineptly ended up reinforcing a naive positivist view of history and privileged documentary sources. In the recordings of a symposium on Nationalism and the Comfort Women Problem held at the Centre for Research and Documentation on Japan's War Responsibility in September 1997, Yoshimi accuses Ueno of making 'rudimentary mistakes' in *Nationalism and Gender* and several articles that preceded the book's publication. He even goes as far as to suggest that she has not properly read his work, which is a criticism that can hardly be taken seriously given the meticulous nature of Ueno's analysis (Yoshimi, 2003:124–125). Despite the heated nature of the debate between Ueno and Yoshimi, the fruits of this kind of verbal sparring between two sharp-minded scholars cannot be overlooked. In the words of Suzanne O'Brien, in her translator's introduction to the English edition of Yoshimi's *Comfort Women*:

> The debates between Ueno and Yoshimi raise critical issues regarding survivors' testimonies and their status in discussions of the comfort women issue. The challenge for survivors' supporters is how to appreciate the varying and productive nature of survivor's testimonies without undermining their power and coherence when they are taken up as evidence in the context of legal proceedings. It is through their testimonies and activism that survivors have been able to create new identities for themselves, and each of their testimonies illustrate that even an individual's or a group's memories of the past are plural. When this multiplicity is then brought to bear on the memories of people with a very different understanding of that past, it becomes clearer that all memories are necessarily limited and contextual, and that no one of them alone can suffice as historical truth. The question for discussion then becomes which memories, whose memories are given pride or place in history and accorded the status of truth (O'Brien, in Yoshimi, 1995:15).

It is this understanding of the multiple nature of historical truth and Ueno's 'feminist curiosity', to borrow Cynthis Enloe's wonderful term (Enloe, 2000), concerning whose memories have been given pride of place in history and how and why they have been accorded the status of truth, that represents not only the beginning but also the powerful conclusion of *Nationalism and Gender*.

Structure of *Nationalism and Gender*

The original Japanese version of *Nationalism and Gender* was divided into three sections, the titles of which have been translated as follows; Engendering the Nation; The Military Comfort Women Issue, and The Politics of Memory. In addition to these, the English version has a completely new section, Hiroshima from a Feminist Perspective: Between War Crimes and the Crimes of War. This is a translation of a paper given at a Symposium on Women, Nuclear Weapons and Peace (Josei, kaku, heiwa shinpojiumu) in Hiroshima in 2000. It was felt that this would provide a fitting conclusion to Ueno's theorizing on the issues of war responsibility and war crimes. The English edition has an updated epilogue and a specially written author's introduction. In translating the original Japanese version of *Nationalism and Gender,* I have contemporised the language to bring it up to date, however, no other revisions have been made.

The first section, Engendering the Nation, considers the way in which the Asia Pacific war, has been understood by historians and other social scientists. Ueno identifies three schools of thought – discontinuity, continuity and neo-continuity – and considers the implications of each for understanding both post-war Japanese society and the issue of war responsibility. The discontinuity school posits a sharp break between pre- and post-war Japanese society. The continuity school argues that there has been continuity in what Ueno refers to as the 'modernisation project,' and views the war as a deviation from this path. The neo-continuity school recognises the through line in many aspects of Japanese society pre- and post-war, but regards the war less as a *deviation*, and more as an *innovation* that furthered certain aspects of the process of modernisation, especially in the strengthening of the nation-state.

Having made clear her own position within the neo-continuity school, Ueno moves on to the field of women's history and examines the shift in perspective that occurred in the late 20th century from viewing women as victims to active participants in history who in supporting the wartime regime bear some of the responsibility for the atrocities that were carried out in its name.

This new approach in women's history that recognises both women's agency and, by extension, culpability in the war, Ueno refers as the reflexive school of women's history (*hanseiteki joseishi*). She offers a critique of Suzuki Yūko and others who call for a reflexive women's history, suggesting that in terms of analysis and conclusions it is trapped within the limitations of its own national history. Ueno asks whether it should be only women in Japan and other Axis countries who are obliged to *reflect* on their country-women's support of the wartime regime, pointing out that women in the Allied Alliance countries similarly supported their governments during wartime playing a very similar role on the home front. Ueno throws out the rhetorical question, If the only difference between women in the Allied and Axis countries is that one group supported a *just war* while the other supported an *unjust war*, then on what basis were the latter able to judge that theirs' was a *bad war* if not after the event?

This exploration of women's history incorporates the feminist project of engendering the nation. The states 'gender strategy' for nationalising women through the mobilisation process is examined showing clearly that, regardless of desperate circumstances, a rigid gendered division of labour was maintained throughout the wartime period, with women given the task of protecting the home front, while their men-folk fought the war on the front lines. The inherent dilemma of this approach is examined, along with the apparent willingness of leading feminist figures to go along with this gender strategy.

The second section of *Nationalism and Gender* deals specifically with the comfort women issue. Ueno examines in turn the various paradigms that have been employed in the discursive battle over the comfort women and, as such, traces the history of the comfort women issue itself. We are told that the former comfort women are the victims of a triple crime: first their forced incarceration and sexual abuse at the comfort' stations; second the near 50 years of silence that was imposed upon them by patriarchal society; and finally the defamation of character carried out by those on the right in Japan, particularly members of the Liberal View of History Group, after Kim Hak-sun and others finally came forward. In looking at the resistance both within Japan and Korea to the former comfort women coming forward and speaking out, Ueno underscores the power of patriarchal values to define rape and sexual abuse as the victim's rather than the perpetrator's shame, and to view it as an issue of male honour. In addition, she also points to the complexity of post-colonial politics where former *Teishintai* (volunteer corps), including comfort women, are apt to be viewed as collaborators with, rather than victims of, the imperial military regime.

The third section takes up the issue of the politics of public memory. Many of the issues that Ueno touches are not specifically Japanese, but universal ones. How does a nation remember its past, particularly when that past includes a recently executed discredited war? Ueno starts by taking on her natural adversaries, the so-called historical revisionists who seek to create a more positive Japanese history, particularly with respect to the Asia–Pacific War. Of particular interest here is the Atarashii Rekishi Kyōkasho o Tuskurukai (a literal translation would be the committee to create new history textbooks, however their official English name is The Japanese Institute for Orthodox History Education, hereafter Orthodox History Group). This is a group created by members of the Liberal View of History Group in 1996 to try and influence government policy, particularly in relation to the content of history textbooks. The group have staunchly rejected 'any need for official acknowledgement of Japanese wartime atrocities, let alone apologizing or paying reparations' (Hein and Selden, 2000:26). They have been especially incensed by mention of the comfort women system in school history textbooks and have campaigned vigorously and very publicly, making full use of the media and Internet, to have all mention of comfort women removed from school textbooks. More recently they have increased tensions between Japan and its Asian neighbours by submitting and having accepted their own history school textbook; a textbook that attempts to restore national pride by whitewashing wartime events.

While the historical revisionists are Ueno's obvious adversaries, her criticism of their approach is brief and blunt. She does not regard them as a serious theoretical challenge, and therefore it is to her natural allies, 'conscientious historians' like Yoshimi Yoshiaki and Suzuki Yūko, that she directs her fullest attention. As already mentioned above, her attack on Yoshimi and Suzuki is on the basis of their positivism and the privileging of documentary sources. She argues for the recognition of *multiple histories* as a reflection of the multifaceted and essentially constructed nature of our experiences. As noted by Jordan Sands, 'In her indictment of the methodology of academic historians, Ueno appears to veer dangerously towards ethical relativism' (Sand, 1999:122). Yet as a feminist scholar, her 'solution to the epistemological dilemma' inherent in her arguments is to focus on 'relations of power' (Sand, 1999:122). Ueno places gender theory at the centre of her analysis and, as a result, she is able to avoid the extreme relativist strain of post-modernist thought while drawing on many of its insights (Sand, 1999:122).

The final part of the English edition of *Nationalism and Gender,* Hiroshima from a Feminist Perspective: Between War Crimes and the Crimes of War, is very different in style and tone from what comes before it. Firstly, it is aimed at a non-specialist audience. Secondly, it is in the form of a paper given at a symposium and, therefore, the audience is addressed directly. In the translation I have kept the chatty and informal style of the original. Finally, while the first three parts focus largely on issues and events within Japan, this final section steps quite consciously outside Japan to address international issues from a feminist perspective.

While the style, tone and focus may be different, the final section takes a step further the tentative conclusion that Ueno reached at the end of the original Japanese version of *Nationalism and Gender*; namely that from a feminist perspective there can be no such thing as war crimes as war itself is the crime. Her argument is simple and quite straight forward, in that she argues that in accepting certain acts as war crimes and, therefore, criminalizing them, we are at the same time legitimising other acts of war and therefore de-criminalizing them. As Ueno points out, rules are created such as 'If we are going to have a war, let's do it in a gentlemanly fashion'; 'Let's not use inhumane weapons'; 'It's okay to have a war, but let's go about it in a fair way', yet this diverts our attention from the reality of war, which has as its intention the murder of those on the 'other side' in order to achieve an end; however 'noble' or 'right' that end may appear at the time. While Ueno takes a no-holes-barred, anti-war position, she does not espouse a naïve pacifism. Her analysis uses the tools of gender theory to ask questions that de-construct the issue of violence and to make clear the links between violence carried out under very different circumstances. Ueno asks, 'Under what conditions is violence criminalized and under what conditions is it de-criminalized'? This question leads to an examination of both the shadowy 'public' domain where violence in the name of the state is de-criminalized and the 'private' domain where the same process of de-criminalization can be seen at work with regards to gender-based violence. Having argued that war is the execution of state violence, Ueno moves on to ask whether feminist activists and theorists demanding gender equality are really seeking 'distribution justice' in terms of equal opportunities to execute such violence by entering the military. In turning her attention to the recruitment of women in the U.S. army, Ueno underscores the cleverly disguised fact that the flip side of the noble act of 'dying for one's country' is 'killing for one's country'. Arguing that the taking of life is the 'folly of all follies', Ueno asks whether this is the extent (or limits) of the feminist vision.

As I translated this final section in the build up to the war in Iraq, Ueno's arguments seemed particularly pertinent and urgent. Her position that feminism should condemn all forms of violence, under all circumstances, is not one that will 'rock the boat' in terms of mainstream Japanese society, where peace and democracy has been the 'great mantra of post-war Japan' (Dower, 1999:30). Yet, I suspect that it will meet with strong resistance from mainstream feminism in the U.S. and perhaps some other Western countries where there continues to be strong support for 'just' wars. I can also hear feminist activists involved in protecting the victims of domestic violence, particularly those supporting women incarcerated for striking back at abusive partners, protesting Ueno's argument that feminists should not support violence under any circumstances. Yet, it is hard to see where lines should be drawn if state or private forms of violence are to be supported under certain circumstances. Ueno's careful analysis of the issue of war and war crimes, by taking arguments for violence to their logical conclusion, makes this extremely clear. As the conclusion to Ueno's arguments surrounding the issue of Japanese war responsibility, this final section also redefines the parameters of the debate in a way that has the potential to open that proverbial can of worms. As such, it is striking piece of theorizing that bravely pushes forward the debate on war memory and war responsibility in the international arena as well as that in Japan.

Notes on the Translation

I have tried as much as possible to keep the original style of Ueno's writing, which moves between an almost chatty style, punctuated with hard-hitting rhetorical questions, to a the kind of academic theorizing that is more familiar to the English reader. The way I was taught to translate text at the University of Sheffield was to account for every word in a sentence and then to re-work the whole thing for readability in English. This is the rule I have followed here, meaning that somebody who cared to compare the two should be able to find everything in the original Japanese accounted for in the English translation.

In terms of general 'housekeeping', to borrow David Askew's terminology (see Oguma, 2002), Japanese and Korean names are written in the conventional order for these countries; family name followed by given name. There are, however, two exceptions to this rule: in the case of a Japanese person living outside the country who has chosen to follow the opposite (Western) order or where the Western order is followed in an English-language publication. Macrons have been used to indicate the long 'o' and 'u' vowel sounds in Japanese, except in words or place names that are familiar in English such as Tokyo or Osaka. The names of Japanese organisations have been given in English with a Romanised form of the original Japanese inside brackets. The same basic principle has been followed for the names of laws or government policies. While translations of names inserted by the translator appear inside brackets thus ( ), any additional comments or clarifications by the translator have been inserted inside the following kind of brackets [ ]. As a matter of policy, I have tried to keep additional comments by the translator to an absolute minimum so as not to intrude on the original text. Finally, although Ueno Chizuko used the Japanese equivalent of quotation marks around the a number of terms, including comfort women, throughout the book to indicate their constructed and problematic nature, I have followed the minimalist tradition of Trans Pacific Press and omitted them on all but the first occasion.

Acknowledgements

I would like to thank Ueno Chizuko for first writing *Nationalism and Gender* and then for entrusting me with the important task of translating it into English. I am also grateful to Yoshio Sugimoto, our publisher, for his confidence in my ability to make a good job of the translation. It was a pleasure working with them both on this project, and I greatly appreciate their support and patience during the translation process. I am grateful to Martin Collick for his advice in the early stages of the project. Graham Healey's close reading of the first section and generous feedback greatly improved the translation. Likewise, I am extremely grateful to Joe Banerjee for reading the remaining sections and offering sound advice throughout. I would like to thank Hiroko Takeda for first introducing me to *Nationalism and Gender* back in 1999 and for working with me to devise a post-graduate distance learning module around it for the School of East Asian Studies, University of Sheffield. Likewise, I am extremely grateful for the stimulating input from students who have taken the module over the past three-and-half years. My heartfelt thanks goes to my husband, Yamamoto Yukishi, who supported me by doing more than his fair share of child care and by explaining some of the more difficult grammatical points. Finally, I would like to thank my two children, Shia Anne Yamamoto aged nine and Yujin David Yamamoto aged seven, who showed interest, patience and understanding well beyond their years.

Beverley A. Yamamoto
Fukuoka, April 2003
(University of Sheffield)

Author's Preface to the English Edition

It has been four years since the first publication of *Nationalism and Gender* appeared, and it is a great joy and honor to now have an English translation of the book. *Nationalism and Gender* provides a feminist intervention into the debate sparked by Japanese historical revisionists. The Japanese version of historical revisionism emerged in the post-Cold War era. It was triggered by, and has taken as its target, the military comfort women issue, and is sexist in nature. The military comfort women system has its roots in the Asia–Pacific War, but only emerged as a high profile issue as the result of the coming forward of living witnesses, Kim Hak-sun and two others, in 1991. In the guise of positivist historians, the historical revisionists have attempted to discredit the testimonies of these and other living witnesses, devaluing such testimony as a source of historical evidence. I took this attack to be a serious challenge not only to the women themselves, but also to what women's history has achieved in recent years by using oral histories and life stories.

The Japanese *historikerstreit*[1] or historians' debate has raised a number of questions including: What is history all about? Is there only one history or multiple histories? Is there such a thing as 'truth' in history? Who judges which history is 'true' in the presence of multiple histories? Are oral testimonies less valuable than written documents? Who is entitled to narrate history? To whom is it narrated? When one history contradicts another, who is eligible to judge the 'truth'? Here, gender matters in relation to the answer to all these questions.

History can be rewritten and re-narrated. In this context I would dare to call myself a feminist revisionist, as I believe that women can revise the past by looking at it with different eyes and by hearing the voices of previously silenced witnesses. This is exactly what has taken place in Japan, when the voice of a survivor of military sexual slavery, Kim Hak-sun, was heard for the first time in history.

Following her testimony, history has been re-narrated and rewritten from a totally different perspective of reality.

As I will argue more substantively in this book, there was nothing new about this issue in terms of its existence as a historical fact since the comfort women system was widely known by soldiers and historians. What has changed is the way we view this fact, from something taken-for-granted as an inevitability of war to an intolerable inhuman act. What I saw here was how a testimony, the voice of a subaltern woman who had been silenced for nearly half a century, could change and challenge orthodox history.

The entire book is dedicated to the effort of revising Japanese women's history in response to the challenge posed by those Korean survivors of the comfort women system who have come forward. The comfort women issue has personally shaken me deeply and forced me to re-examine what Japanese women, both the elite and masses, have done, and made me rethink my own feminist heritage, positive or negative. This struggle coincided with the emergence of a reflexive women's history here in Japan, in which feminist historians tried to restore women's agency within the historical process.

The structure of *Nationalism and Gender* consists of the following four sections exploring the nature of the historical project. Part one, Engendering the Nation, explores the historical heritage of Japanese feminism, a heritage which unfortunately failed to ask questions about the comfort women system until the victims spoke out for themselves. This re-examination of women's history ended up leading me to question the place of women in the nation-state, since imperialism and colonialism are deeply wound up with this crime of the state.

Part two, The Military Comfort Women Issue, examines the variety of discursive strategies that have been used to interpret the comfort women issue, from conservative to leftist and feminist, and makes clear that each contradict each other. Each paradigm is placed according to the chronological order in which it appeared giving the appearance that each new paradigm overcame the problems inherent in the last, but it is not this simple as every discursive strategy has its own possibilities and limitations. The lesson that we learn from this is that we can never avoid the politics of category since we became more sensitive about discursive practice in historical studies since the linguistic turn.

Part three, The Politics of Memory, deals with the Japanese version of historical revisionism focused on the comfort women issue. This is the actual political situation that brought me into a confrontation with conservative historians. I became deeply involved with the Japanese *historikerstreit* from the point of view of a feminist historian, as I took this controversy to be a serious challenge undermining the achievements of women's history based on the use of oral histories and testimonies. The question that I address is rather methodological focusing on how history is constructed. This approach eventually led me to ask two additional questions: 1) *Who narrates history?* 2) *To whom is it narrated?* In the end these merged into a final question; *Whose history is it?* This is a question that inevitably obliges us all to ask questions about our own positionality in relation to history.

Part four, Hiroshima from a Feminist Perspective, was not included in the original publication of *Nationalism and Gender*, but fortunately with the positive support of both the translator and the publisher, we all agreed to include this chapter at the end. It contains a feminist vision of the future, looking at how we can criminalize all forms of state violence. It is particularly appropriate to include this chapter when we eyewitness the illegitimate use of the military force at the beginning of the 21st century by the world's most powerful nation-state, and at this historical juncture when women are trying to gain in the name of gender equality their share in the use of military force. The comfort women issue takes us to a point where it is clear that we need to go beyond the legitimacy of the nation-state.

At the very least, the historical lessons of Japanese women's history teaches us the following, a learning process, which I repeat, was triggered by the breaking of the silence of the survivors of the comfort women system and as such I will be ever grateful to those brave, elderly women who came forward. What we learn is that the feminist goal of gender equality does not lie in the pursuit of the nationalization of women. This conclusion is reached as a logical consequence of engendering the nation. Japanese feminism, coming out of its specific historical context, can contribute to global feminism with this lesson.

Finally, I would like to show my deepest gratitude to my translator, Beverley Yamamoto, and my publisher, Yoshio Sugimoto, both of whom found my book worthy of English publication and who took painstaking efforts with all the detailed work involved in producing this edition. I would also like to give my special thanks for the financial support of the Japanese Council for the Promotion of the Social Sciences, without which this translation would not have been possible.

This book is dedicated to Irokawa Daikichi, a survivor of Kamikaze attackers, and relentless anti-imperialist historian, who guided me to reflect on the war-time experience for which I, belonging to the post war generation, have no memory.

Spring 2003
Chizuko Ueno

Part I
Engendering the Nation

Methodological Issues

Recently, historical revisionism targeting the wartime period has been the subject of considerable controversy. However, revising understandings of the past is not an activity limited to historical revisionists for example, in the German historians' debate[1] or the much-criticised liberal historiography movement seen in Japan. History is something that is always being exposed to revision by those in the present.

History, then, is the constant reconstructing of the past in the present. The naïve view that history is simply an exercise in narrating the events of the past as they actually happened is no longer tenable. Supposing there was only one truth in history, then a definitive history of say the French Revolution or the Meiji Restoration would only need to be written once. Once written, there would be no need to re-write them. In reality, however, our understanding of the past is constantly being revised according to contemporary concerns and interests. For this very reason, the appearance of an official history or an established theory concerning the French Revolution or the Meiji Restoration has not brought to an end the process of writing about these events. The histories of both have been written again and again as times and perspectives have changed. I think, fundamentally, that history is something we re-write. Consequently, as was made clear to me by Kurihara Yukio, I should also be described as a revisionist (Kurihara, 1997). While this may be the case, the question addressed here is: history for whom?

Since the linguistic turn,[2] each area of the social sciences has taken as its point of departure a serious epistemological questioning of the idea of objective fact. History is no exception here. There is a shared consensus within the social sciences that there is no fact or truth, only a reality that has been reconstructed as a result of the problematising of specific viewpoints. This perspective, which we can also call social constructionism, has already become a matter of common knowledge within the social sciences. Again, history is no exception here.

Following on from this, as in other fields of the social sciences, history is also the site of a discursive battle over the politics of categories. My objective here is to join this battle for discursive hegemony, and not to try and establish a single truth. I am not using the term politics here in the sense of politics with a capital 'P', as in class conflict Politics, but, in the sense of Michel Foucault's politics of discourse, to mean politics with a small 'p' that lies hidden within categories and descriptions.[3]

Given these parameters, social constructionism cannot avoid entering the dispute surrounding revisionists who claim, for example, that there were no Nazi gas chambers, or debates concerning the representation of history. If anything, it can be said that history is the site of a discursive battle over whether or not to allow limitless reinterpretation. For example, in response to historical accounts of the Japanese wartime period, there are those who exclaim, 'Do not accept historical fabrication! or 'Do not distort historical truth!'[4] These comments sound to me as though they are tacitly premised upon the perspective of historical positivism, with the idea that there is a single truth in history that has to be discovered. However, do their proponents think that facts remain unchanged regardless of who is looking at them?

Having said that I am a revisionist, it is not the case that I accept the Kantian view that fact is merely an idealised social construct.[5] All I am saying is that those facts that have been positioned as facts, those facts that have been given greater importance than other facts, and that other reality unearthed from behind and standing in opposition to certain facts are all simply constructed viewpoints. Reality as a socially constructed phenomenon is something material, and what we are accustomed to calling fact from within this reality is simply that on which legitimacy has been bestowed.[6]

The construction of reality is a key issue in the study of women's history. How do we reconstruct what amounts to another reality for women, lying behind the official histories written by men, when the possibility of obtaining historical facts is completely absent? The new field of study called women's history, which is a product of second wave feminism that emerged in the 1970s, is a response to this problem. How to unearth this other reality is a particularly pressing issue within the field of medieval history where historical materials from the hands of women themselves are almost non-existent. Even when historical accounts focusing on women do exist, they have generally been written by men and are limited to materials that have survived historical censorship (Perrot et Duby, 1990; Ueno, 1995a). In the field of modern and contemporary history where there are living subjects, the task of unearthing that other reality lying behind what is recognised as historical fact is being carried out with considerable vigour using oral history techniques.

In recent years, there is no example that demonstrates this issue (that is unearthing that other reality) in starker terms than that of the 'comfort women' problem.[7] If we are simply talking about facts, many people have been aware of the existence of the comfort women. It is not something that has been hidden. What has changed is the way that this fact is dealt with. Nobody considered the comfort women system to be criminal until the women concerned defined themselves as victims and reconstructed it as a sexual crime. In more precise terms, the authenticity of historical fact as seen from the side of the assailants, who did not consider the comfort women system a crime (this fact moreover had been maintained by the silence of the victims) was first challenged and then overturned by the victims constructing a very different-looking other reality.[8]

This situation is not limited to the comfort women issue. Recently, as a result of the continuous efforts of a small group of conscientious historians, there is a growing body of painstaking empirical research and the discovery of facts based on primary sources concerning the period of the Asia-Pacific war. This has occurred precisely because 'that war' [meaning the Asia-Pacific], has been exposed to historical revision.

There are still many things concerning this war period that need to be made clear and, whether by accident or design, a considerable amount of material has vanished. My aim is not to even attempt to compete with the successes of such painstaking historical research. Indeed, I am not a historian and my own interest is in analysing why changes in historical interpretation occur and what the implications of this are for history. In other words, I am interested in the changes of narratives of meta-history. My analysis is based largely on secondary sources and, as a result, has its own limitations. It is probably for this reason that sociologists have to suffer the bad reputation of being the usurpers of history using the work of historians as a springboard for their own.

Paradigm Change in Post-War History

The question of how post-war history should be viewed has already been widely discussed and a number of paradigms now exist.

The first of these emphasizes a sharp break between the pre- and post-war periods and should perhaps be called the discontinuity school of history. This viewpoint overestimates the value of post-war reforms. Here it is claimed that oppressive social structures typified by feudal practices and the emperor system were swept away with post-war democratisation and a new era began. Where problems are seen to exist in the post-war era, these are put down to the fact that the so-called post-war democratisation process was not complete and remnants from the pre-war era remain. This line of argument is very similar to the pre-war theory of 'remnants of feudalism'. Given that anything negative is ascribed to the past, this could also be called the developmental school of history; the development being from oppression to liberation.

Words like *tradition* and *national characteristics* are also frequently employed to describe these remnants from the past, a legacy that cannot be easily swept away. As a consequence, they are refashioned into concepts that stand outside history. Tradition is explained in terms of something that cannot be explained [outside the confines of that tradition], therefore a 'magic box' or 'black box' category is invented (Hobsbawm and Ranger, 1983).

Examples of the invention of tradition[9] within the so-called *Nihonjinron* genre are too numerous to mention here. A number of self-referential social science works have appeared concerned with what should be referred to as the meta-history of the *Nihonjinron* (Aoki, 1990; Oguma, 1995), yet none are more stimulating than Oguma Eiji's *A Genealogy of 'Japanese' Self-Images* (1995; 2002). Through the act of re-reading the *Nihonjinron* literature of the pre- and post-war periods, Oguma discovered that both the pre-war theory of a heterogeneous nation and the post-war theory of a homogeneous nation were legitimated in the name of national tradition. Through the process of re-reading secondary sources, Oguma made a discovery similar to that of Columbus's egg.[10]

The pre-war theory of a heterogeneous nation was mobilized in order to legitimate the policy of colonial expansionism by the Japanese imperial state. It was claimed that the Japanese had long been a people successful in bringing about 'peace and harmony between different peoples' and that this was even brought out in the *Kojiki* and the *Nihon shoki*.[11] There was a complete reversal of this idea in the post-war period, with the fabrication of a new history where the Japanese emerged as a homogenous people with a continuous unbroken line of emperors. Furthermore, the post-war *Nihonjinron* resulted in the setting up of a supra-historical homogeneity and group-orientation of the Japanese people, just as if the preceding half-century had been forgotten.

The second paradigm emphasizes continuity between the pre- and post-war periods and therefore should perhaps be called the continuity school of history. This argument for continuity is offered on the grounds of the continuation of the 'modernisation project' since the Meiji era. This theory emphasizes continuity in development from the so-called period of the Taishō democracy through to post-war reforms. Consequently, from the perspective of this continuity school, the principles of post-war democratisation were not simply something imposed on Japan from the outside.

Now, if the *modern* is characterized by legal, political and economic rationality, then that 'irrational war' emerges as a stumbling block. For those proposing a continuity view of history, the war represents an unfortunate interruption in the modernisation project, an exceptional occurrence. Although there has been a modicum of self-reflection on the war, since post-war rehabilitation it is as though the Japanese have been a peace-loving people ever since ancient times and the modernisation project continued as if nothing had happened. Furthermore, the 'miracle' of post-war economic growth is viewed above all else as evidence of the success of the modernisation project.

Yamanouchi Yasushi (1996a) sums up the dominant view to date concerning contemporary Japanese history as follows:

Japanese history during the fascist era followed an abnormal course, straying from the natural path of maturation that a modern society should follow. The trend towards democratisation in the Taishō era (1912–1926) suffered a setback when it came to the period of fascism, and in its place

7

came a system of state power, with irrational ultra-nationalism as its ideological pillar, that forcibly dragged the people down the track of wartime mobilisation. Post-war reforms that began with defeat in 1945 returned Japanese history to the true line of Taishō democracy. From 1945 through to the present, Japanese history takes as its starting point post-war reforms (Yamanouchi, 1996a:33).[12]

For the continuity school of history the war represents a litmus test. The question that it raises is whether in terms of the modernisation project the war was inevitable or coincidental and, following on from this, whether there existed the possibility of some other way than this 'former madness'. In the case of it being coincidental, some factors of unique and external pressure are needed to explain the war. A frequent response, and one found among the familiar clichés of the right-wing, is the suggestion that as a latecomer to modernisation it was Japan's destiny to follow this distorted zigzag course. It is the cliché that Japan's intentions were not bad, only its methods, and that the international environment that forced that course of action on Japan was bad. In contrast, where the answer to the above question is that war was inevitable, theorists of the continuity school need to search for the intrinsic and unique factor within Japanese society that distorted the path of the modernisation project. What the post-war modernists Maruyama Masao and Kawashima Takeyoshi came up with was a kind of fate in the form of intrinsic pre-modern characteristics within Japanese society, in short, Japanese 'uniqueness'.[13]

Maruyama Masao wrote *Chō-kokka shugi no ronri to shinri* (The logic and psychology of ultra-nationalism) in 1946 in the immediate aftermath of defeat (Maruyama, 1946, 1995). In Maruyama's arguments, which equate the modern with the West, even Nazism is regarded as embodying the qualities of individualism and the responsible subject, and Japanese ultra-nationalism is described as second-rate nationalism compared to this. Maruyama's criticism of the irresponsible emperor system set the tone for the post-war *Nihonjinron*. Then the post-war *Nihonjinron*, making use of the same idea of uniqueness and by switching to the explanatory variables of peace and prosperity, was able to transform the thoroughly depressing and masochistic tone of Maruyama Masao's theory into one of opportunism.

What the discontinuity and continuity schools of history (described above) have in common is that they both view wartime conditions as a deviation or abnormality in order to legitimise the post-war system. Challenging this position is what can perhaps be called the neo-continuity theory.[14]

> The understanding of (ultra) state nationalism as a deviation of mass nationalism and its reduction to a problem of the war period is an indispensable and constituent factor in the discursive form that asserts the relative legitimacy of 'post-war' by ignoring the connection between the wartime mobilisation regime and post-war democracy, and by emphasising the abnormality of the wartime period. Recent research on the wartime mobilisation regime has grappled with this problem by paradoxically focusing on the dimension of continuity between the wartime and post-war periods when previously only the discontinuities had been discussed (Kasai, 1996:226; Sakai, De Bery, Iyotani 1996; Yamanouchi, Koschmann, and Narita 1995).

The neo-continuity theory as represented by Yamanouchi Yasushi incorporates the following three points of debate. Firstly, neo-continuity theorists understand the wartime regime not as a deviation of the modernisation project, but as its continuation. Here the wartime regime is regarded as a new stage in the modernisation project and as a consequence is treated as an innovation. The continuities between the two are underscored. Second, they claim that a key variable in this innovation is the process of nationalisation. As a result of going through two world wars, classic modernity centring on the Industrial Revolution and civil society experienced the all-important innovation of nationalisation or the establishment of the nation-state. Today, neither the market nor the family can exist without the intervention of the state. Third, this analysis opens the way for comparative history going beyond the theory of Japan's uniqueness. We are not only talking about the fascist states here as wartime mobilisation regimes were also established in the countries of the Allied Forces during both world wars. If anything, war was the violent opportunity that became the driving force in the innovation of the mobilizing system.[15]

The nation-state is a relatively new concept. Benedict Anderson (1985), Homi Bhabha (1993) and others working in the field of post-colonial studies advanced the idea of the nation-state in the 1980s, and at the same time revealed its illusory nature. It is due to Nishikawa Nagao and others that the term came to be used in earnest in Japan. The market and civil society are not the

9

only actors in the process of modernisation, as the nation-state has also played an indispensable role. The nation-state supplied not only 'a variety of devices for integrating the state', but also a 'powerful ideology for integrating the people'(Nishikawa, 1995:6). In the words of Anderson, the nation-state, by inventing a homogenous people, created an 'imagined community' and this group identity came to form the nucleus of our concepts of culture and the nation (Anderson, 1985). We are not free from this unfinished nationalisation project even today.

The backdrop to the nation-state suddenly being placed under the spotlight as an analytical concept from the 1980s onwards was the tumultuous history of this period, when the nation was denaturalised for the first time and ceased to function as a form of fate. As such, we cannot forget our own position as actors in history. The relativisation of the nation-state resulted from a paradoxical movement questioning the enlarged role of the state and the supposed autonomy of civil society, which occurred as huge nation-states collapsed before our eyes. What was being questioned here was the common-sense notion that modernity establishes an autonomous sphere called civil society. It became clear that state was an important actor from the beginning of the modern period and pushed forward the nationalisation of the social domain. Conversely, only when long-established nation-states started to crumble before us did we realise the extent to which the nation had been regarded as unquestioned given. Moreover, when the nation finally ceased to be viewed as fate analysts did not possess a perspective to enable them to transcend it, and in pointing to the limitations of history they generally had to rely on hindsight (Scott, 1988; Ueno, 1995b).

The merit of using the nation-state as a key concept in our argument is that we can separate the modernisation project from its Euro-centric (more accurately Western European-centric) bias, thus making possible a historical comparison. The modernisation project can be discussed in terms of three components: economic capitalism, political democracy and civic individualism. There already exists within the field of economic systems theory a convergence theory that takes a concept of industrialisation as a variable, and views capitalism and socialism as two versions of this process. However, if we make use of the nation-state as an analytical concept, both the capitalist and socialist states emerge as two different versions of the nation-state. Furthermore, this approach makes possible a comparison of authoritarian states and military dictatorships from within the category nation-state. It is not simply that this approach overturns the idea that only states in one area of the West exhibiting the three components of modernisation are deserving of the name modern states, it also challenges the myth that socialist states are post states and the view that military dictatorships and authoritarian states are pre-modern. In the words of Nishikawa:

All bodies we call 'nation-states' share the same character and structure, and each individual nation-state is no more than a variation on this... I consider the nation-state a historical product that needs to be transcended, and the debate about the nation-state is linked to the search for a way to do this (Nishikawa, 1995:4).

What I would like to do here is not only to make use of Nishikawa's concept of the nation-state, but also to add to this the analytical category 'gender'. Therefore, this book is an attempt to engender [apply a category of gender] to the nation-state.[16]

Gender has also been denaturalised as a result of historical change and is no longer seen as fate. The discovery of gender, through the discovery that the family was not nature but another society, exploded the myth of the 'private' sphere as a holy sanctuary from the public sphere and made clear that the family was not in the least bit autonomous from the state and the market. Here too, paradoxically, one must say that the invisible roles that had once been carried out by the family of 'pre-ordained harmony' became visible to us through the process of its functional paralysis and disintegration. Furthermore, the engendering of the so-called public sphere of state and society made clear the extent to which the public sphere was in fact depending upon a shadowy domain, namely, the private sphere, while at the same time revealing the secret that it had been able to assume the pretence of being public. It was precisely due to the fact that the public sphere was viewed as a public that the private sphere had to be separated from this and naturalized. Gender studies have made clear that not only the private sphere, which we can see even at a glance is gendered, but also the public sphere, has been ingeniously gendered using the rhetoric of gender neutrality (Ueno, 1990).

What we refer to here as the public sphere actually consists of two different realms: the market and the state. If we were to point to the public sphere as a market it would be nothing more than an area of what Marx called 'capitalist private activity'. In contrast, if we were to suggest that the public sphere were only a state sphere, this would not mean that the state would necessarily represent the public interests of its citizens. Indeed, the assumption is that civil society will eliminate as much as possible any interference by the state in the free activities of its citizens. Put another way, we can say that although the state and society were originally different domains, the two were deliberately conflated within a concept of a public sphere defined in terms of its separation from the private. In fact, a relationship of inter-dependency emerged between the market and the state in order to establish a national economy, with the boundary between the two difficult to discern.

If I might draw upon a previous piece of work, in *Patriarchy and Capitalism* (Ueno, 1990) I treated the public/private divide in modern society as equivalent to the separation of the market and the family, and thought that it was sufficient to analyse the dual dialectic between the two. From a Marxist-Feminist perspective, it is clear that the market is by no means autonomous, depending for its existence on the so-called external sphere of the family. Yet, external to the market is another non-market sphere in the form of the state. In response to my argument on the dialectics of the state versus the family, the criticism of Adachi Mariko really got to the heart of the matter when she pointed out that 'Ueno's analysis lacks a concept of the state'. Let us just say that I inherited both the strengths and weaknesses of a Marxist theory that understands the modern almost solely in terms of the capitalist system. However, inherent in Marxist theory is the state as a conceptual device. It is only now with the benefit of hindsight that I realise that I underestimated the state in my analysis[17].

If we are talking in terms of the nation-state, then the modernisation project can be referred to by another name, the 'nationalisation project'. Incidentally, the nation as defined geo-politically or demographically inevitably goes hand-in-hand with some kind of definition of exclusion. On reflection, from the very beginning the nationalisation project was a continuous definition and redefinition of the boundaries of the nation and those to be included in or excluded from it. For example, *Les Droits de L'Homme et du Citoyen* (The Declaration of Human Rights – of the Rights of Man) of the French Revolution, that happened to be translated as *jinken* (human rights) in Japanese, literally amounted to nothing more than the human rights of *homme* (males) and *citoyen* (citizens). Women and workers were excluded from this. To enjoy these rights it was necessary to be a citizen who had been civilised (Nishikawa, 1992).[18] Hence, human rights always go hand-in-hand with a definition of boundaries concerning the scope of the definition of human. Then we have the term democracy, which frequently appears as a partner of the term human rights, and this too amounts to little more than democracy between citizens who have been granted equal human rights. This is not surprising given that the history of the modern era is tied in with slavery, racism and sex discrimination. These social injustices are not simply the vestiges of ancient times or feudalism, neither are they modern 'noise', but essential components of the modern nation-state and national economy and should therefore be referred to as modern slavery, modern racism and modern sex discrimination. Then, concerning the re-definition of boundaries, there are disputes over which group of second-class citizens should be civilised next.[19]

Paradigm Change in Women's History

With the relativisation of the nation-state, the modernisation project emerged as a prominent target of research. When it was realised that the state was not akin to fate, the construction of the nation was problematized for the first time. One after another institutions such as the national language, national history, national literature, national education and the national military ended up being problematized as media of nationalisation. It gave rise to analyses of how events such as imperial visits, state ceremonies and expositions were mobilized to create Anderson's 'imagined community' (Nakamura, 1994; Yoshimi S., 1996), and also to the kind of work carried out by the young historian, Takashi Fujitani, looking at the physical techniques of nationalisation seen in military disciplining of soldiers (Fujitani, 1994).

Looking back, it is clear that the modernisation project did not go smoothly even in the beginning. The fact that there was strong resistance can be understood from the immense effort it took to raise school attendance rates over a long period (after the compulsory education system was introduced in 1872), and the 'blood tax' riots that occurred all over Japan in response to the Conscription Ordinance of 1873.[20] However, Oku Takenori points out that even within the nationalisation agenda, 'there was little awareness of the issue of women as targets of nationalisation' (Oku, 1995). In terms of the task of engendering the nation-state, researchers in the field of women's studies have at least taken up the challenge and have, for example, analysed the relationship between women's suffrage and nationalisation. The work of Tachi Kaoru is representative. Tachi points out that when the Universal Suffrage Law came into effect in 1925, 'Korean and Taiwanese males living in mainland Japan' were included in the category of 'Male Japanese Imperial Subjects' entitled to vote, and concluded that 'in the case of universal suffrage in Japan gender norms came into play more forcefully than those of class or ethnicity' (Tachi, 1994:126–127).[21] In other words, the Universal (Manhood) Suffrage Law, in order to establish among men an equal community that transcended class and ethnicity, denied women the right to vote.

If we understand the nationalisation of women as an unfinished project that has continued throughout the modern era, then it is clear that the war was not an anecdote in the process of the nationalisation project, but an 'innovation' (a variation in the extreme) that actually advanced it.

Modern total war is the largest project a nation-state undertakes, and is the site of geo-political, demographic and symbolic struggle. Aiming at unification, the state in wartime ends up demanding the nationalisation of both society and the family (Wakakuwa, 1995). As a way of putting directly into words this intention, it can be said that the terms 'national socialism' and 'ultra-nationalism' are absolutely appropriate. War achieves a transparent community, and for a long time afterwards people reminisce nostalgically about the excitement of 'togetherness' and 'national unity'.

A number of notable scholarly works have appeared since the 1980s concerned with the nationalisation of women. One reason for this is that the categories nation-state and gender were finally 'discovered' at this time. Yet, at the same time, it is exactly because the limits of the modernisation project became evident that these two categories were, for the first time, revealed to us. Again, this was due to the impact of feminism on women's history in the 1980s. In other words, it was preceded by a paradigm shift in historical viewpoint where women were transformed from passive subjects into autonomous agents creating history. Within Japanese women's history, this transformation went from the *victim* school to a *perpetrator* school of history, leading it to pursue the questions of women's support of the war and war responsibility. This is because, if women's agency in history is recognized, women cannot be exempted from responsibility in relation to history.[22] I will call this new trend since the 1980s in women's history the *reflexive* school of women's history. This is simultaneously both retrospective and self-reflexive. Ironically, the discovery of women's historical agency also leads us to relentlessly pursue women's war responsibility. Yet, at the same time, it also signifies the maturity of both feminism and women's history as both are extricated from the victim school of history. As subsequent examination will make clear, there is a significant difference in the way issues are grasped depending on the target of reflexivity.

The Nationalisation of Women and Wartime Mobilisation

We can consider the various media of women's nationalisation on four levels. The first level is that of the state, namely politics, policy, regulation and public propaganda. The second level is that of ideas and discourses, and here I am referring to areas such as the discourse of the leadership class, and the media, and imagery. The third level is that of campaigns and action, namely the level of mass mobilisation. The fourth level is that of daily life-style and customs. There is now a body of research that has been carried out by women researchers concerned with each of these areas. Here I would like to discuss wartime mass mobilisation by the state, women's policy and trends in state propaganda as one axis, and as another, the reaction of women to this, particularly tendencies within the feminist leadership.

From the early stages of militarization through to total war, the Japanese government was fully aware that the cooperation of women on the 'home front' was indispensable, and pushed ahead with the organisation of the female population. In the year following the Manchurian Incident (1931), the Greater Japan Women's Association for National Defence (*Dainippon Kokubō Fujinkai*) was hastily formed. When the Marco Polo Bridge Incident in 1937 triggered full-scale aggression in the Sino-Japanese war, an 'Outline for the Implementation of National Spiritual Mobilisation' (*Kokumin Seishin Sōdōin Jisshi Yōkō*) was decided on. Then in October of the same year, Yoshioka Yayoi, Ichikawa Fusae and other women's group leaders were appointed committee members when the Central League for National Spiritual Mobilisation (*Kokumin Seishin Sōdōin Chūō Renmei*) was inaugurated. In 1940, a year after the Second World War broke out, the Imperial Rule Assistance Association (*Taisei Yokusankai*) was inaugurated with a Central Co-operation Committee (*Chūō Kyōryoku Kaigi*), also known as the National Family Committee (*Kokumin Kazoku Kaigi*). Immediately after the beginning of the

Pacific War in 1942, the Women's Patriotic Association (*Aikoku Fujinkai*), the Greater Japan Women's Association for National Defence, and the Greater Japan Federated Women's Association (*Dainippon Rengō Fujinkai*) merged to form the Greater Japan Women's Association (*Dainippon Fujinkai*). The Greater Japan Women's Association formed as a part of government policy, and 'all Japanese women over 20 years, except single women' were made members. At the time, the Women's Patriotic Association embraced a membership of 4 million, and the Greater Japan Women's Association for National Defence, 9 million. It is clear that the Greater Japan Women's Association was a military initiative. As has been frequently pointed out, the president was a woman called Marquioness Yamauchi Sachiko, the wife of Marquis Yamauchi, but the Chairman of the Board of Directors was a male bureaucrat from the Ministry of Home Affairs.

Furthermore, as the war situation become more strained, a total mobilisation system began that incorporated women, including the Ordinance on Women's Volunteer Labour Corps (*Joshi Teishin Kinrō Rei*) in 1944 and the National Labour Mobilisation Ordinance (*Kokumin Kinrō Dōin Rei*) in 1945. On the 23rd June 1945, in the closing stages of the war and with the battle for the mainland anticipated following defeat in the Battle of Okinawa, the Volunteer Military Service Law (*Giyūheieki Hō*) was pro-mulgated.[23] This organized all 'men aged 15–60 and women aged 17–40' into National Volunteer Combat Corps (*Kokumin Giyū Sentōtai*), and brought about the Greater Japan Women's Association's dissolution into several sections within this new organisation. Wakakuwa Midori, who has analysed visual propaganda concerned with women's wartime mobilisation concludes, drawing on the words of Kōketsu Atsushi, that 'the total war regime did not demolish the gender division of labour' (Kōketsu, 1981; Wakakuwa, 1995:83).

This raises questions about the definition of the boundaries of both nationalisation and gender. In other words, it would appear that when the nation is defined in terms of masculinity, there are two possibilities for resolving the dilemma of total mobilisation and the designation of gender differentiated domains. If I can begin by offering my conclusion here, it is probably reasonable to say that this resolution can be defined in terms of an integration model and a segregation model. To avoid misunderstanding, let me emphasize that within the limits of both frameworks women are second-class citizens.

In both Japan and Germany the model was that of segregation[24]. At the beginning of the war in both countries women were prohibited from engaging in political activity. In Germany, a law banning women from political activity was approved some time after the Nazis came to power. In Japan, a Women's Civil Right's Law was initially passed by the House of Representatives in 1931, the year of the Manchurian Incident, but it met with rejection in the House of Peers. Immediately after the Sino-Japanese war broke out in 1937, the Greater Japan Federated Women's Association's youth section began campaigning for the formation of a 'young women's volunteer corps'. It is reported that an increasing number of young women came forward volunteering to go to the war front, but the authorities announced that they would not allow this (Wakakuwa, 1995).

Japan did not consider the possibility of female soldiers even in the final stages of the war when there was a shortage of military personnel. At the very end of the war in 1945, women were hired as aviation maintenance staff and were even recruited as medical orderlies for the air force. However, in neither case were they hired as combatants, but as auxiliary staff offering rearguard support. The question of how to interpret the National Volunteers (*Kokumin Giyūhei*) is a delicate matter. However, in Okinawa, which had become the front line, local people had already built up experience preparing for national militarization through participating in the Local Volunteer Corps (*Tekkestu Giyūtai*) and the Women's Volunteer Corps *(Joshi Teishintai)*. The American Army were no doubt surprised when they landed in Okinawa to find that their prisoners-of-war included young boys and old men who were unequal to the demands of war. However, even in these extreme conditions, female volunteer corps like the Star Lily Corps *(Himeyuri Butai)* were positioned as rearguard support corps offering relief, and were not regarded as combatants. With the aim of turning the whole nation, including women, into soldiers, the National Volunteers were, in short, the final self-defence force and blurred the distinction between combatants and civilians in preparation for the battle of the mainland. However, it would arguably be pushing it too far to characterise these women as a kind of female soldier.[25]

When a nation-state makes an increase in military and man-ufacturing capacity a state goal, and reduces the nation to its population (in other words, troop strength and labour power), military service becomes the key to nationalisation. When this happens, the nation is divided into those who have the honour of dying for their country and those who do not, and only the former are qualified as members of the nation. War makes clearly visible those gender boundaries advanced during peacetime. Consequently, women seeking equality of the integration model hope to overcome the gender boundaries of wartime by taking part in the fighting. In reality, in the case of the United States where female troops have been enthusiastically employed and the United Kingdom where a female draft was put into practice, on the state side there has been a positive adoption of a strategy of integration and women have responded to this. The American case refutes the view that female soldiers are a last resort to supplement a shortfall in troop strength. The reason for this is that, unlike Japan and Germany, there was no real concern over the possibility of a severe shortfall in troop strength. If a shortage of troops was not the reason for employing female soldiers, then we must search for another reason. The United States sent female soldiers into battle in the Gulf War, but a long experience of female military participation preceded this. This difference between the strategy of integration or segregation is extremely familiar to us even today in the form of the confrontation between the equality and difference factions within feminism. However, we collide with the unexpectedly deep-rooted reality of the close correspondence between the different routes taken by feminism and the context of the national culture. Thus, we can see that contemporary feminism is bound within the confines of both nationality and culture.

It probably comes as some surprise that faced with total mobilisation Japan, to the very end, did not demolish the system of gender segregation and, moreover, there did not arise from women themselves a demand for integration. When it comes to wartime experiences, there are numerous uplifting accounts of how women could also contribute to the war, but to the best of my knowledge only Morisaki Kazue speaks of the 'the sense of humiliation of women during the war'. In the short phrase 'men with exclusive possession of guns owned the war', she testifies to the shame of women 'who were not able to die in battle' (Morisaki, 1965; 1992:44).

In honour of Morisaki, I would like to add that she definitely was not a militaristic young woman. Far from it, having spent her girlhood in colonized Korea she reacted with a keen sensitivity to the injustices of colonial rule. While everyone was aware of the extreme definitions given to gender by war, to be so totally frank in the face of such an overwhelming reality and to be able to describe the gender asymmetry instead of pretending it was not there suggests, at the very least, that Morisaki had some distance from it.

Whether or not you can become the military hero who turns into a 'god of war' after death, depends on the powerful and, moreover, asymmetrical definitions given to gender by war. The seat reserved for Japanese women by the gender strategy of segregation was not that of god of war but the 'mother of a god of war enshrined at Yasukuni'. In the opening page of her book *Sensō ga tsukuru josei zō* (Images of women created by war) Wakakuwa Midori (1995), a feminist art historian, has placed a picture of a young mother with a baby boy in her arms visiting the Yasukuni Shrine. The illustration shows the solemn picture of a young widow meeting with her late husband who has become a god of war. This was the only colour illustration in the whole book, making it easy to appreciate the high value Wakakuwa placed on the symbolism of this icon. It revealed the resolve of the woman to offer her son to the nation, despite having lost her husband. For the first time, women who carried the humiliation of not being able to die in battle were able to rival the heroism of the gods of war by becoming the mother of a god of war. Wakakuwa indicates that here the child is little more than something belonging to the nation that the woman happens to be looking after; perfectly demonstrating the patriarchal idea of the 'borrowed womb'. Wakakuwa compares this with Michelangelo's Pieta statue of the Virgin Mary returning to god the child she had been entrusted to look after, and comes to the following conclusion:

> The image assigned to Japanese women during the war was not a morale-boosting picture representing war itself, but the figure of motherhood holding a boy child. In other words, it fitted into the genealogy of 'the Holy Mother and Child' (Wakakuwa, 1995:254).

Wakakuwa does not only indicate what is present in each picture, but also refers to images that are not included:

> As part of their image strategy for mobilising women, the state and those leaders with orders from the state, opinion leaders, and propagandists definitely did not offer women 'scenes' of the front line, a battle-in-

progress, or victory. Neither did they proffer women such images as the triumphal return, defeat or occupation. War scenes with a capital 'W' were aimed at men, and bloody scenes of battle that were frequently featured in men's magazines were a male domain (Wakakuwa, 1995:244).

The fact of the matter is that there was a route for women to be worshiped at the Yasukini Shrine. This was the route of being killed in the performance of one's duties as a nurse attached to the military.[26] Drawing on the work of Kameyama Michiko, a historian of medical nurses, Wakakuwa suggests that the masculine virtues demanded of military nurses such as courage, coolness and composure (self-possessed even at the sight of human blood), were perceived as contrary to women's essential femininity. Yet as nurses were persons serving to restore fighting strength in the front line, the role was considered to be the most appropriate to women's 'innate character' (Kameyama, 1984a).

Another group supposedly serving to restore fighting strength were the military comfort women, yet their contribution was overlooked. At the same time, given the sexual double standard (the separation between mothers and prostitutes) it was necessary to distinguish clearly between the category military nurse and military comfort woman. Higuchi Keiko, a renowned feminist social critic, suggests that military nurses were probably exposed to a considerable amount of sexual harassment while working, but the saintliness of the category nurse would have obstructed the problematising of sexual harassment in the workplace. This, then, is the exact reverse of the discrimination towards the comfort women. In reality, many comfort women at the front were required to act as nursing personnel, but the military nurses were not happy about this and demanded that a stop be put to prostitutes acting as nurses.

The Feminist Response

How did women react to the type of policies mentioned above? There has been a rapid accumulation of research concerned with this question, focusing on the ideas and discourses of the leadership class and, in addition, the support and involvement of the female masses.

In terms of questioning the war responsibility of the female intelligentsia of the pre-war period, a paradigm shift has occurred in women's history moving from the *victim* school to a *perpetrator* school of history and, along with this, a re-reading of the literature on the subject. The thoroughness of this process is such that the past of each and every female thinker who bears responsibility for pre-war feminism, without exception, is being examined.

From among these, three leading feminists are frequently singled out; Ichikawa Fusae, Hiratsuka Raichō and Takamure Itsue. I am picking out these three women not simply because they are prominent figures that cannot be overlooked when discussing pre-war feminism, but because they are also stand as representatives of the integrationist and segregationist strategies within feminism. Ichikawa as an advocate of women's suffrage is a classic example of the former, while Hiratsuka as a maternalist represents the latter strategy. As Hiratsuka's maternalist successor and, moreover, as an ultra-nationalist who was an even more fanatical supporter of 'the holy war', Takamure cannot be forgotten. Even so, it is not the discourses produced by these women that I am interested in here. I would like to focus on the meta-history, the interpretations given to the discourses and activities of these feminist thinkers by scholars of women's history, and then the changes that have occurred in the interpretive paradigm.

In 1937 when the second Sino-Japanese war broke out, Ichikawa Fusae (1893–1971) formed the Federation of Japanese Women's Organisations (*Nippon Fujin Dantai Renmei*) embracing eight women's groups including the Women's Suffrage League (*Fusen Kakutoku Dōmei*), and in response to the National Mobilisation Law she created a support structure to 'strengthen the defence of the home front'. In the same year, Ichikawa was appointed committee member of the Central League for National Spiritual Mobilisation (*Kokumin Seishin Sōdōin Chūō Renmei*). In 1939 she became Secretary of the National Spiritual Mobilisation Committee, in 1940 a councillor at the National Spiritual Mobilisation Central Headquarters, and in 1942 an officer on the deliberative council of the Greater Japan Women's Association (*Dainippon Funjinkai*) and a Director of the Greater Japan Patriotic Speech Society (*Dainippon Genron Hōkokukai*).

As a result of this kind of support and participation, Ichikawa was purged from public office by the post-war occupation forces. Her support and participation were highly visible and, moreover, Ichikawa herself and researchers have acknowledged this 'stain' on her career. At the Ichikawa Fusae Memorial Hall wartime documents are open to the public and Ichikawa is respected as a woman of integrity because, if for no other reason, she did not try to cover up this stain. The interpretation is that, given the level of state oppression, Ichikawa had little choice but to cooperate if she wanted to protect the women's suffrage movement.

In contrast, Hiratsuka Raichō (1886–1971) lacked enthusiasm for the 'intergrationist ideal', and it is widely known that she chose from the beginning the segregationist strategy of maternalism. As Hiratsuka did not participate as energetically in public activity as Ichikawa during the war, the question of her 'war responsibility' was not raised until very recently. Nevertheless, through a re-reading of the wartime literature, the underside of Hiratsuka's maternalism, namely her eugenic ideology, has recently come under attack. Unexpectedly, it has become clear that she had written prose enthusiastically praising the emperor and, along with a re-evaluation of Hiratsuka as a theorist, a movement has arisen to re-examine the unique features of the strand of Japanese feminism led by her (Furukubo, 1991; Suzuki, 1989b; Miyake 1994; Ōmori, 1997).

Incidentally, Suzuki Yūko, a scholar of the reflexive school of women's history, raised the following questions concerning the war responsibility of these two leaders typically regarded as representative feminists of, respectively, the integrationist and segregationist models that came out of the first wave of feminism.

Why did somebody who had previously been considered outstanding end up committing such a mistake during the war?...What caused (these

women) to get caught up in cooperating with the imperialist war?
(Suzuki, 1989b45–46)

Behind the words 'the mistake' made by Raichō, Ichikawa and others
is, firstly, the assumption that theirs was a choice based on free will
rather than on the unavoidable compulsion of circumstances.
Secondly, if indeed a mistake was made, the question this raises is
whether the mistake was avoidable or not. If it was avoidable, then
there is the awareness that by learning from the mistake these
women made we should be able to avoid falling into this pitfall a
second time. Finally, the judgement of the war as 'that bad war'
is presupposed within this idea of a mistake, but I would like to
save discussion of this until later.

In taking the standpoint that they want to provide as consistent
an explanation as possible of the inherent logic of this *mistake*, it
can be said that these scholars of women's history have, without
clearly stating the fact, adopted the standpoint of the continuity
school of history.

According to Suzuki Yūko, Ichikawa's path can be summed up
as 'women's rights equalling participation in the public sphere,
which in turn equals women's liberation' (Suzuki, 1989b). Within
these limits, Ichikawa's path can be seen as the consistent life of a
female suffragist with the sense of an outstanding activist. For
Ichikawa this meant consistently supporting the participation of
women in public activities. The mistake made by her turns out to
be her failure to question the content of this public activity (that bad
war!). On top of this, Ichikawa's powerful sense of mission as a
women's suffragist and, the reverse of this, her own elitism meant
that she could not tolerate seclusion from what was going on.

A re-reading of the literature is similarly moving in the direction
of demonstrating the through-line in Hiratsuka's ideas. Eugenic
statements made during the war have been tied in with Hiratsuka's
position on the 'motherhood protection debate'[27] that took place
before this, and are viewed as the inevitable consequence of her
maternalism. Serving the state through motherhood, as a matter of
course, includes the selection of 'superior descendants' from
'inferior descendants', and the position of demanding the protection
of motherhood by the state can all too easily result in approval of
the state's controlling motherhood. In fact, the protection/control
of motherhood by the state through such measures as the passing
of the Mother and Child Protection Law in 1938, the National

Eugenics Law in 1940, and the issuing of Expectant and Nursing Mothers Notebooks in 1942 were welcomed by Hiratsuka, for at last the arguments she had been advancing over many years had been acknowledged. Once again, Suzuki suggests that the background here is Hiratsuka's own elitism (causing her to separate women into those fit to give birth and those who are unfit)[28].

According to scholars of women's history such as Suzuki and Yoneda Sayako, the cause of Hiratsuka moving in the direction of praising the emperor can be found in her anti-modernism. Behind this lies a re-interpretation of the motherhood protection debate, which precedes it as a kind of pre-history, resulting in an understanding of the confrontation between Yosano Akiko (1878–1942) and Hiratsuka as one between individualism and maternalism, on the one hand, and modernism and anti-modernism, on the other. It is well known that even before she launched the journal *Seitō* (Bluestocking), known as the pioneering feminist journal of the first wave in Japan, Hiratsuka was, among other things, a Zen Buddhist who sought enlightenment through the guidance of a priest of the Rinsai sect, someone who emphasized spiritual values, and a great believer in nature (for example, she ate brown rice).[29]

While indicating that she is repelled by Suzuki's 'accusatory view of history', Yoneda also offers her strong support for the notion of Hiratsuka's 'continuity'. She goes as far as saying that 'Raichō was not a traitor [to her cause] who willingly snuggled up to the state; it was the emperor state system that "seized" Raichō!' Yoneda then asks 'Is it not the case that statements made by Raichō represent not a temporary shakiness but something fundamental to her?' and then answers this question herself saying, 'I dare to say yes even with the fear of misunderstanding.'

> Due to her continuous anti-modernism and anti-rationalism, Raichō rebelled against the existence of a total control system (the modernist, rationalist system created by the modern nation-state). However, this kind of critical spirit, that is to say taking on the authority of the state as an adversary, and her own position as an anti-modernist and anti-rationalist made it highly conceivable that she would literally be 'seized', when she found her own ideas in the dominant ideology grounded in the imperial view of history (Yoneda:1996:50).

Suzuki also displays perplexity at some of Hiratsuka's remarks, such as 'the Emperor, living descendant of the Sun Goddess' and 'the imperial policy as devine will', and resigns herself to the fact that it was as if in Hiratsuka 'there was another world that had transcended logic', so that 'from the start it is probably impossible to try and understand her logically' (Suzuki, 1989b:43).

It is worth noting that there are a couple of problems in Suzuki's interpretation. First, there is the question of whether Hiratsuka was truly an anti-modernist. Although there is a repeated tendency to hastily position maternalism as anti-modernism, on the basis that it rejects modern individualism, recent feminist research on the subject has made clear that motherhood is also an invention of modernity. The view taken is that maternalism as product of the modern era is one possible form feminism can take. This position can be verified through a detailed re-examination of Hiratsuka's arguments in the motherhood protection debate.[30] In response to Yosano Akiko's calls for 'the complete independence of young women', Raichō insisted that, 'the claim for the protection of motherhood was not one for dependency'. At this time, Hiratsuka's target for the 'dependency' of motherhood protection was not the husband but the public sphere of the state. It is exactly because women could contribute to the public sphere of the state through motherhood that women had a right as citizens to be provided with motherhood security by the state. This line of thinking would have been inconceivable before the foundation of the state as a public body. Hiratsuka and Ellen Key [1849–1926][31] shared similar ideas about motherhood security and, tied in with this, the role of the welfare state. In the context of the times, these ideas in many ways constituted the development of a progressive argument, because they amounted to nothing less than placing hopes on an enlargement of the public sphere at a time when this kind of public aspect of the state had yet to be fully established. Consequently, we can understand Yosano and Hiratsuka's argument as a battle between Yosano's realism, as a self-supporting person, and Hiratuska's 'idealism divorced from reality', which placed its hopes in a public realm that did not yet exist. Following on from this, what Hiratsuka saw happening during the war years was, in a manner of speaking, the enlargement of the 'public domain'.

Yosano was able to see through Hiratuska's overestimation of the state:

Although Hiratuska placed great hopes in the state...the 'state' that Hiratsuka was talking about was not the state as it actually was, but refers to a state that has been re-modelled in an ideal way (Yosano 1918a; Kouchi, 1984:102).

Incidentally, the Scandinavian women's theorist and maternalist feminist, Ellen Key, acquired an even higher standing in Japan among leading participants in the motherhood protection debate, than in the West, by virtue of the enthusiasm with which she was introduced here by Yamada Waka [1879–1957] and Hiratsuka. However, it would be incorrect to take the view, simply for this reason, that first wave feminism was an imported ideology brought from the West. Translation as a means of introducing culture always includes a screening process.[32] From when it was first established, Japanese feminism held an affinity for Scandinavian maternalism and rejected Anglo-Saxon individualism and egalitarianism. For example, Hiratsuka translated Ellen Key's work in *Bluestocking,* but this was less to do with Key's influence over Hiratsuka and more because Hiratsuka discovered shared ideas in Key's writing. At the time, Charlotte Perkins Gilman's[33] Anglo-Saxon ideas of individualism were also widely known, but were not introduced into Japan with such enthusiasm.

As part of a fascinating attempt to locate the motherhood protection debate within the context of contemporary international feminism, Miyake Yoshiko (1994) discusses the Yosano-versus-Hiratsuka debate, referring to the differences in the ideological backgrounds of Ellen Key and Perkins Gilman. Pre-dating this, Anglo-Saxon feminism, that is individualistic feminism aiming at economic independence and political equality, was already known in Japan through the writings of Mary Wollstonecraft [1759–797] and Olive Schreiner [1855–1920].[34] From the beginning, Key-style maternalistic feminism was something that appeared at the second stage within the current of first wave feminism as a criticism of individualistic feminism. 'Western feminism' itself was not a single stratum. Feminism in Japan, a late-comer to capitalism, was, in the words of Yosano, like 'the momentary springtime blossoming of all flowers at once in a cold country', but there did undoubtedly result from it a selective acceptance of 'Western feminism'.[35] The debate between Yosano and Hiratsuka was not a war by proxy for Western feminism to be played out on the Japanese stage.

Secondly, a question has arisen over whether Yosano (who is viewed as the voice of individualism within the motherhood protection debate) was really an advocate of modern individualism.

The following statement is frequently cited from the motherhood protection debate:

> I do not believe a child is either a 'thing' or a 'tool'. I consider each child an individual with his or her own independent character. A child belongs to his or her self. In contrast to Hiratsuka, I certainly do not view a child as the property of 'society' or 'the nation' (Yosano, 1918b; Kouchi, 1984:188).[36]

This is offered as proof of Yosano's 'individualism', but surely it is worth investigating whether her position pre- or post-dates the state. For example, Yosano's famous anti-war poem *There's Nothing to Die for, Brother!*, written during the Russo-Japanese war, can be understood as an expression of the values of pre-modern familism, the fore-runner of nationalism. In a sense, Yosano's intuition is correct when she describes her impression of Hiratsuka as a nationalist who expresses herself like a high-handed militarist. Conversely, it is conceivable that the reason Yosano was able to distance herself from nationalism was her embodiment of the communal ethic that preceded the state.[37] In 1918, at the time of the motherhood protection debate, the women's suffrage movement was still not established. It is well known that the maternalists, starting with Hiratsuka, were indifferent to the demands for women's right to vote. In 1920, Hiratsuka joined with Ichikawa Fusae to form the New Women's Society (*Shin Fujin Kyōkai*) and set about demanding political rights for women. 1924 saw the start of the Association for the Promotion of Women's Suffrage (*Fujin Sanseiken Kakutoku Kisei Dōmei*) by Ichikawa Fusae and Kubushiro Ochimi among others. In the course of the motherhood protection debate it was suggested to Yosano by the male socialist Sakai Toshihiko, popularly known as Sakai Kosen, that she 'set up a women's suffrage movement and take a leading part in it', and that '[Yosano] was most qualified to be an advocate', but she firmly declined on the basis that her present lifestyle left no room to avail herself of such an opportunity (Yosano, 1919; Kouchi, 1984:223–9). It is clear from *Dear Sakai Kosen Sama* (Yosano, 1919) that Yosano supported women's suffrage, and that it is appropriate to position her along with Ichikawa in the genealogy of the integration model.

The third problematic point is that as a result of their emphasis on Hiratsuka's consistency and still more the irrationality of the wartime regime, both Suzuki and Yoneda presume a rupture in the modernisation project during the crisis of wartime. Then in order to demonstrate the inevitability of feminist thinkers' support for the war, they adopt the position that the war was a deviation from the modernisation project. As a result, Suzuki and Yoneda end up going back once again to the old paradigm where the war is viewed as an irrationality or moment of madness in Japan's modern history. In this sense, the view of these women, which emphasizes the consistency of pre-war feminists, falls within the former Continuity School paradigm and is unrelated to the neo-continuity theory.

The Feminist Version of 'Conquering the Modern'

I would like to consider one more important figure here, Takamure Itsue [1849–1964]. In a sense it is much easier to see why Takamure was treated as an anti-modernist, because of her fanatical glorification of the war and support of the emperor ideology. Moreover, as the self-professed ideological successor of Hiratsuka and due to her emphasis on a 'maternal self' that transcends modern individualism, Takamure is considered the most enthusiastic female promoter of ultra-nationalism. In a way, she has been regarded as the ideological leader of the feminist version of the 'conquering the modern' school and on this point her treatment in critical biographies leaves little room for her defence (Kano and Horiba 1977; Kanō, 1987, 1995d; Nishikawa, 1982a, 1990; Yamashita E., 1988).

> From the period when everyone felt cowed into silence through to the revival of the 'Japanese spirit', many thinkers went down the road of enthusiastically involving themselves in the Imperial Rule Assistance system during the fifteen years of war…When one considers the results of Takamure linking together women's liberation and the quest to 'conquer the modern', and that she pursued these with all her heart and soul, I cannot help feeling sorry for her (Kanō, 1987, 1995d:180–1).

However, there is room for a re-investigation of Takamure's so-called anti-modernism. From when she made her debut as a poet in *Jitsu getsu no ue ni* (Above the sun and the moon) in 1920, Takamure presented herself as an enemy of the evils of urbanisation and capitalism, and protector of nature and the rural and pastoral. Incidentally, the history of modernist discourse reveals that the 'rural ideal' is itself a reactionary ideology born out of opposition to the newborn modern age, which creates as its subject a nostalgia for a non-existent past, a point of view that is nothing more than a by-product of the modern era. Consequently, Takamure's anti-modernism (anti-industrialisation and anti-urbanisation) is an ideal that, like maternalism, made its appearance in the second stage of modern feminism.

Within a structure of Orientalism in which the West represents the modern, this reactionary idealism towards the modern had a character extremely well suited to Japanese nationalism. In addition, Takamure's own attempts to skilfully use the emperor system discourse to legitimise her own position bore fruit in her voluminous work *Bokeisei no kenkyū* (A study of matriarchy) (1938, 1986).

In 1931, Takamure entered her legendary life of scholarship at the *Mori no Ie* (*House in the Woods*) in Setagaya, Tokyo, where it is said that she put up a notice saying 'Never leaving the house; refuse all visitors', and adopted a regime of ten hours study a day over a ten year period. A Takamure Itsue Support Group was formed with the intention of supporting Takamure's life centering on her research over this period. However, it is not the case that all the names on the membership list, which included Ichikawa Fusae and Hiratsuka Raichō, necessarily got along well with each other. Nishikawa Yūko suggests that the motivation for supporting Takamure among a group of the leading feminists was their fervent desire for theoretical legitimation of wartime collaboration. These women regarded Takamure as a theorist who could provide them with this. Takamure regarded the ancient family as a matriarchal family in which the husband joined his wife's household. She thereby challenged the pre-war patriarchal view of history. At the same time, however, in treating the ancient emperor system as the period when women's status was at its highest, she tied women's history to the imperial view of history, and through the logic of 'marital harmony' legitimated the ideals of the Greater East Asia Co-Prosperity Bloc (*Dai tōa kyōei ken*) (Kōno et al.,1979; Nishikawa Yūko, 1997; Kurihara, 1997; Ueno, 1996). This is why Takamure was able to publish *A Study of Matriarchy* during the wartime period and continue her serial essays in *Nihon Fujin* (Japanese women), the bulletin of the Greater Japan Women's Association, which embraced a membership of 20 million.

Takamure's statements praising the war have been carefully deleted from *The Collected Works of Takamure Itsue* published between 1966–1970 (Rironsha Publications). Judging by this, at the very least the editor, her husband Hashimoto Kenzō, considered Takamure's past a 'blemish'.[38] I would like to cite one section of a piece that appeared in the January, 1944 edition of *Japanese Women* entitled *Taoya-me* (Graceful, delicate ladies) but was not included in Takamure's *Collected Works*.

> The graceful, delicate ladies of this country make the family the centre of their existence, and have an unquenchable longing for the whole world to become one large family. Thus, as our holy war has been launched against that which obstructs this, it can be said most positively that this is a war for women. Women's unfaltering purpose should be to encourage our children, our husbands, our older brothers, our younger brothers, and never to yield. In this great war we are not taking a stand 'even though we are women' but 'precisely because we are women'. (Kōno et al., 1979:262).

There are many scholars studying Takamure, but few go back to and examine the primary sources that she used in her women's history. It would take a huge effort to verify the more than ten thousand ancient genealogical records that Takamure is said to have written out on cards in preparing the original text of works such as *Shinsenshōjiroku* (Newly Compiled Genealogical Records). Kurihara Hiroshi spent more than ten years himself doing this and, on the basis of case-studies of 500 families from the mid-Heian era that Takamure had made an object of study, claims that she 'falsified, and deliberately fabricated, historical documents' (Kurihara H., 1994). Kurihara's conclusion of Takamure's fictitious reporting of women's history caused shock waves among Takamure scholars. For all this, Kurihara has not simply criticised Takamure, but also offers us an understanding of the concealed intentions of Takamure's women's history that is sympathetic but intellectually sound. According to Kurihara, 'Takamure's ultimate motive' was to 'realise women's liberation within written history' and to 'dispel the gloom of Japanese women since the dawn of history' (Kurihara H., 1994:244).[39] As far as Takamure is concerned, if we take it that her women's history itself was an 'illocutionary speech act'[40] done for the purpose of the liberation of women then she continued – regardless of direction – to encourage women through her discursive practice even during the war.

Female Socialist or Socialist Feminist?
The Case of Yamakawa Kikue

I would like to touch upon another leading actor in the motherhood protection debate, the only socialist, Yamakawa Kikue (1890–1970). Whether pre-war socialists should be counted as feminists is itself a topic of debate. The *Bluestocking* group consciously used the term 'feminism', but among socialists their movement was dismissed as 'bourgeois feminism'. In the eyes of those taking a class perspective, the first wave feminism that was sweeping the world at that time was nothing more than another version of bourgeois liberalism, and there is no evidence that women in the socialist camp identified with it. If we distance ourselves from the self-definitions of the persons concerned, here again, in terms of world history the socialist women's liberation movement formed one current of feminism, but further study is needed to decide whether an individual woman activist was a *socialist feminist* or merely a *female socialist*.

Of course, what we call feminism varies depending on the perspective that we take. If I can offer a provisional definition here, for a movement to be feminist the following two conditions are necessary. First, it has to be an autonomous women's movement. Second, gender, or femininity defined in the given context, must be problematized. The first of these two conditions is necessary, but it is not the case that all movements where women are the torch-bearers are, simply for that reason, instances of feminism.[41] If we make a judgement on the basis of these two criteria, firstly the socialist movement, as a male-dominated movement, lacks the condition of being an autonomous women's movement. Secondly, the socialist camp does not recognise women's demands for independence and, moreover, dislikes it when women create an separate movement, calling it 'factionalism'. For socialists, women's liberation is dependent on the liberation of the working class, and is something that is expected to be accomplished automatically along with the socialist revolution. Consequently, women should join the class struggle in order to bring about working class liberation, and an independent fight by women is regarded not just as meaningless, but as a hindrance to working class solidarity. Furthermore, the women to be liberated are those who belong to the working class, and a feminist movement seeking to 'demonstrate the talents concealed within one's self' (Hiratsuka 1911; Horiba, 1991:18) can only be called a bourgeois diversion.

In the confrontation between Yosano and Hiratsuka in the motherhood protection debate Yamakawa came between the two, summing up her comparison of their theoretical stances with the words 'Yosano is the Japanese Mary Wollstonecraft...Hiratsuka is the Japanese Ellen Key (Yamakawa 1918; Kouchi, 1984:137). By the tender age of 28, Yamakawa had established a reputation for herself as a theorist. From her perspective as a socialist,'Yosano's social criticism started with the bourgeois and ended with it'(Yamakawa, 1918; Kouchi, 1984:136).Yet, Yamakawa concludes that, 'in the end Ellen Key is nothing more than an advocate of outdated social policies', which makes hers a'reactionary ideology...based on an exaggeration of sexual differences' (Yamakawa, 1918; Kouchi, 1984:118). A brilliant young theorist, Yamakawa, argued that women have both 'a right to work' and a 'right to a life (including a family life)' and maintained that both the value of women's paid and unpaid work should be properly evaluated. Yamakawa criticised Yosano and Hiratsuka on the following points:

> Along with refusing women the right to work, conventional society also denies them the right to a life. That being so, it was the conventional women's rights movement that emerged stressing the former by shouting for equal opportunities from start to finish and as a proposed amendment to this are the mother's rights campaigners who have risen up as advocates of the latter. The fault of the former is that in demanding all out for the right to work they forgot to demand the right to a life. While a shortcoming of the latter is that they did not advocate the right of all people equally to a life, but tamely limited their demands to mothers (Yamakawa, 1918; Kouchi, 1984:146).

Yamakawa's own policy solution was 'a higher, more thorough-going conclusion', namely 'taking an axe to the evil foundations of current economic relations' (Yamakawa, 1918; Kouchi, 1984:146). Given the times, only an ambiguous style of writing would have been permissible, but it would have been clear to everybody from the context that 'a change in contemporary economic relations' meant a socialist revolution.[42] In addition, Yamakawa believed that women's liberation was dependent on the liberation of the working class and would come about automatically when that was achieved.

Be that as it may, Yamakawa was the most aware of the unique demands specific to women among the socialists. In 1925, with the formation of the Communist Party, she requested the party headquarters insert a demand for equal rights for men and women into the manifesto. This comprised the following six items:

1 Abolish the patriarchal household system. Abolish all laws that enforce inequality between men and women.
2 Equal opportunities in education and employment.
3 Abolish the system of licensed prostitution.
4 Guarantee an equal minimum wage, regardless of sex or ethnicity.
5 Equal pay for equal work.
6 Protection of motherhood.[43]

According to Yamakawa's post-war memoirs, the deliberations of the Communist Party leadership resulted in the third proposal (to abolish the system of licensed prostitution) being left undecided; the leadership being split fifty-fifty. The 'remainder were rejected because they were regarded as anti-Marxist' (Yamakawa, 1979:66). On the basis of Yamakawa's own perceptions, 'these items were fundamental demands of the women's liberation movement; unexceptional, commonsense items, acknowledged world-wide and accepted without dissent by the Second and Third International and the International Labour Organisation (ILO); and opposition to them cannot have been anything other than conservative reactionism' (Yamakawa, 1996:66).

However, such was the character at that time of the male-dominated Communist Party. Nor did the female party members, as comrades, question this male control. Yamakawa reports that in response to her demands, 'the same reply came from the female executive officers'(Yamakawa, 1979:66). Should we then call the female party members 'socialist feminists' or simply 'female communists'?[44] At the very least, it is certain that the women did not attempt to overturn male domination in the Communist Party. On the contrary, within the outlawed movement, the women's role as 'housekeepers' ended up being exploited[45].

In the same year, 1925, the Universal Manhood Suffrage Law (*Danshi Futsū Senkyo Hō*) came into effect, but curiously women's suffrage was not specifically included in Yamakawa's six-point demand. She held a cynical view of the women's suffrage movement.

> There was such wariness of the granting of universal male suffrage...that it was feared that it would 'undermine the national polity'...Conservative forces considered the problem of women's suffrage to be something akin to a child wanting somebody else's toy, and it was not feared in the way that male suffrage had been...This was probably because, as a result of its baptism overseas, women's suffrage, unlike the extension of the male franchise, was not regarded as something unusual or likely to bring sudden change, but was seen rather as something that would have many benefits for the conservative forces. There were no politicians nervous enough to oppose it because they foresaw changes in the national polity.
>
> I was extremely fearful that the end result of simply wanting the right to vote without deciding the purpose of this or the kind of society that we wanted to create, would not be women's liberation but the use of women as weapons of the military-bureaucratic dictatorship. Because already at the time there were numerous government-controlled women's groups, such as the Young Girls Association (*Shojokai*) and the Women's Patriotic Association, and working-class women and women from farming communities were being mobilized in the same way and were under their influence...In the past, women's activists in the West have suggested that wars would be prevented if women had the vote, but history speaks clearly and most painfully of the fact that this alone will not prevent war (Yamakawa, 1979:73).

It has to be said that, even allowing for the fact that this was written after the war, Yamakawa's observations were penetrating.[46]

During the war, the socialist movement was made illegal and it was forced into silence. Yamakawa's husband, Hitoshi, a Communist Party leader, was also imprisoned. Yamakawa experienced all kinds of hardships. In order to support her husband in prison and make a living, she tried raising quails in the place she was evacuated to [during the height of the war]. Nevertheless, according to recent research by Beth Katzoff (1977), far from keeping silent, Yamakawa was a prolific writer during the war. Those around her did their best to ensure that she could earn money from her writings, works such as *Buke no josei* (Women from

Samurai Families) (1943), which she wrote at the request of Yanagita Kunio, and she derived most of her income from her writings.[47]

As the war situation deteriorated, the opportunistic tendencies in Yamawaka's work became stronger (Katzoff, 1997). Yamakawa had always backed women's labour participation and thought long and hard about the protection of women in the work place, but in her writing at least, she ceased to ask whether or not this labour was being used to pursue a war of aggression. For a brief period after the war, during the period that the socialists were in power under the Katayama Tetsu cabinet, Yamakawa was asked to serve as the first head of the Women and Minors Bureau within the Ministry of Labour. For Yamakawa, who took great pains over women's protection in the workplace, there was a consistency throughout her life in her aspirations.

The War Responsibility of Ordinary Women

Another outcome of the reflexive school of women's history has been the pursuit of the 'war responsibility' not only of the elite leadership class, but also of ordinary women. From works that dig into the history of ordinary women, such as Kanō Mikiyo's *Jūgo shi* (The history of the home front), it is clear that the female masses did not necessarily take a negative view of the war. Women's participation in the public sphere, made possible by war, was both exhilarating and brought with it a new identity for women, and this is remembered as a feeling of spiritual uplift.

Among women's historians, it was Murakami Nobuhiko (1978) who first pointed out the liberating aspect of the war, and Kanō also comments that 'women being on the "home front" was one form of women's liberation' (Kanō, 1987, 1995d:84). Kanō cited the section from Ichikawa Fusae's autobiography (*Jiden*) where she comments on the appearance of women at the gathering for the inauguration of the Women's Defence Association, who seemed both embarrassed and delighted', that 'for the female masses from agricultural and mountain villages who previously had no time of their own, just being able to leave the home for half a day and listen to a lecture was women's liberation' (Ichikawa, 1974; Kanō 1987; 1995d:84). According to Kanō, 'there were many women who as executive officers of the Women's Defence Association worked day after day forgetting food and sleep, and are [now] left with passionate memories in their minds of this period as 'the best days of our lives' (Kanō, 1987; 1995d:96).

In addition to this, we should not overlook the unearthing of documents concerning oral history practices such as life-histories and personal autobiographies conducted by the efforts of Local Women's History. Among memories reconstructed as the *recalled past* (the past reconstructed in the present), there are few examples of women who have an awareness of themselves as perpetrators. Even the personal accounts of returnees from Manchuria focus on their own hardships, with little awareness of themselves as invaders protected by military strength. Indeed, there was a tendency to disregard the rape of Chinese women or the sufferings of the comfort women on the grounds that 'we all suffered' or that 'these things were only to be expected given the times'.

In her valuable work listening to and recording the experiences of Japanese women who had gone as colonists to Korea, Tabata Kaya (1995) discovered that their recollected past of these Korean experiences was that of a privileged class, filled with nostalgia, and there was absolutely no interest among these women in questioning the injustices that brought about this privilege.

The feminist paradigm change, within which women emerged as subjects rather than objects of history, also brought about awareness that women are not simply the victims of war, but also active perpetrators in prosecuting it. Now, from what kind of perspective is the judgement of wrong doing made? Here, once again, we must confront the question, on what grounds and with regard to what should we reflect?

As we have seen, most feminists in some way or other welcomed the plan for the nationalisation of women through modern, total war. The same can be said of other women's activists, including Yamataka Shigeri, Yoshioka Yayoi and Oku Mumeo.

It should not be forgotten that for women's activists the nationalisation of women project was not in any way considered a reverse course or action, but was received as an *innovation*. Women received this new system that both demanded and made possible women's activity in the public sphere with excitement and something resembling a sense of mission.

In 1937, at the start of the Sino-Japanese War, Hiratsuka Akiko (Raichō), attending a meeting held by the magazine *Bungei Shunjū* under the title *Round Table Discussion on the Problem of Women during Wartime*,[48] made the following comments:

At any rate, I feel that there has been a massive change in the lives of women given that the female masses have been mobilized, that they are having to work for society and the state outside the home, and that husbands are having to accept their wives leaving the home to do this kind of work...In a variety of senses, I think that the habits that the ordinary housewife will form during these troubled days, and, in addition, the experience of cooperating in group projects can only leave behind a positive legacy. For example, they will come to understand the intimate relationship between the family and society/the state, and will be able to look at their own households through new eyes and will probably come to free themselves from their hitherto selfish focus on the home (Maruoka, 1976:647).

Here Hiratsuka treats society and the state as virtual synonyms.

In the course of the same roundtable discussion, Yamakawa Kikue had the following question put to her by the journalist who was chairing it: 'Is not the most remarkable thing about the ideological trend brought about by the [China] Incident...that the conflict between men and women has disappeared and women have begun to think about things from the standpoint of women as members of the nation?' Yamakawa replied that 'within the women's movement both these points are evident' and went on to point out that:

Ordinary women who until now lacked awareness are as a result of the Incident acting like mobilized persons for the first time...They have been mobilized as members of the state and in the process have been found to have a special function as women and are receiving new training relating to this (Maruoka, 1976:653).

During the roundtable discussion, the journalist in the Chair suggested that 'state compulsion' since the Incident 'appears to me to be in accordance with the movement for women's liberation'. In their replies to this, the women's activists were, if anything, unable to conceal their irritation at the incompleteness and half-heartedness of the reform of the government's women's policy. Hiratsuka argued that, 'the Central League for Spiritual Mobilisation should demand even greater participation from women and should work to mobilize all women's groups' (Maruoka, 1976:648).

As a way of promoting 'women's cooperation during the current situation', Ichikawa Fusae advocated a 'unification of women's organisations' that would overcome the opposition between the Women's Patriotic Association and the Women's Association for National Defence (*Kokubō Fujinkai*).[49] She then pointed to the lack of a 'women's section' in the Imperial Rule Assistance Association (*Taisei Yokusankai*) inaugurated the same year, making the following criticisms:

To us, the fact that the Assistance Association ignores women or puts them on the back burner is the result of the way in which women have always been thought about, the fact that they are devalued...As a result, I demand that...the Assistance Association quickly...establishes a women's section... I would like to offer the following warning, that if the authorities within the Imperial Rule Assistance Association...leave the old system as it is, without considering women, they will definitely not be able to establish a new system and the strong defence of the state will collapse at its foundations (Ichikawa, 1940; Suzuki, 1986:124–5).

When it came to the female draft, Ichikawa was more enthusiastic than the government. She made the following criticisms in response to incumbent Prime Minister Tōjō's statement that 'due to the fact that the female draft would cause the collapse of the Japanese family system we shall not institute it at the present time' made to the Diet [the Japanese Parliament] in October 1943:

I do not think there is any need to hold back if women's labour is indispensable to the state in order to increase productive capacity... When it comes to female labour, I would like the government itself to have a much clearer view of women's work...I am deeply vexed that, even having reached this current stage, the way that almost all men, at all levels of society from the government down, think about women has not advanced a single step from the feudal age (Ichikawa, 1943a:6; Suzuki, 1986:132–133.

Ichikawa's comrade in the women's suffrage movement, Yamataka Shigeri, took an even harder line. At the July 1943 assembly of the Imperial Rule Assistance Association's 4th Central Support Conference (*Chūō Kyōryoku Kaigi*) she stated: 'I would like to request that the draft of single women is carried out without hesitation'. She also stated her 'earnest desire' that 'the state show its might' and 'make the establishment of motherhood protection facilities in all factories compulsory' (Yamataka, 1943; Suzuki, 1986:154–7).

Ichikawa Fusae argued that 'the female draft is not at odds with the family system'. Rather, the compatibility of work and motherhood, and the establishment of a policy of motherhood protection in the workplace had been goals of the women's movement for a long time.[50]

At the very least, the general mobilisation system as seen through the eyes of women's activists was an innovation that solved at a stroke the obvious women's problems to date, including women's participation in the labour force and the protection of motherhood on the one hand, and women's public activities and the raising of women's legal and political status on the other. These women berated the authorities' lack of thoroughness and weak attitude, and made it their mission to 'compensate for the insufficiencies and inadequacies of the government's women's policy' (Suzuki, 1986:157).

'Conservatism in thought and innovation in action – isn't that what fascism was?' writes Kanō (Kanō, 1987; 1995). However, fascism was definitely not a conservative ideology. Even the ideology of the national polity (*Kokutai*) was not presented to the people as another name for a partially realised, incomplete state project. Deceived by the rhetorical flourish of ascribing tradition to the polity, subsequent generations of historians have called this *conservative* ideology.

The Dilemma of the Nation-State's Gender Strategy

At a time of total war, with its unprecedented and inflated expectations of the public sphere, there were two options for the reorganisation of gender. One was to aim at the nationalisation of the private sphere while maintaining the gender role assignment, and the other was to dismantle the gender role assignment itself. The former, we can refer to as the 'gender segregation model' (hereafter segregation model) and the latter, the 'integration model'. These two gender strategy options, perceived as two paths to women's liberation, have long been debated in feminist discourses as a confrontation over the question of 'equality versus difference'.

Japan, Germany and Italy, the fascist states of the Axis Alliance, all opted for the strategy of segregation. The Nazis publicly declared their partiality for 'manly men, and womanly women', and placed limits on the public activities of women. It is curious that in all three countries maternalism was very prominent and the rhetoric of 'different but equal' dominated the ideology of the women's liberation movement. Of course, a spectrum of ideas from segregation to integration can be seen everywhere in modern feminist ideology. However, from within this variation in the internal line of feminism we can see a process of adjustment in the liberationist rhetoric in an effort to conform, as it were, to the discourse of those in power.

In *Kindai Doitsu no boseishugi feminizumu* (Modern Germany's maternalist feminism)(1993), Himeoka Toshiko outlines the process by which the dominant strategy of integration during the Weimar Republic gave way to a separatist or segregationist model, in short, maternalism, under Nazism. This was a kind of survival strategy for feminism and, speaking from the perspective of activist tactics, it was a 'persuasion technique' that appealed to dominant cultural categories. The reason that I say that feminism is culture-bound is because feminism too has profoundly yielded its vocabulary to cultural categories.

Based on the gender strategy of segregation, what the state expected of women on the home front was that they would play the roles of 'reproductive soldiers' and of 'warriors in the economic war'. These were, to use technical terminology, the roles of 'reproducers' (procreation) and 'producers' (labour), in other words the promotion of fecundity and the mobilisation of labour. We can add to this the role of consumer, or put another way 'life-style reform' (the name for frugality and contribution). In the words of Kanō:

> Men to the front line overseas and women to the home front...In a situation of a total war that was also a war of aggression, norms concerning the existing gendered division of labour that made a distinction between the 'inside' (the home) and the 'outside' were, at a stroke, expanded to the whole of the state' (Kanō, 1987, 1995:67).

There are already a number of studies concerned with population control policies during the war (Nagahara, 1985; Kondō, 1995). The Mother Child Protection Law (*Boshi Hogo Hō*) came into effect in 1938 after the China Incident. In the same year, the Ministry of Welfare was established in order to plan population policy and bring about an improvement in the physique of the nation. In 1940 the National Eugenics Law (*Kokumin Yūsei Hō*) was passed and along with this, Eugenics Marriage Counselling Centres were established in every area. In November of the same year, the Ministry of Health and Welfare held the first round of awards for Excellent Families with Many Children (ten or more). In 1941, just before the outbreak of war between Japan and the United States, the Outline for the Establishment of a Policy on Population (*Jinkō Seisaku Kakuritsu Yōkō*) was approved by the cabinet. This proposed that a population of 73 million in 1940 should 'increase by approximately 27 million over the next twenty years, reaching 100 million by 1960'[51] (Kondō, 1995:492).

Among the measures recommended to bring about population growth were an increase in births, encouragement of marriage, support for a wholesome family system, the fostering of motherhood, a ban on contraception and abortion, and the eradication of venereal disease.[52]

Ichikawa Fusae welcomed the government's Outline for the Establishment of a Policy on Population in the following terms:

> Through this piece of national policy women have reached the point at which, for the first time, their status as the mothers of the Japanese race is recognised, and their consciousness and cooperation are sought by the state...The fact that giving birth and bringing up children are treated [in this plan] not as a private matter of concern to the mother alone or to the family, but as a public matter of concern to the state and the nation, brings the greatest pride and joy to those who are able to give birth (Ichikawa, 1943b; Suzuki 1986:128).

It has also been pointed out that population policy was never a matter solely of managing the quantity of the population but also concerned itself with quality, and that behind the policy of increasing the population lay a eugenics policy. It has also been pointed out that eugenic ideas circulated among Japanese feminist thinkers concerned with principles of selection for motherhood: who was qualified for motherhood and who was not? (Furukubo, 1991; Suzuki, 1989b). Furukubo Sakura uses the following statement by Hiratsuka to point out her 'intimacy with eugenics':

> The new task of motherhood is a matter not simply of bearing and raising children, but of bearing sound children and raising them well. In other words, the great mission towards humankind that women who eternally pass on that most holy flame, life, are charged with is to contribute to, above and beyond the mere preservation and continuation of the human race, its evolution and improvement. (Hiratsuka 1920: 165; Furukubo, 1991:78).

In *Hinin no kahi o ronzu* (On the rights and wrongs of contraception), Hiratsuka takes her argument a step further:

> From a eugenic point of view, it is desirable that in this country too, and as soon as possible, certain individuals should be forbidden by law to marry and a sterilisation law should be put into force. (Hiratuska, 1917; Furukubo 1991:78).

If we consider the context, there is no doubt that Hiratsuka was aware of the Nazi sterilisation laws. For many years she had been petitioning for a law circumscribing the marriage of men with venereal disease, and had also been advocating that men and women about to marry should be tested for sexually transmitted diseases. Hiratsuka was concerned that syphilis would be transmitted from husband to wife, and that children would be born with congenital syphilis. She believed that a man with a sexually transmitted disease (regarded as evidence of relations with a prostitute) was not qualified to become a father. Hiratsuka welcomed control of reproduction by the state.

Women's activists like Yamataka Shigeri and Oku Mumeo enthusiastically involved themselves with 'life-style improvement' campaigns for housewives. For some time these women had been involved with campaigns summed up in such slogans as 'simplification of rite-of-passage ceremonies', 'elimination of waste and frugality', and 'rationalisation of life-style'. These ideas were passed on unchanged to the post-war Housewives' Federation (*Shufu Rengōkai*) and to consumer movements. After the war, Oku Mumeo was appointed Chairperson of the Housewives' Federation, and in this respect there was no discontinuity for her between the wartime and the post-war period. Narita Ryūichi (1995) has shown, through an analysis of Oku Mumeo's autobiography, that she carried out her mission and demonstrated her capacity as a women's activist mobilising the masses with complete consistency both during and after the war. There is not the slightest indication of a 'conversion'.

Women's roles as reproducers and consumers fall within the framework, in everyday terms, of 'wife' and 'mother'. What Wakakuwa calls the 'nationalisation of the family' (Wakakuwa, 1995) can also be said to be state control of the roles of wife and mother.

Incidentally, there is a blind spot in the population policy that is euphemistically referred to as 'the family system'. In addition to raising the marriage rate and the rate of childbirth within marriage to increase the population, there is also the option of increasing the incidence of childbirth outside marriage, or extramarital childbearing. Here, the state is faced with the final choice of whether it should, ultimately, dismantle the private sphere of the family.

In the final stages of the Second World War, Nazi concern that women of the 'Aryan race' were having difficulty in finding husbands (because of a gender imbalance among men and women of marriageable age), led them to propose 'the encouragement of single motherhood' in order to increase the population. This included 'encouragement of illicit relations' between members of Nazi elites, such as the SS, and unmarried women. However, this proposal was cold-shouldered by conservative women's groups, who rallied to the chorus of 'defend marriage and the family', and was inevitably withdrawn (Yonemoto, 1989; Koonz, 1987, 1990). The Nazis built 'death factories' to exterminate 'inferior races', but their eugenic ideology, as a logical corollary, made it possible to imagine 'reproduction factories' employing birth quality control (QC).[53]

Although it was not openly discussed, another aspect of the defence of the home front was the control of wives' chastity. One of the duties prescribed for the Women's Association for National Defence was to support the 'childbirth soldiers' left alone at home and to care for the families of soldiers who had been wounded or killed at the front with the same level of concern as if they were their own mothers and sisters. Kanō does not forget to point out that one part of these duties was the role of preserving the 'morals of Japanese women which are second to none in the world' and of giving 'protective guidance' to ensure that the 'problem of loose conduct' did not arise:

In 1938, as a result of a request from the military, the Kobe Women's Association for National Defence issued a directive to all its chapters concerning 'protective guidance' to the families of soldiers who had been killed and, more particularly, the wives of soldiers serving at the front. This directive ordered them to implement, under a cloak of secrecy, effective and appropriate measures to ensure that the moral conduct of the wives of soldiers in the Imperial Army should not give rise to the slightest suspicion. As a result, in Hyogo prefecture a Wives of Heroes Society (*Yūshi tsuma no kai*) and Mothers on the Home Front Society (*Jūgo haha no kai*) were inaugurated. These bodies gave 'protective guidance' to the young wives of soldiers at the front, or assigned officials to individual wives of soldiers away on active service with instructions to establish close relationships with them and keep a watch on them, so as to ensure that their chastity was not compromised. It is recorded with pride in the History of the Head-quarters of the Kobe District of the Greater Japan Women's Association for National Defence (*Dai-Nippon Kokubō Fujin Kai Kōbe Chihō Honbu Shi*) that as the real aim was kept totally secret from the wives, 'there was nothing to trigger

any kind of negative reaction, and the successful prevention of the
problem of lewd conduct that we had been concerned about was an
accomplishment beyond measure' (Kanō, 1987; 1995d:73).

The sacredness of Japanese women as wives and mothers had to be
maintained using any and every method available. Calling the
population policy 'protection of the family system' had already
gone beyond mere euphemism. This was because the family itself
was the stronghold where the masculinity of the soldiers of the
Imperial Army was defined. In its shadow were the military comfort women who were forced to carry the burden of 'whorishness'
as opposed to motherhood, the dark side of the sexual double
standard.

The Paradox of this Gender Strategy

Under the total mobilisation system, the strategy of gender segregation began to show cracks. It was fine while the role of the 'warriors in the economic war' was limited to consumer activities within the household, but once women's labour was demanded in the domain of production (due to a shortage of male labour) a conflict between this and motherhood emerged. Women's policy under the total mobilisation system showed plainly the difficulties of this gender strategy. For example, in order to encourage early marriage and childbearing the Outline for the Establishment of a Policy on Population adopted a policy of placing considerable restrictions on the employment of women workers aged 20 and over, while at the same time took measures to relax or improve employment or working conditions likely to be an obstacle to marriage. Again, as already indicated, women leaders such as Yamataka were critical of the indecision shown by the government over drafting women, and urged it to institute a female draft without hesitation. Even in Yamataka's case, however, the target for the draft was to be limited to unmarried women to ensure that it was not incompatible with population policy. Social history research, concerned with women's labour during wartime, tells us that even the severe shortage of labour did not lead to a dismantling of the system of gender segregation in the labour market. Between 1930 and 1945 the female workforce increased fivefold, but the increase in married women in the labour force was not as great and the scope of women's work was limited. Even under the total mobilisation system, gender segregation was maintained. The integrationist ideal that promoted the female draft was fitted within the gender strategy of segregation. This was because those who promoted the integrationist ideal were, at the same time, wedded to the belief that women's productive labour should not conflict with motherhood. At the same time, those promoting the gender strategy of segregation were least likely to take the plunge when it came to the issue of the female draft. Women's participation in combat would have dismantled crucial gender boundaries that served to define the national subject and, as a result, would have undermined the self-definition of soldiers as masculine.

I indicated that the allied nations of Britain and the United States followed an integrationist gender strategy that was accompanied by female enlistment. However, overemphasising the differences between the segregationist and integrationist gender strategies may invite misunderstanding. The difference between these two strategies is only one of degree. They are rooted in the same configuration of gender within the nation-state. In both Britain and the United States, female service personnel were an exceptional minority and their role was limited to rearguard support.[54]

Even in the campaign urging women to engage in productive labour, the issue throughout was how to avoid damaging women's femininity while they participated in the labour force. Anna Davin, a British writer on women's history, describes persuasively in her classic work *Imperialism and Motherhood* how motherhood emerged as a keyword during the period of imperialist aggression in Britain and other imperialist nations right through to the 19th century.[55]

Among the Allied countries, France is renowned for its pronatalist policy of openly encouraging childbearing. The population policies of the fascist states came to be treated as taboo after defeat. Nevertheless, in France, which was on the winning side, wartime population policies continued into the post-war period. As a matter of fact, defeat in the war against Germany was put down to defeat in the population war. A policy of promoting population growth was adopted immediately after the war, and has continued to this day. It is also noteworthy that the decrease in the birth rate that has affected all the advanced industrialized countries occurred first and progressed more rapidly in France than in other country. In Germany, too, the birth rate had started to decline even during the Nazi period and Nazi population policy achieved no great results despite all the rhetoric.

In this sense, an integrationist gender strategy that included the drafting of women as combat personnel, a move that would ultimately dismantle the gender boundaries of the nation-state, was not adopted in any nation-state, and neither was it advocated even by proponents of women's liberation. The ultimate goal of 'one-nation gender equality' (*ikkoku danjo byōdō*) premised on the existence of the nation-state,[56] has to be equality between men and women in the military. Yet, when the Equal Rights Amendment (ERA) was in the process of being debated in the United States in the 1970s, those opposed to it mounted a pernicious campaign to prevent the passing of the ERA, suggesting that if men and women were equal, then women would also have to shoulder the burden of military service. At the time, a young soldier just about to be despatched to the frontline in Vietnam was asked in a television interview how he would feel if the fellow-soldier standing next to him was a woman. His answer revealed his dilemma:

> We've been taught that we're fighting to protect our wives and sweethearts at home, but if the wives and sweethearts we were protecting turned up on the front line I wouldn't know what we were fighting for (Ueno, 1991).

Without a doubt, the success of the anti-ERA campaign was that it attacked the secret yet decisive alliance between 'the nation' and 'masculinity'.

At the end of the Vietnam War in 1973, conscription was abolished in the United States and participation in the armed forces became voluntary. Along with this, the number of female service personnel increased and their participation in combat emerged as an issue. Eventually, at the time of the Gulf War in 1991, (a war the majority of American citizens enthusiastically supported as 'good war' fought to check Saddam Hussein's 'madness') the National Organisation for Women (NOW), the largest women's organisation in the country, sought the removal of the ban on women's participation in combat in the name of equality. Yet, should we view this as women's liberation or as the ultimate nationalisation of women?

Women and the Issue of Conversion

In emphasising the historical agency of feminists, the reflexive school of women's history also emphasizes that the wartime support of these women, whether active or passive, was based on 'free will'. As a result, the question that presents itself is; did these women in fact undergo a 'conversion'?

Here the word conversion incorporates two meanings. The first is a conversion from the principles of first wave feminism to supporting the goals of the war. The second is the conversion from supporting the war to promoting post-war peace and democracy.

Scholars of the reflexive school of women's history deny the first conversion. Here, war support was not something forced upon feminists. What, then, about the second conversion? It is pointed out that Ichikawa, Hiratsuka and Takamure were all quick to adapt to changing circumstances after the war. For these women, it was as though the statements they had made during the war had never been and there is no sense of reflection or discontinuity.

After defeat, Ichikawa wasted no time in resuming her suffragist activities. Indeed, she welcomed female suffrage brought about by the occupation authorities. For a period after the war, Ichikawa was purged from public office by the occupation forces, but after a comeback she stood successfully in the elections for the House of Councillors (*Sangiin*).[57] Ichikawa's support of and cooperation in the war was evident to everybody. It was regarded as a blemish on her career, but that too has been legitimised as an unavoidable choice made to protect the women's suffrage movement. Until the close of her long life in 1981 at the age of 87, Ichikawa, as a female Diet member who served five terms over a period of 25 years, filled the role of the figure who symbolized post-war women's liberation. It can be said that only with her death did any real criticism of her become possible.[58]

Suzuki Yūko cites the following from Ichikawa's post-war recollections:

Since I was a national subject living under the conditions of that time, although I wouldn't go as far as saying that it was only natural, I don't feel any sense of shame. I wonder if I am wrong? (Ichikawa, 1979; Suzuki, 1989b:103).

In her quotation of this section, Suzuki underlines the words 'Seeing that I was a national subject', and indicates that this 'is a key point when we consider the issue of her nationalism based on the emperor system' (Suzuki, 1989b:65). The conclusion that arises from this is that Ichikawa did not go through a conversion after the war, and consequently did not reflect on what she had done either, which serves to convict her still further.

Hiratsuka also participated enthusiastically in peace campaigning after the war. When there was a resumption of nuclear arms testing after the war, along with Yukawa Hideki, a Nobel Physics Prize winner, and Shimonaka Yasaburō, she became a member of the Seven-Person Committee Appealing for World Peace (*Sekai Heiwa Apīru Shichinin Iinkai*), and sent a protest letter to the President of the United States. She also became a director of the World Federation Establishment Alliance (*Sekai Renpō Kensetsu Dōmei*) and acted as a leader in the post-war peace movement. To Hiratsuka, the ideal of pacifism, linked to the conquest of overcoming the egoism of the human race, was something that she had adhered to consistently from the beginning. She felt that the conviction that she had held all along had only deepened post-war, and it cannot be said that she was conscious of a need to convert.[59]

In the case of ultra-nationalist Takamure Itsue, it appears rather difficult to defend her defection. Takamure wrote the following in her diary on the day after hearing the imperial declaration of surrender:

I felt a deep pain that cut right through to my heart and all I could do was weep and moan. Prostrating myself, all I could do was weep and moan. At night I slept fitfully, and could only weep and moan. In the morning too, all I could do was weep. For a long time my tears did not cease. Tears of profound suffering. Tears of grief. What did this pain mean? We still had not found words to express our feelings. Yet, we suffered. The pain went on and on (cited in Kano and Horiba, 1977).

After this, Takamure showed herself quick to adapt to the changed circumstances in a manner that can only be called opportunist. She revised sections of *Dai-Nippon Joseishi* (The history of the women of greater Japan) that had been serialised in the magazine *Nihon Fujin* (Japanese women) during the war to remove the emperor-centred nationalistic view of history. This was published it in 1948, at the same time as the classic cannon of women's history, Inoue Kiyoshi's *Nihon Joseishi* (The history of Japanese women).[60]

Kanō Mikiyo, who criticised Takamure for being 'the state shamaness', comments that, along with the 'high priest' Emperor's renunciation of his divine status, Itsue the 'child of god' was reborn as Itsue the 'human child':

> It is difficult to say that Takamure's comeback as the 'human child' was fair play. Just as in the case of the Emperor's renunciation of his divine status...(Kanō, 1979:175).

Should we call this Takamure's 'conversion'? According to Nishikawa Yūko, Takamure's position of 'being with the female masses' was at least consistent. In that sense, it is perhaps fair to say that Takamure was opportunistic to the same degree as the 'female masses', and that she underwent a 'conversion' to the same degree. However if, as Kurihara Hiroshi (1997) suggests, Takamure achieved the liberation of women within her historical writing, her position as an independent scholar of women's history was consistent and in this sense there was no conversion.[61]

Incidentally, the perspective that raises the issue of conversion, rooted as it is in the continuity school of history, reveals a strange twist. If there was continuity in the modernisation project between pre- and post-war, why was it necessary for a conversion to take place? From the viewpoint of the continuity school, it would be correct to say that there was no conversion. Now what does the reflexive school of women's history rescue from a re-reading of the texts? Just as we would expect, they find the consistency and agency of pre-war feminists thinkers.

Accepting that this is the case, just who was it that made a mistake? To condemn women's support for the war as a mistake, two conditions are necessary. It is necessary, first, to judge the war itself a mistake and, second, as a consequence of this, to point out the ignorance and historical limitations that prevented these women from seeing that the war was a mistake. A perspective that points to this variety of mistake must always be both retrospective and transcendental. For example, Suzuki criticises Ichikawa for the limitation of not foreseeing the trap of nationalisation, and Hiratsuka for the ignorance of idealising the Emperor. This is an absolutist viewpoint in which nationalisation and the emperor system are judged wrong in their aftermath, in other words, this is given as a post-war perspective.

Suzuki is included in among the 'post-war faction whose departure point is the self-evident premise that the fifteen-year war was equal to an aggressive war, which in turn equals a bad war' (Kanō, 1987; 1995:166). But here again, the self-evident nature of this premise is something formed by history[62]. As the limits of the state and the evil of the emperor system have only been pronounced retrospectively, is it not unfair, as a historian, to convict an individual living in the midst of it for not being able to overcome historical limitations? The reason why Suzuki's women's history (while recognised as having raised many excellent questions and as making an important contribution to women's history) is often called the prosecution school of history, is simply that it adopts these transcendental standards of judgement resting on this 'vacuum zone' of history.

Ideas Capable of Transcending the 'State'

In his essay about the war generation *Wadatsumi sedai*, Yasukawa Junosuke raised the question 'what footholds would have made it possible for anyone to get through the period?' His answer was that to 'live through the period without being swept away by the times, fate or conditions, demands that one holds a particularly dependable tenet or principle' (Yasakawa, 1996:104).

By offering examples of individuals living in the same era who did not make the mistake of supporting the war, Suzuki emphasizes the 'responsibility' of those who made a mistake that might have been avoided. As examples, she includes communist, anarchist, Christian and pacifist women. Just what were the grounds upon which these women were able transcend the state?

Communist women were able to transcend the nation-state by relying on the internationalism of the Comintern,[63] but their idealism was betrayed by the actual socialist state. The state egoism of the Soviet Union under the rule of Stalin meant that internationalism was hastily cast off for national interests, and the state did not even decline to enter a non-aggression pact with Nazi Germany. And this was not all. Communist women were prevented by their prioritising of the class struggle above all else from problematising the oppression they themselves experienced as women. These women may have transcended the nation-state, but they were not able to transcend gender. This was due, moreover, to their loyalty to a socialist internationalism that had been tailored by men.

What about religion? It is a well-known fact that not only Japanese Buddhist groups but other religious groups, including Christian ones, became involved in the imperial rule assistance system.

Claudia Koonz offers the example of the resistance of Christian women's groups under Nazism (Koonz, 1987). What is extremely interesting is that she points out that Protestants, who emphasize internal ethics, were easily caught up in Nazism, while Catholic women demonstrated greater powers of resistance to it. Now, what was it that Catholic women had that enabled them to transcend the National Socialist regime? It was simply the fact that another source of authority, a 'state within a state', the Vatican, existed as a concrete presence. Ought we not applaud the historical irony that this obedience to another authority, an authority that was itself extremely discriminatory towards women, was in the end what enabled these women to resist Nazism, which had been declared evil.

Suzuki introduces the example of Hasegawa Teru who could be called a traitor for carrying through her anti-war intentions. As an Esperantist, Hasegawa took an absolute anti-war position. She went to China and turned on her own homeland, taking charge of anti-war broadcasting aimed at Japan. Since hers has been acknowledged as an inspiring career, there are two questions that I cannot repress asking. Firstly, was Hasegawa against all wars without making a distinction between good and bad ones? This is closely tied in with the question of whether an imperialist war of aggression is automatically bad, while a war fought for national liberation (or to support it) is good. This is in turn tied in with the confrontation between 'good nukes' and 'bad nukes' that divided the post-war anti-nuclear campaign. Secondly, what if the broadcasts to Japan that Hasegawa was engaged in had not been for China, but from another country? What about the case of Okada Yoshiko, who was similarly engaged in broadcasting work targeting Japan, but this time from Moscow? Okada's cooperation is regarded as having been forced. But while Okada, who cooperated with Stalin's regime, a regime already judged to be bad, is said to have been used, Hasegawa, who assisted the Chinese people in their fight against Japan, in other words in a 'just war', is regarded as a hero.

What about anarchists like Kaneko Fumiko and Itō Noe who were killed by the authorities? It is hard to guess what these women would have done had they not died before the Sino-Japanese war began. If the task of examining the pasts of feminists closely were carried out painstakingly, it is most likely that the majority of feminist leaders would fall from their seats of honour and the only ones left at the end would be those who had the good fortune to die before the war, thus leaving their reputations unsullied.

It was not only women, but also ethnic minorities and down-trodden groups who were dragged into the nationalisation project of total mobilisation. Kim Chonmi has fully exposed the process by which, in Japan, the National Levellers' Society (*Zenkoku Suiheisha*), the forerunner of the Buraku Liberation League (*Buraku Kaihō Dōmei*), and its leader Matsumoto Jiichirō enthusiastically supported the nationalisation project and cooperated with the war of aggression (Kim, 1994). Tomiyama Ichirō asked the same question in relation to Okinawa, delving into the trap that caught the people of Okinawa; their expectation of nationalisation leading them to fight in the battle of Okinawa (Tomiyama, 1990).

It is widely known that even in the United States, the victor nation, black and ethnic-Asian soldiers welcomed 'equality within the military' and enthusiastically went to the front. The nationalisation project created Anderson's (1985) 'imagined community', and certainly in the course of historicising this it is a difficult task for anyone to criticise this from a transcendental, extra-historical perspective.

A Critique of the Reflexive School of Women's History

Total war required the nationalisation of women (*josei no kokuminka*) and so advanced the process. As we have already seen, many women's activists welcomed this new regime, and indeed energetically promoted it. Study of modern total war demonstrates that irrespective of whether we look at the situation in the countries of the Allied Powers or those of the Axis Alliance the 'nationalisation of women' was similarly advanced. There must have been female leaders in the victor countries of the United States and Britain – Wakakuwa Midori calls them 'war cheerleaders' – but as theirs was an anti-fascist war for 'freedom and democracy', does that mean that the nationalisation of women in this 'legitimate' cause is excusable?

When the reflexive school of women's history raises the question of the perpetrator responsibility of women, just what is it *reflecting* on? Just by asking what the scope of the object of reflection is, we also ask whether the reflexive school of women's history can transcend the boundaries of national history. This question brings with it three secondary areas of inquiry.

Firstly, when the reflexive school of women's history raises the question of what war responsibility women bear because of their support for 'that war of aggression', does this mean that the object of its reflection extends to war in general? While war is the largest project that a nation-state undertakes and modern wars share the characteristic of being total wars that demand total mobilisation of all citizens of all classes, is it the case that the same act of war support requires women who belong to fascist states to reflect, while there is no such necessity for women who are citizens of the Allied Powers? If this is the case, it means that wars can be divided into good wars and bad wars, and the culpability of Japanese women lies in the fact that they did not have the foresight to realise that they were supporting a bad war. When it comes to distinguishing between good and bad wars, how is this to be done, if not after the event?

Secondly, is it the case that the reflexive school of women's history supports the nationalisation of women, but rejects war as an undertaking of the nation state? This way of thinking fits well with the one-nation pacifism embodied in Article Nine of the Japanese Constitution, which declares that the Japanese people do not recognise the right of belligerency of the state and forever renounce the threat or use of force as a means of settling international disputes. At the same time, it brings in its wake all the limitations that accompany one-nation pacifism. For all that, how are we to evaluate the fact that the modern nation-state was established on the basis of the disarming of its citizens and the monopolisation of violence by the state?

In the modern era, the nation-state is the sole legal entity for which the use of violence has been legalised. Furthermore, how should we view the fact that military service is the basis of citizenship? In contrast, if the nationalisation of women is to be the object of criticism regardless of the circumstances, then the question that arises is, on what basis can or indeed must women transcend the state? Does the perpetrator historical viewpoint of the reflexive school of women's history include this question within its range of fire?

Thirdly, while there are versions of the nationalisation of women between the integration and segregation models (whether as a result of historical accident or historical necessity, the countries of the Allied Powers correspond to the integration model and those of the Axis Alliance to the segregation model), can it be said that the segregation model is more oppressive for women and the integration model more liberating? In addition, is it possible to criticise the women of the fascist states who, having accepted the gender boundaries of the segregation model, meekly accepted cooperation with the system in the role of second-class citizens, as backward beings who submitted to the patriarchal state?[64] However, the integration model strategy of gender equality leads to female soldiers as the inexorable conclusion of the nationalisation of women. Moreover, it cannot even be said that the achievement of the kind of gender equality aimed at by integrationists would necessarily be liberating for women. This is because the model of a human being is based on a male standard and as such women's reproductive function can only be a handicap. While the segregation model confines women to a female domain, the integration model forces women to deny their own femaleness. What is more, even if the integration model is fully realised, women end up being treated as a second-class fighting force. In the Gulf War, American service women made the nightmare scenario of soldiers getting pregnant and giving birth and soldiers going on maternity leave come true before our eyes. Besides this, we can also expect to see female prisoners of war subjected to sexual degradation to 'humiliate the bitches'.

The differences between the integration and segregation models reflect the dilemma of the modern age's designation of an allotted domain for women, yet we can say that both are versions of the nationalisation of women. In the Soviet Bloc countries, which in a sense maintained in peacetime the state-regulated economy of the war years, the integration model was realised in terms of women's labour. The capitalist economies of the Allied countries, on the other hand, returned to the segregation model in peacetime. If we look at the position of women in the communist countries we see that there is no guarantee that the integration model is more liberating than the segregation model. The generous maternal protection policies of the communist countries were implemented with the aim of relieving women of the additional burdens of maternity by having the state shoulder them but, if anything, they preserved traditional ways of thinking concerning the family and gender roles. It should be noted that the socialisation of childcare was originally a labour policy aimed at mobilising women's labour, and was not established as a part of some generous policy on gender equality and even less as a child welfare policy aimed at securing children's right to be cared for (Ueno, Tanaka, and Mae 1994).

As it happens, the problem of the nationalisation of women carries within itself the possibility of its own solution. Just as the emperor system was relativised as a target to be overthrown by the very fact that the term *emperor system* established it as a thesis, so too the term *nationalisation of women* highlights at a stroke the ludicrous inconsistency of the categories *nation* and *women*. Firstly, from the very beginning the nation was defined, through the exclusion of women, in masculine terms. Secondly, women were only later discovered as a single community through the category *gender*. To rephrase this, both 'nation' and 'women' were denaturalised as a result of the deconstruction of these categories. Furthermore, what the paradigm nationalisation of women, obtained by gendering the nation made clear was, firstly, the all too obvious fact that women were not citizens and, secondly, the acuteness of the dilemma that the state faced in order for the nationalisation of women to occur; should gender boundaries be maintained or transcended?

Post-colonial analysis has persistently exposed the way in which a category, by creating an imagined community, in turn becomes something oppressive. In this sense the category 'women' is no exception. Oppression inevitably surfaces because each category involves an exclusiveness; if you are not this, you are that. Now the category *nation* is nothing more than one type of exclusive category. War makes this exclusiveness even more visible. The nation demands that one belong exclusively to just one state. People with dual nationality or indeterminate beings who are neither enemy nor ally, are not recognised. The post-colonialist's response to this is not to reject categories, but to multiply them; let's have more categories! Only a multiplication of categories to match the complexity of the individual can check the absorption of an individual into the community of a single category. The reason why the nation is oppressive is that it demands an exclusive jurisdiction that recognises no higher category. Setting up another transcendental category in order to overcome this would mean that even if individuals fled from the state they would be gathered up into another community. The lesson learned from the tumultuous international history of the 1980s was that the state has lost its transcendency, and that the state does not have a transcendency sufficient to 'lay down ones life' for it. In other words, the state had been relativised.

Going Beyond the 'Nationalisation of Women' Paradigm

Having considered the above, it is possible to place the various versions of the nationalisation of women in a more general frame.

There are two strategies for the nationalisation of women, that of gender segregation (the segregation model) and that of disregarding gender (the integration model). As a dilemma of 'difference versus equality', these two roads have been all too familiar to feminism since the beginning. If we go along with gender segregation we must adhere to norms of femininity, but as the converse of this we are able to acquire an autonomous domain inside a women's ghetto. At first sight, equality appears to be achieved by the strategy of disregarding gender. However, for as long as the public sphere is defined in terms of masculinity, women who become producers or soldiers have to resign themselves to being second-class workers or soldiers. Otherwise, all that awaits them is a choice between denying their femaleness and seeking to become male clones. This means taking on a double burden and doing their best to maintain their womanly role while being reduced to an auxiliary labour force. Both paths are all too familiar traps within modern feminism.

This dilemma persists today as an unresolved problem. On the one hand, military base prostitution, Peace Keeping Forces (PKF) prostitution, and rape in wartime are as much problems now as ever. While on the other, feminists are calling for debate concerning the problem of female soldiers participating as combatants in the Gulf War.

When I posed the question, can feminism transcend the state?, I came face-to-face with a much simpler and more fundamental question: Why *must* feminism transcend the state? Although I think that feminism must and can transcend the state, the reasons for this have only now become clear to me. Feminist analysis of the nation-state has made clear that gender equality is impossible in principle within a framework of modernity, patriarchy and the nation-state.

Ehara Yumiko, a contemporary feminist theorist, has pointed out that among the complex questions that surround feminism and modernity the opposition between 'equality' and 'difference' is a 'false problem' forced on women by modernity itself (Ehara, 1988).

The post-structuralist gender historian Joan Scott, looking back at the history of French feminism in her book *Only Paradoxes to Offer* (Scott, 1996), questions the fact that the individual born of modernity was gendered. The fact that the individual was created in the mould of man has lead women to face the dilemma of equality versus difference. Yet, whichever one they choose, it is a trap for women. Feminism is nothing more than modernity's demon child, there simply to embody this paradox. Scott's intention is precisely to deconstruct the fact that modernity has forced upon women a false problem.

The modernisation project was itself the cause of the rise of the 'woman question', and feminism demonstrates that within this historical analysis there can be no solution to the woman question within the framework of the modern. In this sense, while feminism is a product of modernity, it has in its sights the possibility of being able to transcend the modern. What feminist analysis of the nationalisation of women has shown is the fact that feminist studies, which began with the private sphere, has ultimately extended itself to an examination of the state and the public sphere. As a result, the state and the public sphere have been deprived of their outward appearance of gender neutrality. Having pursued research into the nationalisation of women I can say that the nation-state is gendered. The nationalisation of women embodies the paradox that was imposed on women by the modern nation-state, and the total mobilisation system, in displaying this paradox in an extremely grotesque form, proved conversely that women's liberation was impossible within the framework of the modern nation-state. As a result, we can point to the basis for women to transcend the state.

Nevertheless, is it not possible to say that the reverse is true? That the category 'women' is itself the creation of modernity, just as civil society and the nation-state? The nationalisation of women, their participation as women in the nation-state, whether in accordance with the segregation or the integration model, means nothing other than women share a common fate with the nation-state while still burdened with the paradox that 'woman' does not equal 'citizen'. For men who equal citizens, this situation is probably a trap that is even harder to escape.

Dismantling the category *women* is the same thing as dismantling the category *men* as a gender category. If feminism is a product of modernity then the end of the modern should also bring an end to feminism. Yet, feminism was the demon child that was paradoxically born out of the innate contradiction of the modern period. The discovery by feminism of the gender category had the dismantling of this as its ultimate end.

Part II
The Military Comfort Women Issue

A Triple Crime

Back in the 1990s, there was no more fundamental line of inquiry challenging us in the debate concerning nationalism and gender than that of the military comfort women issue[1]. This same issue has forced upon us fundamental questions regarding historical methodology in the construction of public memory.

The conclusive problematising of the military comfort women within Japan occurred in December 1991 when Kim Hak-sun[2] and two other former Korean comfort women filed suits against the Japanese government at the Tokyo District Court demanding a formal apology and individual compensation. Even though the fact of the military comfort women was on occasion raised as an issue after the war, this never went beyond regarding the women as wretched or pitiful, and was naturalised as the kind of cruelty or 'going too far' that accompanies war, or even as a sacrifice to male lust (Senda, 1973; Kim I., 1976; Yoshida, 1977). The courageous testimony of these three female victims contained the power to shift in a single stroke the paradigm surrounding the military comfort women. From the immediate period after surrender through to the present day, military pensions, annuities for bereaved families and wartime postal savings have all emerged as issues in the debate surrounding the post-war compensation of nationals from former colonies, yet the military comfort women have never emerged as targets for compensation, and the historical fact that it took half a century for their suffering to be problematised is shocking.

The historical fact of the comfort women was known. Moreover, without the slightest hint of any sense of shame concerning their experiences, many soldiers left behind written testimony in diaries and memoirs. Nevertheless, the comfort women system was not problematised as a crime by anybody until very recently. The facts were there, but they were indiscernible. In short, as far as history was concerned it was as though they did not exist. There are as many as 30,000 war diaries and memoirs, some official and others unofficial, of former soldiers collected in The National Diet

Library, including some that were published privately. At last a re-reading of these is taking place.

The ramifications of criminalizing the military comfort women system go well beyond a redefinition of the past. In reply to those who ask, why after half a century has passed should we talk about this now?, I would like to say that this is not a problem of the past but a present day one; a crime that we are continuing to play some part in. The double crime surrounding the military comfort women is firstly the crime of rape during wartime and secondly the crime of silencing the victims for half a century after the war. In terms of the second crime, as a result of failing to acknowledge the suffering of the victims on a day-to-day and on-going basis and letting half a century pass, we can say that this is a contemporary problem. Added to this, we can call the repudiation of the victims' testimony by conservative factions today a third crime. What we have here amounts to considerably more than the suffering that these women underwent in the past, as there is the long silence forced upon them concerning their experiences and accusations of 'telling lies for money' when their silence was eventually broken. If these do not amount to a second and third crime, what are they?

When considering the background to the paradigm shift that led to the military comfort women problem emerging as a sexual crime, the influence of the women's movement in Korea since the 1980s should not be forgotten. Prior to Kim Hak-Sun's lawsuit, and for the first time since the war ended, Korean women's groups issued a statement to coincide with the former Korean President Roh Tae Woo's visit to Japan in May 1990 demanding a resolution to the *Teishintai* (Women Volunteer Corps) problem.[3]

In June 1990, responding to questions in the National Diet, the Japanese government issued a statement denying government involvement stating that the comfort women system was something that was organised by private entrepreneurs. In response to this reply, 37 Korean women's groups sent letters of public protest to the Japanese government. In November of the same year, the Korean Council for Women Drafted for Military Sexual Slavery by Japan (hereafter Korean Council) was established at the centre of these women's groups. In August the following year, Kim came forward in a response to an appeal made by the Korean Council. The way had already been paved for a paradigm shift to 'the one's who ought to feel shame are not the former comfort women' due to the efforts of Korean Council representative Yun Jong-ok and others. Over a 10-year period prior to the establishment of the Korean Council, they recorded the testimony of former comfort women (Yun, 1992; Kim and Yang Ching-ja, 1995).

What is shocking about the testimony of former comfort women is firstly the cruel historical fact itself and second the fact that the victims were forced to remain silent for a period of 50 years. Until very recently, most former comfort women treated their experiences as their personal shame and buried them in the depths of their memories. They had put a lid on their past, not even revealing it to their closest family members. Many were not able to return to their native towns and villages. It was this past that these women made public and redefined as assault. Here we had a drastic change in historical understanding and a paradigm shift.

It was the Korean democratic movement and women's movements in the 1980s that brought about this shift. To put it another way, the background to the Korean women's movement was the rise of a worldwide feminist movement. In 1991, when Kim Hak-sun first came forward as a victim we felt deep shock. As background, two things prepared the way for her testimony. Firstly, there was the testimony in the 1980s of a victim of sexual torture under the military dictatorship. Kwon In-suk, an activist in the student movement, was subjected to sexual torture while in a prison cell and came forward for the first time, openly declaring herself a victim. As a result of this, the ground was laid for a shift in the paradigm surrounding rape from the 'shame of the victim' to the 'crime of the perpetrator'. Kwon In-suk's testimony became possible for the first time when she received the support of women around her. Secondly, at the time the former comfort women came forward, the testimony of many victims had already been collected and the appeal by Yun Jong-ok, representing the Korean Council, had already occurred. It was precisely because the paradigm had already shifted that, in response to this, witnesses materialised before our eyes. The testimony of the comfort women would not have been possible without the existence of the women in the support group.

According to *'Ianfu' mondai Q&A* (The comfort women issue; Q&As) edited by the Asia-Japan Women's Resource Centre, the 'first time post-war that the issue [of the comfort women] was raised in Japanese society was in the 1970s when Korean women criticised Kisaeng tourism'.[4] They protested that 'during the war

Japanese men used their military strength to rope in fellow country women as female Volunteer Corps, and without reflecting on this, are now using their economic power to play about with Kisaeng women' (Asia-Japan Women's Resource Centre, 1997:24).[5] It is easy to understand how, based on a direct association of ideas, Kisaeng tourism can be taken as a form of sexual invasion by the Japanese. This view is not limited to Korea. Another example of where an analogy has been drawn between the sex tours for Japanese men and the military comfort women can be seen in the Philippines (Go, 1993).[6] Nevertheless, this criticism of Japanese sex tourism does not go hand-in-hand with criticism of prostitute discrimination or the general atmosphere of tolerance of prostitution within Korea. We can understand this criticism of sex tourism within a framework of nationalism. What has been violated here is national pride and the indignation in response to this is not necessarily linked with respect for the human rights of the Kisaeng women.

It is appropriate to position criticism of Kisaeng tourism within the pre-history of the comfort women problem, but this is because from the beginning the comfort women problem included as components both national/ethnic discrimination (*minzoku sabetsu*) and sex discrimination. Nevertheless, it was only possible to tie in a criticism of Kisaeng tourism with an indictment of sex discrimination in the 1980s through the medium of a paradigm shift concerning the victims of sex crimes.

The Patriarchal Paradigm of National Shame

The paradigm used for discussing the military comfort women issue has changed rapidly in a very short time. The first to appear was the patriarchal paradigm of the 'nation's shame'. The patriarchal paradigm denies women's agency, and reduces the infringement of women's sexual human rights to a dispute over property rights between fellow men within the patriarchal system. What is more, here lies the exact cause of the second crime; that of silence being forced on the victims.

Initially a truly patriarchal voice of suppression arose in reaction to the testimony of the women's suffering both in Korea and Japan. 'Don't expose our nation's shame' was the catch cry (Yamashita Y., 1996; Ehara, 1992). Firstly, this reaction can be explained in terms of Confucian ethic, which turns the fact of having suffered sexual abuse into the woman's shame. Secondly, the women's testimony exposed to the public gaze the cowardice of Korean men, who had not been able to protect the chastity of their country women. Thirdly, there is the 'loss of face' associated with not being able to suppress indictments of this nature by women that put men to shame. Here chastity emerges as a form of male property, with the focus of discussion the interests of the patriarchal systems of Japan and Korea regarding the infringement of these property rights, and the dignity of the women totally ignored. Even after the movement for compensation had begun, 'there was widespread sympathy for the opinions of those opposing the seeking of compensation from Japan on the basis that it would injure the pride of the [Korean] people' (Yamashita Y, 1996:43). Haga Tōru, a conservative Japanese male intellectual made the following comment:

> One would have expected Koreans to be a people with a stronger sense
> of pride…Bringing out into the open a past that in truth they should also
> be ashamed of, publicising it to the world, and even pressing for

hundreds of millions of yen in compensation...Will this not add to their shame? (cited in Ehara, 1992:39).[7]

While drawing attention to statements like the one above by Haga Tōru, Ehara Yumiko points out the similarities in the thinking of Japanese and Korean men. These include, 'the sense that it is natural for women who have been sexually violated by force to feel shame, and the sense that it is natural for men to feel shame if their women have been taken by other men'. Ehara speculates on the implications of this:

Supposing that both Japanese and Korean men assume that the women of a nation belong to the men of that nation and that rape of a country woman by those of another nation stains male honour, would this not create sufficient pressure for them to force the victims of the military comfort women problem to keep their mouths shut? (Ehara, 1992:30).

She goes on to argue that: 'attempting to suppress the testimony of the victims of sexual violence because it will bring shame upon themselves can of itself be considered a form of sexual violence, and is inexcusable' (Ehara, 1992:40). Here too, Ehara is pointing to the double sexual violence of patriarchy.

We have a history rich in examples of rape being used as a symbol in disputes between two patriarchal regimes. In 19th century India the rape of local women by British colonists was similarly used as a symbol to arouse nationalist fervour and encourage mobilisation. An Indian historian, Aparna Basu writes:

In the late nineteenth century rape and racism were inter-twined, with rape used as a weapon by nationalists to oppose British law. The cry of we will protect our women from the British soldiers...rose furiously. Rather than view rape as violence against women, they viewed it as an infringement of national honour (Basu, 1993; 1995:75).

Here we have a patriarchal logic that dictates that women's sexuality is the most fundamental right and property of men, and any infringement of this is not only an insult to the woman herself, but ends up being the most supreme insult to the male group to which she belongs.[8]

Rape in China by Japanese soldiers was a frequent occurrence even before the Nanking Massacre in 1937, which acted as a direct catalyst for the comfort women system. It is also referred to as the Rape of Nanking due to the large number rapes that took place. It is reported that the rape of Chinese women by Japanese soldiers triggered 'powerful anti-Japanese sentiment beyond all expectation' among Chinese men (Kim and Yang Ching-ja, 1995:92). As intended, they naturally took these rapes to be a supreme insult to their masculinity. Even after the comfort stations were established, rape by Japanese soldiers in the occupied territories did not cease, manifesting the patriarchal logic that women are the 'spoils of war'.

Self-acknowledgement of sexual suffering in a sense means that a woman establishes an identity of herself as sexually self-determined. It brings with it an awareness of agency to the extent that it is recognised that the right to make decisions in relation to one's sexuality – put bluntly, in relation to one's body – belongs to oneself and not to the patriarchal authority of a father or husband. In terms of the comfort women lawsuits, the Japanese government has continued to insist that the matter of post-war compensation was settled with the 1965 Korea-Japan Treaty, however, the logic of individual claims cuts through the patriarchal logic embedded within this stance. Yamazaki Hiromi, a member of a comfort women's support group, asks:

> Suppose that a woman was raped today and the rapist informed you that the matter had been settled on the basis of a mutual agreement between the husband or the father, would you accept this? No you would not (Yamazaki H., 1995).

If we replace the word 'husband' or 'father' with 'state', it is easy to understand the situation with the former comfort women. By refusing to recognise the right to make individual claims and by supporting the views of the Japanese government, the Korean government has reduced the individual to something belonging to the state. On the basis that the state does not represent the (interests of the) individual, the logic of the right to make an individual petition contains the clue for transcending the state. As a consequence, the opponents that the female victims and their supporters must take on are simultaneously the patriarchal regimes of Japan and Korea.

The 'Purity' of Korean Women

In the early 1970s reports on the military comfort women were published in rapid succession. Two of these were Senda Kakō's *Jyūgun ianfu* (Military comfort women) original and sequel (1973, 1984) and Kim Il-myon's *Tennō no guntai to chōsenjin ianfu* (The Imperial Army and Korean comfort women) (1976). Senda's writing overflows with compassion for the military comfort women and their 'pitiful existence'. However even prior to this, we had the memoirs of a soldier who took the position that he and his colleagues had acted cruelly towards the comfort women. He wondered what had happened to the women. As for Senda, he did not see the comfort women system in a way that would have constructed it as a crime and there were no victims who we should apologise to and compensate.

Fourteen years after his last publication and responding to a request from *Ronza* [a monthly magazine from Asahi Newspaper Company], Senda wrote *Jyūgun ianfu' no shinjitsu* (The truth of the military comfort women).

It was 1973 when I published the book entitled *The Military Comfort Women* (original and sequel) with Futabasha publishers. The original and sequel combined sold in excess of 500,000 copies, but the only place to print a *bona fide* book review was the [Communist newspaper] *Akahata* (Red flag). It did not gain much social attention either. When someone investigated the matter for me, they found that the readers were largely former soldiers who had been sent to the front line in China or South East Asia and had bought [comfort] women themselves. Apparently upon finishing the book, these readers gave a deep sigh, put it away at the back of their bookshelves and there it ended without them speaking a word about it to anybody...Sadly, the book did not seem to grab the interest of historians of modern and contemporary history either.

In 1984, Kodansha Bunko republished the book in the form of paperback but the situation was no different…From the standpoint of it not becoming a social issue, the situation in Korea was no different. Soon after being published by Futabasha in 1973, *The Military Comfort Women* was translated into Korean. One newspaper critic wrote that; 'for a Japanese, this is well researched and well written', but that was about it (Senda, 1997:52–54)

Senda notes that; 'It was in December 1991 after the former "comfort women" had filed their lawsuits that the situations in Japan and Korea were transformed'. None of us can reproach Senda for his historical limitations. There were many people in Japan and Korea who were aware of the existence of the comfort women but chose to do nothing especially in the face of the silence of the former comfort women. [9]

Senda further wrote: 'It is rather curious…but the response of women was also close to zero' (Senda, 1997:53). He suggests that the only exception was Takahashi Kikue from the Japanese Christian Women's Association Against Prostitution (*Nihon Kirisutokyō Fujin Kyōfūkai*). [10]

Senda does not refer to it, but there is another exception. This is Maruyama Yukiko, a freelance woman writer. In her writing, Maruyama pursues the cause of the 'uncomfortable feeling' she was left with after reading the reports of Senda and Kim (Maruyama, Y., 1977, 1995). While evaluating Korean writer Kim Il-myon's *The Imperial Army and Korean Comfort Women*, which she describes as 'the product of considerable labour which should also be called a crystal of anger and revulsion', Maruyama does not overlook the male logic within this anger. She notes the more Kim 'emphasised the purity and chastity of Korean women' the more she 'felt that something was not right'. Maruyama argued that:

A society that relentlessly demands 'purity' from women is certainly not a happy society for women, and it cannot be said that simply because women have been obedient to the male demands of such a society that the women of that nation possess outstanding qualities as human beings (Maruyama, Y., 1977, 1995:194).

She then offers a rebuttal to Kim, who compares Japanese women who, he suggests, went overseas as prostitutes by choice and Korean women who, he argues, were pulled into it as a result of the violence of the soldiers of the Imperial Army'. Referring here to the tradition of *karayukisan* [Japanese women sent overseas as indentured prostitutes], Maruyama's counter to this comparison is as follows:

> In Korean society, even if a woman who has been violently abducted, taken to the front line, and then forced to become a prostitute manages to return to her homeland, having narrowly escaped death, she will not be able to tread the earth of her native village again. Compared to this, there can be no doubt that a happier life awaits a [Japanese] woman who could at least go back to her island homeland, erect a grave for herself while still alive, and live in a society where she could speak openly about having earned her living doing 'women's work' or prostitution (Maruyama Y., 1977, 1995:194).

Although her wording over exaggerates the situation to some extent, what I believe Maruyama is intending to say here is that from the standpoint of the oppression surrounding women's sexuality, patriarchy within Korea stands just as guilty as that of Japan.

It is not difficult to point out the limitations of Maruyama's arguments from the perspective of today. Firstly, Maruyama considers military comfort women simply to be prostitutes. She asks, 'what exactly were the military comfort women?, and then answers that, 'they were women who accompanied the Japanese military into all parts of Asia and worked in their brothels there' (Maruyama Y., 1977, 1995:187). Secondly, it was originally Kim Il-myon himself who compared the Korean comfort women to *karayukisan*, but this comparison was way off target because the historical contexts of both cases were too different to compare. Nevertheless, we can also point to the nationalist bias of Maruyama in her strong rebuttal of this unfair comparison. Her line of argument here is that both societies are Confucianist and male-centred, but at least Japan is more generous to prostitutes. Thirdly, while showing compassion for the Japanese comfort women, Maruyama does not consider the possibility that they may have faced the same fate when they returned home. If we are going to compare what happened to the Korean comfort women afterwards, surely the comparison should be with the Japanese comfort women rather than the *karayukisan*. Were the Japanese comfort women accepted when they went back to their native villages and towns? Could they speak about their past when they got back to their home towns and villages? Alternatively, did they become local legends proud of the way they offered themselves for the nation? Through to today, there has been a heavy silence from the Japanese comfort women.

Nevertheless, from the standpoint of problematising the stigma that women who have been prostitutes receive in a patriarchal society regardless of whether force was used or not, Marayama's perspective took her right to [the reason for] the silence of the former comfort women. It was not until the 1980s as a result of feminism that there was finally a shift in paradigm from prostitution being a woman's problem to it becoming a man's problem. Nevertheless, Maruyama came very close to a paradigm shift on the basis of her own insight and language.

The Military Rape Paradigm

The military rape paradigm is a variation of the patriarchal paradigm. Of course, rape of non-combatants as an act of assault is not only a contravention of international law, but also a breach of military regulations. Military rape is sufficiently common for it to be pardoned, along with the slaughter of civilians, as a fact of war; a 'going too far' that accompanies this kind of emergency situation.

The view that rape is something that inevitably accompanies war, something that occurs in all countries in wartime, further exempts the assailants from responsibility. Until very recently, this form of rape was explained in terms of the lust of soldiers living for long periods in an all male society separated from women. However, since it has become clear that a male assailant does not move from sexual desire to rape, little by little we are being released from the peacetime rape myth[11] and a new understanding of rape in wartime is also in the process of being established from the perspective of Men's Studies. Hikosaka Tai, a male social critic, criticises the myth that men cannot control themselves, arguing that men rape in order to display their hold on power. He makes clear that, above all else, rape in wartime is distinctive for its multiplicity (gang rape) and it is a ritual that establishes group solidarity through the assault of a more vulnerable person (Hikosaka, 1991). It is now realised that in reality rape in wartime frequently occurs in places where there is an audience.

On its own, the above is an insufficient explanation of wartime rape. This assault by soldiers is directed above all else at the sexuality of women, because the assailants know that it is a display of their own power, symbolically acting as the ultimate insult to the men on the enemy side. It is exactly for this reason that rape stirs up such vehement rage in the men of the enemy country.

Historian Hirota Masaki (1995, 1996) has attempted to make sense of the comfort women by extending the paradigm of wartime rape. Hirota holds up as one distinctive feature and cause of wartime rape, 'the inability [of those involved] to understand each other'; 'in other words there is from the beginning the presence of two different cultures and no way to establish communication'. However, this is not applicable to the case of the Korean comfort women. Under the assimilation policy of turning Koreans into Imperial subjects, former comfort women would have been given official Japanese names and made to wear *yukata* (cotton kimono) and take on the appearance of Japanese women. Korean comfort women were welcomed by the soldiers exactly because they could act like Japanese women. Among Japanese soldiers there are those who speak nostalgically of their communication with comfort women, and there were comfort women who committed double suicide with Japanese soldiers. Of course, among the latter, there be those who were forced to commit suicide in this way.

Even if we look at this from the perspective of historical reality, it is impossible to make sense of the comfort women using the paradigm of military rape. This is because the comfort women system went beyond casual, unorganised wartime rape. Of course, there were many victims who were first victims of wartime rape who then ended up being abducted, gang raped, systematically and under continuous supervision [as comfort women]. In the occupied territories in the south such as Philippines and Indonesia, this was likely the case.

In reality it is difficult to draw a line between wartime rape and the organised comfort women system. However, simply reducing the comfort women to a case of wartime rape leaves hidden within the comfort women system itself problems that are difficult to solve.

The Prostitution Paradigm

The prostitution paradigm is frequently mobilised to legitimise the comfort women system. In Japan, this is the argument used by conservative female critic Kamisaka Fuyuko, and more recently Tokyo University professor of pedagogy, Fujioka Nobukatsu and comic writer Kobayashi Yoshinori of the *Atarashii Rekishi Kyōkasho o Tsukurukai* (The Japanese Group for Orthodox History Education, hereafter Orthodox History Group). On the basis of 'the involvement of business agents' and 'the giving and receiving of money', this viewpoint presumes the voluntariness of the women concerned. Undoubtedly among former comfort women there were those who came along on the basis of honeyed words that they would be able to make a good living, and there are also cases where the families, rather than the woman herself, received compensation. There are also stories of women carrying home close to their bodies the military scrip they had saved up until the time of their withdrawal from the front. It is necessary here to separate the issue of whether recruitment was voluntary or not, from the question of receiving money. Of the 19 Korean women who gave testimony there were 12 cases of 'employment by deception' (Korean Council, 1993). As the agents doing the recruiting told them that there was a 'job vacancy' or that there was 'a job for women providing board and meals', the women did not imagine that what they were being led into was forced prostitution. It is also possible for money to be received on the basis of coercion. If payment is forced on a woman after rape it does not mean that the crime of rape is erased. In a similar vein, according to the testimony of the 19 former comfort women, three received payment (Korean Council, 1993). Even here they were paid military scrip issued by the Japanese army and after the war it was as good as rubbish paper.

Hikosaka Tai writes the following on the basis of testimony concerning Korean comfort women at Luzon Island in the Philippines in the final stages of the war:

Ultimately, the money that they so carefully took with them was earned and saved as a result of coerced and relentless labour, regardless of their own will. In spite of this, even at the time [they were taking the money back home so carefully] the money had already become absolutely worthless bits of paper (Hikosaka, 1991:70).

If the comfort women system was a variety of compulsory recruitment and sexual labour, this 'offering oneself for one's country' would have ended with the women applying for compensation for the no-longer valid military scrip after the war was over, but the comfort women were most definitely not treated as though they were a part of the general forced labour compensation problem. The reason for this is 'prostitute discrimination' in that prostitution was regarded as 'shameful occupation' or 'dirty work', and if this involved 'free will' then the degraded ones were the women themselves.

On this point, one of the victims, Moon Ok-chu's, 'Military Postal Saving's Lawsuit' is deeply significant. In this lawsuit that superficially appears to be a demand for compensation for sexual services, the case is phrased in terms of Moon not wanting to leave with her assailants, the Japanese government, money that she had torn herself into shreds over in order to receive.[12] However, based on the same logic as in other postal savings suits, the case has been beaten down by the position of the Japanese government which says, 'the matter was settled with the Japanese Korean Economic Cooperation and the Right to Claim Agreement'. In October 1996 Moon passed away with the case still unsettled.

I have a number of reservations concerning this prostitution paradigm. Firstly, in terms of the question of whether the comfort women were recruited by force or not, it was not admitted publicly that forced recruitment carried out by the Japanese government included sexual labour. Secondly, it is doubtful whether forced recruitment was 'work for pay'. The reason for this is that, whether sexual or other forms of labour, forced recruitment in the majority of cases only involved nominal wages and it was usual for those recruited to be made to work under slave conditions.

I would like to indicate one more fundamental misunderstanding that is an inevitable part of the prostitution paradigm. Whether it was forced or voluntary, prostitution is not 'sex in exchange for money' between a woman and a man. Prostitution, as a part of the sex industry, is an exchange between the seller (agent or manager who is frequently male) and the (male) buyer. Here the woman is not the agent or central player in this exchange but simply and nothing more than an object, a commodity. As a commodity, the prostitute does not have the right to choose her customers. Those who made a living at the comfort stations were not the individual women but the operators. No doubt while military scrip was still of value there were agents who became successful men (and sometimes women) by taking away with them fortunes that had been amassed. However, there must have been those who harboured within themselves a sense of shame at exploiting these women who were comfort women.

The prostitution paradigm contains within itself a viewpoint that exempts men from responsibility by implying that women have agency. Women who 'sell sex,' by this very act, are stigmatised. Those women themselves who work in this 'shameful occupation' are considered to be unclean.[13] In terms of making into an issue the volition of the woman herself, at a glance the prostitute paradigm appears to recognise the woman's right to self-determination but, given that it is supported by a sexual double standard that draws a line between prostitutes and all other women, in reality it can be said to be another version of the patriarchal code. The discrimination within the prostitution paradigm has deprived many former Japanese comfort women of their voice.[14]

It has become clear that there are a number of deceits within the prostitution paradigm. Firstly, there is the clear involvement of the military in the comfort stations. There were three versions of comfort station: comfort stations that the military directly managed, comfort stations assigned for exclusive military use, and local comfort stations used by the military. All three versions were placed under military control. Secondly, in contrast to the appearance of prostitution, there is the point that what we are actually talking about is forced labour under conditions of confinement.[15] Soldiers had to pay military scrip each time they used a comfort woman. However, to avoid misunderstanding it is important to stress that it was the agent that received this military scrip and that there was no direct exchange relationship between the soldier and the comfort woman. Thirdly, far from the procurement of the comfort women involving free will, visible and invisible pressures accompanied procurement with women violently taken by force or abduction. Many were lured by the lies of the agents and/or they were victims of human trafficking.

The transformation of existing 'pleasure quarters' into those for exclusive military use, those for use by the military or comfort stations, the trick of setting up payment for each time of use, and the use of a euphemisms like comfort station and comfort women by the military meant that the reality of confinement and coercion was concealed. Further, the military was able to give the impression that this was a business activity.[16] In fact, within Japan in Okinawa where there were Korean comfort women, a request was received from the military to turn into an exclusive comfort station a pleasure quarters of high standing from a long time ago known as Tsuji, but this request was turned down with great pride. The continuity between the conventional pleasure quarters and the comfort stations was categorically constructed.[17]

When it comes to the Korean comfort women in Okinawa, we need to consider the issue of discrimination of the Okinawans by the soldiers from mainland Japan. In response to the complaints from local women's groups that establishing a comfort station would corrupt public morals, the military employed the logic that it would protect the chastity of women from good families and on the basis of this, women's groups accepted a comfort station (Kawada, 1987). Here, because of the likelihood of rape by soldiers of the Imperial Army, the chastity of the women of Okinawa was 'defended' at the sacrifice of Korean women. The fact that for women of Okinawa the soldiers of the Imperial Army were potential assailants suggests the possibility that Okinawa was being treated as a quasi-occupied territory.

Moreover, the fact that the military was systematically involved in the military comfort stations was something that was shameful to them. While it was recognised that the military comfort women system was a 'necessary evil', it was also regarded as a source of embarrassment for the Imperial Army. The transportation of comfort women was carried out on military ships and the military even transferred the women to the front line. As civilians were prohibited from riding on military ships, the women were treated as freight (military goods) and as a result no passenger lists for them remain. Of course it can be said that this reveals the extent to which these women were deprived of their character, but at the same time, in hindsight, we can see that there was also concern not to make public the transportation by the military of 'goods' for the purpose of sexual comfort.

At the end of the war, documents concerned with the comfort women were scrapped along with most other military documents. However, there is no indication here that this was because the military feared that the comfort women problem might be judged as a particular war crime. In reality, it was the abuse of prisoners of war and the slaughter of civilians that emerged as problems, and at the Tokyo Trials (The International Military Tribunal for the Far East) the Occupation Forces did not pass judgement on the comfort women issue.[18] One reason for this is that the Tokyo Tribunal Court did not invite Korea on the side of those issuing indictments against Japan. At that point in time, the problem of Korea as a colony was regarded as an internal affair with Korean people continuing to have Japanese nationality for the time being. The Tokyo Trials were trials of the war crimes of the defeated Japan brought by the Allied Nations. The many Asian nations that were the victims of Japan's aggression – China, Korea, Taiwan, Indonesia, the Philippines among others – were not central players in the indictment process. In the bilateral agreement between Japan and Korea concerning post-war compensation, Korea did not raise the matter of the victimisation of the comfort women. These conditions have opened the way for right-wing popular comic writer Kobayashi's kind of faultfinding, which have continued over a long period of time. His argument has been that if it was such an important issue why did the Korean government keep quiet about it for so long. As Senda Kakō testifies, we had to wait for the paradigm shift that occurred in December 1991 as a result of the victims 'coming out'.

The Sexual Violence Paradigm

The military sexual slavery paradigm clearly denies the voluntarism of the prostitution paradigm. This paradigm has become firmly established since the United Nations World Conference on Human Rights held in Vienna in June 1993. The United Nations decided to create a Special Rapporteur on Violence Against Women within the Human Rights Commission, and chose Radhika Coomaraswamy from Sri Lanka. She energetically carried out an investigation that included listening to the testimony of victims, and submitted the Coomaraswamy Report in April 1996.[19] The Human Rights Commission adopted the report unanimously. In addition to positioning the military comfort women system as a form of sexual slavery, details of the Coomaraswamy Report's proposal, recommending that the Japanese government offer an apology and compensation, are widely known. However, the official position of the Japanese government to-date is, firstly, that the comfort women system cannot accurately be described as a system of sexual slavery, and, secondly, that it is not the job of the Human Rights Commission to retrospectively pursue questions of past responsibility.

At the time, news of the rape camps in the former Yugoslavia after the collapse of the Communist Bloc had shocked the world. We were shocked by the fact that these were not simply casual, unregulated rapes triggered by war, but systematic sexual crimes by the military. Another shocking aspect was the racial genocide type strategy of ethnic cleansing that was carried out. This involved the restraint of women who had become pregnant as a result of rape until abortion was no longer a possibility. The sexual slavery paradigm was applied to the comfort women from an analogy of current issues, and not the other way round.[20] Forming a background to this were the arguments of human rights politics and feminism problematising 'violence against women in armed conflict'.

The reason that the comfort women issue has not ended with the scars from the past of a group of already elderly women, but gained considerable sympathy from the international solidarity of the women's movement, is that there is recognition that the issue is deeply connected to current problems of violence against women. This connection is not limited to the kind of blatant war crimes that occurred in the rape camps of Bosnia. Neither is it simply the problem of 'violence against women in armed conflict' highlighted by the United Nations (UN). Instead, it is understood that the comfort women issue is tied in with the considerable suffering caused by what is regarded as the infringement of women's sexual self-determination, such as ordinarily occurring rapes and sex crimes, domestic violence and child abuse. For many women, the pain is shared as if 'the violence was inflicted on my own body'. In addition, based on the same sexual domination, prostitution is understood as an outcome of structural violence against women. At the 1995 United Nations Fourth World Conference on Women held in Beijing, the comfort women issue was one of the principal focuses of the Non-Government Organisation (NGO) forum, and brought together activists opposed to sexual harassment, domestic violence and military-base prostitution.

Key concepts in the sexual violence paradigm are women's human rights and sexual self-determination. However, this paradigm itself is also loaded with problems. Firstly, human rights is not a supra-historical, universalistic concept. The content of human rights has not only changed historically, but socially it has been limited by categories such as gender, class and race. In addition, the human rights concept is burdened by the boundaries of the historical period, in other words the modern era. A concept of women and human rights is one of the achievements of feminism and, moreover, made possible the switch to the sexual violence paradigm. Yet, at the same time, it has exposed the concepts of human rights and self-determination to a fresh examination today (Scott, 1996; Tateiwa, 1997).

Secondly, as the term human rights diplomacy suggests, there is the issue of human rights being UN focused. Under the post-Cold War system with the United States as the central axis, it is impossible to naïvely evaluate the role carried out by the UN as simply that of international police. While the United States has used human rights as a diplomatic trump card on the one hand, it has shut its eyes to its own war crimes and military invasions, on the other. The UN is not a synonym for justice.

Thirdly, the concept of sexual self-determination is likely once again to draw us back into a debate over the presence or absence of voluntarism surrounding sex work.

Military sexual slaves does indeed seem to be appropriate terminology for understanding the comfort women given the systematic and continuous rape of the women under conditions of forced capture and confinement. Nevertheless, by overemphasising its opposition to the prostitution paradigm, the military sexual slavery paradigm falls into exactly the same kind of dilemma as that of rape trials where the agency of the victims has to be assiduously denied. For example, the purity of the victim's sexual past, whether there was any resistance or not, and the denial of any economic motivation are all symbolically utilised, with the image of the model victim. For instance, it is easier to accept as a victim the image of a young woman who was a virgin at the time that she was taken away, and either completely duped or captured by force. In this kind of story, the woman would have planned to escape or commit suicide, but she was prevented from doing so and somehow survived. Needless to say, for the victims who speak out in public about these kinds of dreadful experiences, the application of a concept of model victim, which is a manipulative category, is truly discourteous. The problem lies not with the narrator but the listener who only hears what he or she wants to hear. Moreover, the political effect of this paradigm is that it makes it difficult for anybody who deviates from the model victim to come forward. It is much harder to gain acceptance in a case where at the time of being rounded up the victim had an experience of prostitution; or due to poverty the victim went for economic reasons although vaguely aware of what was going to happen; or alternatively that the victim had been hoarding military scrip, even if these were survival strategies from among limited choices by the women to avoid certain death. Stated more clearly, this paradigm functions to place a boundary between the 'pure' and the 'impure' victim. Furthermore, as a result of creating the image of the 'immaculate victim', it is capable of becoming the unintended accomplice of the patriarchal paradigm, which demands women's purity.

Historian Kurahashi Masanao divides the comfort stations into two types, the civilian-run model (prostitution model) and the military comfort women model (sexual slavery model), but if this is the case then once again a distinction has been drawn between the victims (Kurahashi, 1989, 1994).[21]

Another political consequence of a military sexual slavery paradigm that distinguishes itself from the prostitution paradigm is that it creates a division between Japanese comfort women and non-Japanese comfort women. The sexual slavery paradigm refers to systematic sexual crimes carried out against the women of enemy or occupied countries. Consequently, it functions to exclude from this victimisation those comfort women who were fellow nationals or military-base prostitution of allied countries. For example, there has been a tendency to pardon as economic activity based on free will the military-base prostitution of Korean soldiers who participated in the Vietnam War and American military-base prostitution within Japan. Yet, surely the rape of a 12 year-old girl in 1995 by three American soldiers that so enraged the residents of Okinawa prefecture is contiguous to military-base prostitution and everyday structural violence against women?[22]

Yamashita Yeong-ae, a feminist activist, points out the prostitute discrimination within the logic of the Korean Council:

Within the logic of the counter-argument of the Korean Council for Women Drafted for Military Sexual Slavery, that the comfort women were not prostitutes and were very definitely not state licensed prostitutes, there is the danger of reinforcing the view that the comfort women were forced, while for prostitutes it was free-will (Yamashita, 1994:45).

On the other hand, in an effort to transcend this kind of division, Suzuki Yūko has developed the logic that the pre-war system of licensed prostitution was also sexual slavery (Suzuki, 1996b). Given that a concept of sexual slavery has been applied to the traffic of women, including the 'white-slave' trade, then the system of licensed prostitution as an act that violated women's human rights was certainly such a system. By 1925 Japan was already a signatory to The International Agreement for the Suppression of White Slave Traffic (1904), The International Convention for the Suppression of White Slave Traffic (1910), and The International Convention for the Suppression of Traffic in Adult Women and Girls (1921), and in 1932 Japan ratified the International Labour Organisation Treaty No. 29 (the Convention Concerning Forced or Compulsory

Labour). While the comfort women system was an even bigger infringement, the system of licensed prostitution was already in violation of these conventions. While on paper it looked as though the women had entered into a contract of their own free will, it was an open secret that binding debt and working under surveillance meant that actual conditions were those of slavery.

Conservative historian Hata Ikuhiko, in a discussion of the 'contested points and blind spots in the Four Major Affairs' (*yondai jiken*), meaning the Marco Polo Bridge Incident, the Nanking Massacre, Unit 731 and the comfort women, raises the following three questions in relation to the comfort women issue. First, was there a system of *forced recruitment* by the authorities? Second, were living conditions harsher than for licensed prostitutes during peacetime? Third, why have no Japanese comfort women come forward? In response to the first two question, Hata gives the answer 'no' (Hata, 1997:39). Of course, Hata's argument is cleverly devised. For example, in his first question he asks whether there was a *system* of forced recruitment and not whether forced recruitment occurred. Would the answer still have been 'no' if he had phrased the question in this way: did systematic, forced recruitment on the instructions of the military occur? If not, would it be a case of there is no substantive proof that the military participated systematically? In terms of the second question, the implication is that if the comfort women were given an equally miserable lifestyle as licensed prostitutes, at least it meant that their treatment was the same as the Japanese. This inter-connects with question three; if this was the case, why have no Japanese comfort women come forward? Although Hata takes what appears to be great pride in indicating that this question is one of the 'blind spots' in the debate, of course he refrains from pointing out that this is also a contested point. It is exactly Hata's type of conservative discourse that provided the reason for the existence of the comfort women, and the reason for their continued silence until today. Turning this around the other way, this problem is surely evidence of the powerlessness of Japanese feminism.

The Nationalist Discourse

The shift in our understanding of the comfort women issue from national shame to gender discrimination and national discrimination was one of the achievements of the Korean women's movement. Nevertheless, from the very beginning the tendency was to construct these within a nationalist discourse.

Activist and brilliant theorist Yamashita Yeong-ae, while close to the Korean Council, has provided an extremely perceptive critique of the nationalism embedded within the movement. She has not only criticised the gender discrimination embedded in the Korean nationalist discourse, but has also shown how discourses surrounding the comfort women have been constructed on the basis of their exposure to this national discourse and suggests that these too 'may be tinged with gender discrimination' (Yamashita Y., 1996:42).

The first thing here, as already discussed, is the distinction between 'forced' and 'voluntary', and which itself is based on prostitute discrimination. As we have seen in the example of the model victim, as a result of stressing force the chastity of Korean women is also being emphasised. Secondly, the distinction between forced and voluntary is equivalent to matching Korean comfort women against Japanese comfort women, with the result that a division is brought into play on the basis of nationality.

Yamashita cites a section from the Korean Council's *Nihon seifu no kyōsei jyūngun ianfu mondai dainiji shinsō chōsa happyō ni taisuru wareware no tachiba* (Our position in relation to the Japanese government's second truth-finding survey into the forced military comfort women problem) published in August 1993:

> The character of sexual slavery of the forced [Korean] military comfort women was clearly different than that of the Japanese women. Japanese comfort women were prostitutes within the existing state-regulated system of prostitution, and they received money, had a contract, and when the contract came to an end they could quit their life as a comfort

woman...The [Korean] comfort women were different from the
Japanese female prostitutes under the state licensed system of prostitution existing at that time. They were sexual slaves forced by the state
and public authority to give sexual comfort to the military (Yamashita
Y., 1996:44).[23]

Here, the military sexual slavery paradigm was mobilised for the
purpose of anti-Japanese Korean nationalism. National confrontation has been emphasised within the Korean Council with one
theory even locating the comfort women system as a policy of
ethnic genocide.

Yamashita states emphatically that the nationalistic discourse
concerning the comfort women issue is ethnocentric and erects a
wall between Korean victims and those from other ethnic groups
and from other regions, thus bringing a division between them.
Yamashita considers the nationalist tendency within the Korean
women's movement to be 'a survival strategy aimed at having the
women's movement acknowledged within the national democratising movement'. However, she also takes the view that
'compared to its enthusiastic reception as a women's issue within
the international solidarity movement, the comfort women issue's
influence on the domestic women's movement and human rights
movement has been extremely small...The reason for this is
that...to begin with it was approached largely as a nationalist issue
within Korea. On top of that, there was little effort made to overturn
the nationalist discourse' (Yamashita Y., 1996:51).

According to Korean feminist Kim Eun-shil, who Yamashita
introduces:

By conferring greater symbolic meaning to the signifier sexual violation,
the nationalist discourse denies the specificity of the women's
experiences and universalises it into a national issue. To rephrase this, it
was not the women but the Korean nation that was sexually violated by
the rapist Japan. Due to the fact that it was the nation itself that was of
issue here, the crime of rape was not endowed with any meaning until
perpetrated by the Japanese Empire (Kim, 1994:41; cited in Yamashita
Y., 1996:44).

By subsuming women within the 'national subject', or more
precisely through the unification of women's interests with men's
(in reality they are subordinate), the nationalist discourse could be

used to mobilize nationalism. It is also a cliché among the right wing in Japan to use the rape metaphor to express a violation by another nation, however, this does not mean that they necessarily respect women's human rights. Far from it, there is a tendency to criticise the assertion of women's rights as an act that serves the enemy by bringing about divisions. Seen from this perspective, the nationalist discourse can be considered a variant of the patriarchal paradigm. We can understand this within the context of the nationalisation of women as discussed in Part One. The patriarchal paradigm by objectifying women understands rape as the infringement of male property rights, while the nationalist discourse, by turning women into national subjects, understands rape as the violation of the nation. In both instances the norm for the nation is based on the male subject and there is an identification of female interests with male interests. From this standpoint, there is little difference between them.

The Grey Zone of Collaboration with Japan

It is necessary to point out that behind the nationalist discourse and concealed by it is another latent issue, that of Korean collaboration with Japan. Currently nationalism within Korea is suppressing the surfacing of the issue, but the problem of collaboration with Japan under imperial rule is a deeply rooted and smouldering one, in the same way as the issue of the Vichy government's collaboration with the Germans is in France.

For example, on June 23rd 1997 a memorial service was held by the Cornerstone of Peace Memorial to mark the 52nd anniversary of the end of the Battle of Okinawa. The Cornerstone of Peace Memorial was the former Governor of Okinawa, Ōta Masahide's, cherished project. Completion was planned for the 50th anniversary of the end of the war with an inscription of the names of all the war dead from the Battle of Okinawa, military and civilian, regardless of nationality. Included among these were Korean war-dead who had been taken to Okinawa by force. The job of tracing back and identifying the original Korean names of those who had been recorded under the Japanese names imposed on them as a result of the renaming policy was an extremely difficult one, but it was given to On Jon-biru, a leading figure in Okinawan history in Korea and a Professor at Korea's Myongji University. Professor On's investigations revealed 50 names. Of these, seven of the bereaved families refused the inscription on the Cornerstone of Peace Memorial. The same day, June 23rd, the *Ryūkyū Shinpō* newspaper covered an interview with Professor On:

> The general view in Korea is that those people who were led away by force supported the Japanese military during the period of the Japanese Empire…There are those who fear that the descendents of families who collaborated with the Japanese army will be labelled. Even in the villages they are looked upon as dishonourable, and this ends up having an effect on such things as marriage prospects (*Ryūkyū Shinpō,* 23 June, 1997*)*.

This article shocked me. If the compulsory draft was equivalent to collaboration with Imperial Japan, then following the same logic it was possible that the comfort women would also be dealt with in this way. The name of not even a single comfort woman was inscribed on the Cornerstone of Peace Memorial. As pointed out by Kawada, 'the real names' of these women 'to say nothing of their numbers or whether they are alive or dead, are unknown' (Sensō giseisha o kokoro ni kizamukai, 1997:162). However, even if names were known, would the bereaved families give their consent for the inscription to be carried out? Even if they are able to rid themselves of the dishonour of being prostitutes and come to be regarded as victims of war, treated as equivalent to Korean civilians attached to the military, next they will probably be viewed as collaborators with Japan.

On the basis that the Volunteer Corps were 'offering themselves for the country', it could be taken that they were serving the Imperial Army rather than volunteering under coercion. At the scene of fierce battle these women served as nurses, and it is said that when an enemy prisoner of war was to be executed they would stand in line wearing their Women's Association for National Defence sashes.

At the trials of class B and C war crimes, Korean and Taiwanese military and civilian personnel were tried as Japanese. Needless to say, Korean agents who profited from the procurement of comfort women or from operating comfort stations were subject to disdain as collaborators with Imperial Japan, but under colonial rule it is difficult to draw a line between what is coercion and what is free will. The movement questioning the perpetrator responsibility of the comfort women crime has demanded legal action be taken against the criminals, however, by exposing the issue of collaboration with Japan within Korea it will probably function to intensify anti-Japanese nationalism still further.

A Uniquely Japanese or Universal Phenomenon?

Historian Hirota Masaki introduces the historical research of Kurahashi Masao, Yoshimi Yoshiaki and Suzuki Yūko, commenting that from the standpoint that 'all three overemphasise the uniqueness of Japan', such as 'the uniqueness of the military of the emperor system', 'the uniqueness of the modern system of regulated prostitution', and 'the uniqueness of Japanese patriarchy', one is left with a feeling that something is wrong (Hirota, 1995). Hirota suggests that we should refrain from 'narratives of the comfort women issue that are confined to the unique problems of the battlefield or the unique problems of Japan'. While I agree totally with this suggestion, even so what narrative should we use in its place? The danger lurking for those who seek to escape a thesis of uniqueness is that they will once again revert to universalism.

The paradigm that reduces the comfort women issue to the uniqueness of the Imperial Army (in contrast let us call it the unique emperor system paradigm), possesses a character well-suited to the theory of Japan's cultural uniqueness. According to this theory, an oppressively dominating regime unprecedented in the world was created due to the 'limping along' of modernisation, and this in turn gave birth to the comfort women system, a cruel and sexually abusive system considered to have no historical parallel. The uniqueness of the Japanese military is emphasised with the suggestion that, although there are examples of prostitutes accompanying the military, there is no other example of the military organising prostitution itself. Ironically, those theorists most likely to strongly insist on the uniqueness of the emperor system as a target that must be opposed are those who are against the emperor system, and they tend to overestimate its importance.

This argument immediately calls to mind the German *Historiker-streit* or historians' dispute. If the Holocaust is made into an act of cruelty unprecedented in history, the end result is that the German people cannot escape this 'original sin'. Historical revisionist Nolte provoked an angry counter-response from Habermas when he argued that the Holocaust was an ordinary war crime. Given that we already have the rhetoric that the comfort women system was Imperial Japan's policy of extermination of the Korean people, it would not be so unimaginable to draw an analogy with the Holocaust.

Historian Tanaka Toshiyuki, while undertaking a comparative study of military controlled systems of prostitution during Second World War in a number of countries, including the United States, Britain, Germany and Australia, and also on the basis of what happened in the First World War, was able to demonstrate that control of sexually transmitted disease among soldiers was a priority task for the military. It was not simply a case of having prostitutes attached to the military, but of the military managing prostitution with the aim of preventing sexually transmitted disease that was regarded as a necessity. Tanaka then posed the question: 'Why did the American military ignore the issue of the comfort women at the Tokyo Trials?' (Tanaka T., 1996) He then went on to give the following reply:

> From the very beginning among the American military, who during the war and in the early days of post-war Occupation took military controlled prostitution for granted, there was a complete lack of any awareness or discernment that the military comfort women problem, one of the serious war crimes committed by Japan and from the stand point of history one example of the most grave of all Crimes against Humanity, actually was a crime (Tanaka, T.,1996, Part II).

In 1993, at the Australian National University where an international Japanese Studies Conference was being held, Tanaka argued for the universality of military prostitution, saying that he would probably have gone to such a place himself, invoking a furious response from a Korean participant who by chance was in the audience. In addition, by exposing rape by Australian servicemen during the Second World War, he also received protests from the Australian Veterans' Association. Tanaka's argument that it was not only the Japanese who did it takes us towards a universal theory, and as a consequence allows for the recovery of a logic that exempts Japan from responsibility for the crimes that it has committed. However, it should not be forgotten that Tanaka pointed out not only the commonalities of the military and sex, but also the differences in the comfort women system. 'It is clearly a mistake to regard as absolutely the same the military comfort women issue and managed prostitution carried out first by the United States and then by the militaries of other Allied countries' (Tanaka T., 1996 Part II:277). This is because there is a crucial difference concerning criminality, but here again Tanaka reduces this difference to the presence or absence of voluntariness (the difference between prostitution based on free will and forced prostitution). A division is brought between comfort women and prostitutes. Those who he calls 'commercial prostitutes' suffer discrimination as their very existence is such that, due to the exchange of money, they are not expected to complain regardless of the extent to which they suffer human rights violations. Will this logic not be appropriated by a similar logic that in reality the comfort women were prostitutes? In addition, will this logic not end up condoning military base prostitution by allied nations?

On the one hand there is the argument that reduces the uniqueness of the comfort women problem to the uniqueness of the Japanese culture and society or the uniqueness of the domination of the emperor system, and on the other, an argument that universalises it as a general problem of the 'military and sex'. It is not a matter of which one of these is correct. What we need is to locate this issue within its specific historical context in comparative history and then, as a result of this, to be able to understand it and surmount it.

Gender, Class and the Nation

In *Sei no rekishi gaku* (Japanese history of sexuality), which describes one point of arrival for women's history in the 1990s, Fujime Yuki places at the beginning a section entitled 'Introduction, Perspectives and Methodology'. Here she writes:

> In the study of women's history within second wave feminism, any methodology that fails to take into account class and nation (race) and attempts to only make an issue of sex (gender) is regarded as invalid. Interest is focused on finding a unified understanding of these and a new methodology (Fujime, 196:17).[24]

The military comfort women issue also requires a unified understanding that includes sex, class and nation. However, in order to achieve this it is necessary to transcend the type of theories that we have seen to date, such as a male-centred historical view point, the national-centric, one-country historical view point, and the reverse side of these, universalism.

If we try and unravel the comfort women issue using these three categories as an axis, in line with the historical context of the times, we can categorise six social groups: Japanese men, Japanese women, men from the colonies, women from the colonies, and then men in the occupied territories and women in the occupied territories. It is also necessary to add to this, discrimination towards prostitutes from the lower classes. Due to the sexual double standard, the category of 'woman' can be further divided into wife/mother (this includes virgin girls who are eligible to become wives and mothers) and 'prostitute'. People from the occupied territories are, regardless of sex, the 'enemy' therefore they are targets for slaughter if they are male and rape if they are female. The problem then is the treatment of people from the colonised territories. During the war, Korea was treated as one part of the territory of Japan, with the Korean people made into imperial subjects. With total war, men from the colonised territories were forced to bear the burden of unwelcome duties such as the military draft and the draft for war work. Women from the colonies were also required to 'offer their bodies for the nation' but, already subject to discrimination even as second-class citizens, they were allotted duties appropriate to their lower status. In Korea, the term *teishintai* (volunteer corps) is often used as a synonym for the comfort women. That comfort women were recruited using roundabout methods under the name *Joshi Teishintai* (women's volunteer corps), which literally means 'women offering themselves for the nation', reveals an aggressor's logic. For the Imperial Army sexual service amounted to just one more way of 'offering oneself for the nation'[25].

In terms of the category itself, there was no difference between Japanese and Korean military comfort women. Although Japanese and Korean comfort women were allocated on the basis of the class of the soldier – Japanese women were assigned to commissioned officers and Korean women to the regular troops – and there was a disparity in the treatment they received, they both shared the fate of the military and when necessary were assigned to carry ammunition or nurse the wounded.[26]

That this was the case can be confirmed by the fact that, despite finally abandoning the women on the battlefield, when the Japanese army took flight from all areas of South East Asia they took the comfort women along with them until the very last moment. Of course we could view this as the Japanese military not abandoning 'carnal lust' even in the face of death. At the same time, these women did not necessarily treat the Allied Forces as a 'liberating army' having been told by Japanese soldiers that if they became prisoners of war then rape by the 'enemy' awaited them and, perhaps because of this, they threw their fate in with the soldiers and under pressure committed suicide, due to an anticipation frequently found to be the case in reality.[27]

Then, above all else, is the historical fact that the Tokyo Trials did not bring judgement on the comfort women issue. It was not simply that a perspective that would have understood the military comfort women as a crime was lacking on the side of the Allied countries. The Japanese government that welcomed the Occupation Forces immediately established comfort stations for the Occupation Forces, and here again the state faced with the unprecedented national crisis of defeat and occupation demanded that Japanese women 'offer themselves for the nation' (Yamada, 1991, 1992).

On this point, the patriarchal logic of the Japanese government did not change in the least between pre- and post-war.

Nevertheless, in contrast to the Japanese women who from the beginning were recruited from among prostitutes, Korean women were made to shoulder the burden of sexual duties befitting of women who were second-class citizens. In keeping with the sexual double standard of the 'wife/mother' and the 'prostitute', it was expected that Japanese and Korean women would offer themselves for the nation corresponding to their respective sexual duties. Stated more clearly, Korean women, who were reduced to 'public lavatories' and 'Ps' (Chinese slang referring to female genitals), were even stripped of the romanticising symbolism associated with the prostitute. On the one hand, this was the practice of designating sex segregated public and private spheres. Yet on the other, through the creation of a sexual double standard, it was also a harsh means of solving the dilemma of patriarchy that had broken its own rules. While the sacredness of the home and motherhood was something that should not be violated, a 'sexual sanctuary' was required for men and the creation of such areas was not something to be brought out into the open. Then, because this 'shame' was something that was collectively shared in Japan, Korea and on the side of the Allied countries, the comfort women system was not problematised by any of the patriarchal states.

In addition, assigned to be the 'mothers of the god of war' or 'sacred mothers', it was Japanese women who internalised patriarchy's prostitute discrimination due to their heightened expectations concerning nationalisation. This prostitute discrimination has remained unchanged post-war, continuing to find expression in the discriminatory views directed towards Japanese comfort women, including those who served the Occupation Forces, and in the spirit of the Anti-Prostitution Law. The contemporary perpetrator responsibility of Japanese women depicted within this reality is that at no time have we been able to problematise the Japanese comfort women, including those who served the Occupation Forces.

The class factor is also tied into this prostitute discrimination. Women who dared to enter this 'shameful calling', assuming they were paid, were considered to have existed as a breakwater to protect the chastity of women from good homes. Whatever treatment they received was regarded as part and parcel of their role. If the Korean nationalist discourse is tied in with indignation that women who were not originally in this lowly position (the chaste Korea argument) were made into prostitutes, then we can conclude that this amounts to prostitute discrimination. But what if we accept, as Tanaka Toshiyuki suggests, that the comfort women system is a variant of military controlled prostitution that can be seen in any modern military? Treating it as a slight deviation from what usually happens in war zones similarly leaves the way open for it to be viewed as something that no-one has any business complaining about. The reason that I am persistently dwelling on the distinction between 'forced prostitution' and 'voluntary prostitution' based on the presence or absence of self-determination, and the division of women based on this, is because the prostitute discrimination contained within this view has a direct impact on the modern oppressive sexual double standard.[28]

Sitting in the background of the comfort women issue is the nation-state and imperialism; colonial rule and racism; patriarchy and discrimination against women; and furthermore, the oppression that continues day-to-day concerning the division and control among women brought by the sexual double standard. Our struggle is not over questions that belong to the past, but over questions concerning contemporary oppression, which belong to the present.

'Truth' Amidst Multiple Histories

If the interpretive paradigms regarding the comfort women contain this much plurality and complexity, what is the truth of the comfort women issue? With such a gap between interpretative paradigms it appears as though nobody knows the truth. However, in reality this way of posing the question is a trick. This is because it is premised upon the idea that truth is something singular that nobody would deny; something that looks the same to everyone. What actually exists are multiple realities experienced by the parties involved, and these are constructed into multiple histories.

There is a gap difficult to bridge between the reality of former Japanese soldiers who speak with an apparent sense of nostalgia of their 'communication' with comfort women and the reality of the female victims who speak of their experiences as comfort women as ones of suffering and oppression. When there is such a gap between one set of involved parties compared to the other, can it really be said that both parties share one experience? However, if we think this way does it mean that this struggle concerning the truth is a Weberian type 'divine struggle', one that carries on to eternity without a conclusion?

Acknowledging multiple histories does not mean that we choose one truth from among these different interpretative paradigms. It is acknowledging the possibility that history can take on an appearance completely different from that which we have seen with our own eyes. It is accepting that history can simultaneously be more than one thing. There is always the possibility of history being compositive and pluralistic. Here, the idea of an 'official history' has to be abandoned. From within history it is possible to write 'another history' of minorities, the weak and the oppressed, even if it amounts to only one person.

The comfort women issue confronted us with another history not known within the official history. Official history was shaken by the testimony of the former comfort women and in a single stroke was relativised. What is even more important is the discursive practice of creating the history for these women who were formerly comfort women. This was a past that had been silenced and sealed. They have attempted to recover their past as a part of their own lives and tell the story of it again. This was a past that if spoken about in the dominant language of patriarchy was thoroughly stained with humiliation. The impact of their speaking out was another revision of history. When witnessing the present that history is re-making, it is not only the victims who were former comfort women who must carry out the task of questioning what kind of narrative we should formulate and proceed with from here.

Part III
The Politics of Memory

The Japanese Version of Historical Revisionism

In December 1996, the Japanese Group for Orthodox History Education (*Atarashii Kyōkasho o Tsukurukai*; hereafter, the Orthodox History Group) was launched with those calling themselves the Liberal View of History Group (*Jiyū Shugi Shikan Kenkyūkai*) at its centre. The Orthodox History Group demanded that all descriptions of the comfort women be removed from the 1997 edition of Japanese history textbooks approved by the Ministry of Education, in turn performing the role of the Japanese version of historical revisionism in a dispute very similar to its German counterpart.[1]

There is a revealing line-up of names among those who put out the initial 'appeal' to start the group and their supporters. Of course there are names like Nishio Kanji and Etō Jun from the old right, but also younger generation conservative male intellectuals like Kawakatsu Heita and Ōtsuki Takahiro, and anti-feminist women such as Kimura Harumi and Hayashi Mariko.[2] Another anti-feminist I would have expected to have seen on the list, Nakano Midori, is not included, but through another media she wrote, 'I support the objectives of the appeal'.[3] While discovering other surprising names on the list, I could not help think that this issue of the removal of descriptions of the comfort women in history textbooks splits public opinion in two, and that it has come to be a kind of loyalty test that separates Japanese commentators into two camps.

In the background here are the nationalism and the superpower consciousness of the Orthodox History Group and their supporters. Their logic is syllogistic: (1) Western powers were equally bad; (2) Western powers have not apologised; (3) therefore, how can it be wrong for Japan, an empire standing shoulder-to-shoulder with the Western powers, to act in the same way?

Four key points in the arguments of the Orthodox History Group can be identified. The first point is their assertion that there is no substantive proof of forced recruitment of comfort women. At a glance, this would appear to be the orthodox position of positivist history, which privileges documentary evidence. However, this stance is no different from that of the Neo-Nazis. (The Neo-Nazis claim that the Holocaust did not happen on the grounds that there are no documents signed by Hitler ordering the extermination of the Jews.) The danger of privileging documentary sources with regard to such problems should be plain to anyone. The reason for this is that it is clear that a defeated nation will destroy any documents unfavourable to itself ahead of any post-war requisition of such documents. It is necessary to consider what kind of trap you will fall into by adopting the apparent scientific methodology of positivist history.

The second point is that, as a result of positivist history's privileging of documentary sources, there are doubts about the trustworthiness of victims' testimony. A particular feature of the comfort women issue is that it came to have the appearance of a 'victimless' crime due to the silence of the victims, despite everyone being aware of its existence. Similarly, in the case of the Holocaust, because not one person who was sent to the gas chambers and survived spoke out when they returned home, there were no witnesses of what happened inside the gas chambers even if there were witnesses to what happened in the vicinity. If witnesses can be liquidated or completely silenced, the crime can be erased. In the case of the comfort women issue, women who experienced being comfort women were successfully silenced. When these victims finally opened up their sealed lips and testified about their experiences, the suffering itself was denied on the grounds that oral testimony is untrustworthy as historical evidence.

The Group's third claim is that it is inappropriate to teach junior high school students about the darker side of sexuality. Yet, when the media the children learn from about the various forms of sexuality in reality, is it the student or the teacher who ends up feeling embarrassed? This argument is nothing more than adults projecting their own feelings of embarrassment and unease on to children, a feeble attempt to avoid reality. But I suppose that many teachers, who are doubtless struggling to deal with their own sexuality, sympathise with the Group's position as a result of this shared feeling of 'discomfort'. In addition, this argument presumes the sexual innocence of Japanese junior high school students. It is an awful hypocrisy to assume children's innocence when we are all inundated with sexual information from the media.

There is one more assumption being made here and that is the underlying premise that sex has to be something good. In reality, sex can take the form of something good or evil. Sex, as just one kind of relationship that can be established between human beings, can take a variety of forms. Sex can be an expression of the joy of life, but unfortunately it can also be used to violate another person. As one type of human evil there is murder, but it makes absolutely no sense when we are teaching about the darker side of human history in terms of wars and massacres in history textbooks, not to be able to teach about the darker aspects of sex.[4]

In actual fact, the age of junior high school students who would be taught about sex is not so different than the average age of pre-war licensed prostitutes or contemporary prostitutes in Southeast Asia. It is said that sixteen was the peak age for prostitutes making a living for themselves in the licensed quarters in the Edo period. The majority of prostitutes in Southeast Asia are young women in their teens. Moreover, female junior high and high school students are exposed and sexually accessible through telephone dating clubs (*terekura*) and 'compensated dating' (*enjo kōsai*). Just what is the educational efficacy of averting the eyes of Japanese children from this reality? What we must re-examine here is the modern myth of youth that confines the teen years to being ones of childhood innocence and fashions the bodies of young people in such a way that 'use is prohibited' (Ōtsuka, 1989; Ueno, 1998a).

The fourth point, and for the Orthodox History Group the most crucial, concerns the task of recovering national pride. They argue that it is high time that we rid ourselves of this 'self-hating, masochistic view of history' (*jiko akugyaku shikan*) and restore an official history that gives us pride in our country. But just whose official history is this and what purpose does it serve? By creating one legitimate national history, an official history serves to cover and conceal the diversity and conflicts within a nation.

Posing as 'patriotic' in the game of who is the most patriotic, they open the way for all kinds of arbitrary purges by drawing a border between those on the side of the the nation and the unpatriotic. The compulsion and temptation of identifying with this 'imagined community' (Anderson, 1985, 1987) we call the 'nation' – that can be defined in any way the speaker likes – is a trap that we must avoid. Given that many on the side of the rival forces have similarly posed as 'patriotically minded' surely signals the recovery of nationalism.

The Challenge to Gender History

Historians such as Yoshimi Yoshiaki and Suzuki Yūko, who have vigorously problematised the comfort women issue, have for some time now been developing counter-arguments to the violent discourse of the Orthodox History Group (Yoshimi Y., 1997; Suzuki, 1997a). Furthermore, it is not only historians, but a large number of people in various positions have entered this discursive battlefield, turning it into something akin to a 'civil war over memory' *(Impakushon*, No 102). In addition, it has the aspect of a media war with specific media appointing commentators from each of the various positions.

The key issue for me personally is the significant challenge made to the accumulated achievements of feminist scholarship and gender history over the past quarter century by the Japanese version of historical revisionism. In addition, there appears to be few from among us who have offered counter-arguments to the Orthodox History Group that actually take this position. Indeed, due to the way in which counter-arguments have been formed, there is a danger that the line of reasoning may well undermine the foundations of gender history to an equal degree as that of their opposition.

From the perspective of gender history, the comfort women issue is tied up with a fundamental questioning of what is historical fact and is thus concerned with historical methodology. There is no other case that reveals this more intensely than the comfort women issue. If it is simply a matter of fact, well everyone was aware of the existence of the comfort women even before it emerged as an issue. What has changed is the way in which this fact is viewed. Put more precisely, it can be said that the fact itself changed from being one of prostitution to that of rape. It required half a century for the paradigm shift from 'the shame of the victims' to 'the crime of the perpetrators' to occur.

The comfort women issue itself confronts gender history with some serious challenges. Hand in hand with this, those who are trying to deny this can no longer simply ignore the challenge that has been thrown out by the issue. Next, I would like to discuss methodological questions raised by gender history concerning the comfort women issue. Firstly, there is the myth of objectivity and neutrality in positivist history and scholarship. Secondly, there is the issue of the relationship between gender history and national history, or put another way, the relationship between feminism and nationalism. Pertaining to the second point, I will also discuss reflexive women's history. Finally, I would like to discuss the seductive and dangerous trap of identification with the national subject (*kokumin shutai*).

The Positivist Myth of Objective and Neutral History

The cut and thrust of the present debate over the comfort women appears to be primarily a dispute over standards of proof concerning whether forced recruitment occurred or not, and whether official documents demonstrating the involvement of the Japanese military exist or not. Of course we can dismiss as being out of hand the logic of those calling for a liberal view of history, being 'absolutely ridiculous academically' (Ienaga Saburō, cited in Kasahara, et al., 1997:225). In fact, while one group of conscientious historians has developed counter-arguments, most historians (including historians of modern history) have avoided getting caught up in the dispute and have maintained silence. The reason for this is that most of them do not share the same fundamental stance on historical scholarship, that of being in awe of the truth. It is easy to reject the Liberal View of History Group by calling them demigods, propagandists, and inadequate adversaries. However, if the myth of objective and neutral scholarship servicing the truth, which forms the background to this perspective, is going to be preserved untouched, then the dangers of this need to be pointed out.[5]

It is not my intention here to enter into a debate with the Liberal View of History Group. I do not think it is even possible to argue on the same wavelength as them. However, the dispute is open to more contemporaneous audiences with much wider horizons than theirs. If the Japanese version of the historical revisionism debate begins and ends with standards of proof surrounding facts, then one of the fundamental questions thrust upon us by the comfort women issue [concerning the nature of the historical project] will be overlooked. Up until this point, the oppositional discourse from conscientious historians in response to the Liberal View of History Group has been to chant, 'do not distort historical truth' and 'do not allow historical falsification' (Suzuki, 1996a; 1996b). Here we have view of history that appears to consider historical fact to be something that takes absolutely the same appearance regardless of who is looking at it, and it is perceived as an objective reality.

The forms of evidence that positivist history accepts as historical fact are documentary historical sources, archaeological (material) sources, and oral historical sources. Among documentary historical sources, official documents are valued more highly than private ones. Even among those who emphasise the importance of oral historical sources, oral tradition and testimony begins to have credibility only when they are backed up by other forms of proof, such as material evidence or documentary sources, and its value is considered secondary and supplementary to documentary historical sources. Positivist history is centred on documentary historical sources, and views the researcher as an objective outsider. In the guise of positivist history, the Liberal View of History Group have made into an issue the lack of official documentary sources to prove forced recruitment of the comfort women.[6] In this respect, Yoshimi Yoshiaki, the historian who has contributed more energetically than anybody else to the excavation of historical materials relating to the comfort women issue, was driven into a corner by popular comic writer Kobayashi Yoshinori on the TV Asahi show *Asa made nama terebi* (Live TV discussion through 'til the morning) during a special feature on the military comfort women aired on January 21st, 1997). Yoshimi was forced to admit that documents that he himself had discovered in the Self-Defence Agency's National Institute for Defence Studies Library, that led directly to the Japanese government issuing a formal statement of apology in 1992, while offering collateral evidence of forced recruitment, did not back-up the fact of forced recruitment itself.

Of course, Yoshimi is not some naïve positivist historian. Behind his untiring inquiry lies an intense sense of mission concerning the question of Japan's war responsibility. Yet even here, it was not until after the former comfort women's testimony in 1991 that Yoshimi himself rediscovered the value of the said historical documents referred to as 'Yoshimi's discovery'[7]. It was the paradigm shift that led to these documents (documents that would otherwise have probably gone unheeded) being suddenly reappraised as something valuable.[8] Had they been discovered 10 years earlier, they would probably not have been noticed or been thrown into the spotlight.

Although her name does not appear in the line-up of the Orthodox History Group, TV reporter Sakurai Yoshiko constructed the following logic concerning the comfort women: there is no proof to back-up the idea of forced recruitment, therefore the fact of forced recruitment itself cannot be verified, and it is not appropriate to include unverified matters in school textbooks (Sakurai, 1997). Many people appear to be persuaded when faced with what, at first sight, appears to be objectively constructed, positivistic logic.[9]

What we refer to as official documents, are in fact sources that indicate the way in which bureaucracy has managed affairs. In this questioning of their presence or absence, to take the position that facts cannot be verified without official documents is nothing less than identifying with those in power.

It is known that most documents concerning the execution of the war were destroyed towards the end of the war. Documents concerning the comfort women were included among these. Yet there is nothing to suggest that in the disposal of documents concerning the comfort women that the military took the comfort women system to be an especially serious war crime. Rather, documents relating to the comfort women system were disposed of in the same way as other military documents. In 1991, in response to the Korean Council's demand for an 'investigation of the truth', then Chief Cabinet Secretary, Katō Kōichi, remarked when attending a news conference that: 'We cannot find any documents indicating that government institutions were involved', and to prove that officials had not cut corners added defiantly: 'If they can be found, I would like you to find them'. Depending on how you view this, his statement could be taken to mean that Katō is entirely confident that the Japanese army effectively destroyed all evidence. In such a case, what function does the privileging of documentary sources serve with regards to the victims?

The greatest problem with the privileging of documentary sources is that the evidence potential of verbal testimony is denied, or at best it is regarded as having some value as a secondary source. Those who privilege documentary sources dismiss verbal testimony not backed up by documents on the basis that it has insufficient evidence potential. The testimony of Yoshida Seiji, about the only person on the side of the perpetrators to give testimony under his real name, was deemed to have weak credibility and was not accepted by either camp. What is much worse, is that testimony from the victims' side failed to be accepted on the grounds that evidence to back it up was lacking. This amounts to nothing less than the worst possible challenge to the reality of the victims. Half a century after the war, when those who experienced being comfort women gave testimony as victims, their 'lost past' was for the first time recovered as 'another reality'. We can say that history was re-written at that moment. This revision of history only became possible for the first time 50 years after the end of the war. Separated from the reality of these central actors is the arrogance of positivist historians who think that they can judge certain historical facts just as they are from a third-person standpoint.

When the victims testified to the fact of their suffering by stating that: 'I was forced to have sex' and 'I was raped', they were challenged to bear the burden of proof and provide material evidence as well. To the positivist, sources such as the private notes, diaries, memoirs or the oral history of the persons concerned are only acknowledged to have value as secondary sources complimenting documentary historical sources due to their vagueness, subjectivity and because of lapses of memory. However, here the term 'documentary historical sources' is just another name for sources that have been legitimated by authority; the sources of the dominant power. In a case where the dominant power is motivated to conceal or legitimise its own crimes, then surely we must question the credibility of such documentation.

There is also a problem concerning who should bear the burden of proof in relation to a crime. By way of an example, Japan's Anti-Pollution Law sets a precedent internationally by taking a progressive stance towards the extending of aid to the vulnerable by shifting the burden of proof concerning the fact of damage from the victims to the offending company, which has to provide evidence that will disprove any accusations of wrongdoing. Normally, in a case where the perpetrator is an institution like the military or a corporation, the victim ends up utterly powerless in social terms compared to the accused. In Japan's Anti-Pollution Law, legal doctrine is overturned with the accused having to bear the burden of providing evidence to the contrary rather than the powerless having to prove their own suffering.

The same can be said of court cases where there is an indictment of sexual damage. I believe that legal logic should be recomposed so that it is not the victim who has to provide proof of sexual harassment, but the person who stands accused of harassment who should bear the burden of providing counter-evidence. The reason for this is that from the outset with sexual harassment a difference in power exists between the parties involved, and it is a crime committed by the strong against the weak. This being the case, it should be quite clear which party benefits in a court battle when both the strong and weak are treated as though they are on an equal footing.[10]

Historicization versus an Ahistorical Approach

The idea that history is a constant revision of the past in the present is tied in with the question: is it possible to somehow judge the past from the present? In response to this question, there are two positions: one is that judging it within its historical context (historicization[11]) and the other is to take an ahistorical, universal standpoint. Whichever route you take, they are both fraught with problems.

The argument for historicization is that you must understand the events of a time in terms of the historical context of that time. This argument, which is honest and well-intentioned, has been distorted in the context of the comfort women issue in the following way. It is stated that at the time state-licensed prostitution was legal in Japan. Alternatively, we are told that, although state-licensed prostitution was based on a contract system, in reality there were many wretched cases where the women were victims of human trafficking and coercion. Following on from this, it is argued that from the perspective of this historical background, although the situation of the comfort women was pitiful, their wretchedness was no worse than that of Japanese licensed prostitutes and that we must understand their plight against this historical backdrop.

There is an agreed framework that is common to both sides in arguments surrounding the historicization of the comfort women system, namely that the military comfort women system was established precisely because state-licensed prostitution already existed. Understandably, today when state-regulated prostitution is no longer legal, we have not seen the appearance of arguments legitimating this system. Nevertheless, we have seen the entry of narrative that end up legitimating it just the same. We are told that, considering the context of poverty and hunger, there were plenty of young women in Japan in pitiful circumstances and because of the times such things could not be helped.

Against these arguments that, at first sight, seem entirely plausible, there was suddenly a counter-argument. For example, Maeda Akira, a specialist on the international law, indicates that by 1925 Japan had already signed up to the International Agreement for the Suppression of White Slave Traffic, the International Convention for the Suppression of White Slave Traffic and the International Convention for the Suppression of Traffic in Women and Children, and that in 1932 it became a signatory to the Convention Concerning Forced or Compulsory Labour (International Labour Organisation Treaty No. 29). Consequently, the logic framed by Maeda is that, even in line with international treaties of the time, the comfort women system was a treaty violation.

> The argument that contemporary human rights theory denies the comfort women system invites misunderstanding. The human rights theory of the time also denied the comfort women system. This was a minimum normative premise (Maeda, 1997a:12).

This historicization has as an exact reverse argument in the thesis of Suzuki Yūko who asserts that the comfort women' system is nothing less than pre-war state-regulated prostitution and forced labour. Furthermore, she notes that pre-war state-regulated prostitution has also been condemned by current standards of human rights. From the standpoint that the military comfort women system was an even crueller form of slave labour than pre-war state-regulated prostitution, Suzuki has constructed a super-historical continuity between human rights violations against women and the victims, yet the background to this is a universal value, human rights.

In a passage written as a counter-argument to those opposed to the comfort women campaign, Suzuki locates this confrontation as 'a bitter battle over an awareness of history and an awareness of human rights' (Suzuki, 1997a:4). For Suzuki, an awareness of history means questioning whether a single truth is acknowledged or not, and it is something that is generated by reality. There is no perspective of history as something that is constantly being reconstructed. Likewise, for Suzuki an awareness of human rights equals a super-historical questioning of whether human rights, as a form of 'universal justice', is acknowledged or not. Yet, a concept of human rights is not a super-historical given. The content of human rights has changed along with history and when adopting a concept of human rights we must also take on, at the same time, the historical limitations that it carries with it.

Should we use the human rights doctrine of the time to judge the history of that time, or should our present day human rights doctrine be used to judge the history of a past time? As outlined in Part One, the act of judging the past from the present can only ever amount to historical hindsight. This being the case, what happens if we follow Maeda's advice and consider things on the basis of the human rights standards of the time?[12]

It is a fundamental principle that questions concerning responsibility should not be applied retroactively to a time before a law or treaty was established. There are those who take the line that *ex post facto* there is no statute of limitations in international law. In a court battle, there is no option other than to construct legal principles based on laws and treaties. A human rights lawyer or a specialist in international law will no doubt construct an argument based on legal principles within the parameters of their specialism, which is exactly why they are specialists.

A legal dispute has to be constructed on the basis of legal principles. I do not want to deny the significance of court battles, however, it is important to remember the following points. Firstly, a legal battle is an extremely limited dispute. Secondly, if legal principles are created for the convenience of policy makers then, before it even starts, a court battle is the locus of a dispute where one is disadvantaged by being forced to play on the opponents home turf. Thirdly, it is always possible to change legal principles, which are the rules of battle, if those in power are so inclined even in the midst of the dispute.[13]

Supposing, as Maeda suggests, our argument should be premised on treaties and international law, then trafficking in women and forced labour that took place before the conclusion of any treaties would not be illegal. It is common knowledge that international law is the product of give and take in power politics between the great powers of that era. Arguments that are dependent on international law have no option but to construct their logic taking the existing international order as a given standard of judgement. As we have to fight according to the logic of the people in power, we have to accept their logic, however temporarily, and are forced to employ it in the art of persuasion. As a result, there is a tendency for the realism of those who specialise in international law and international politics to end up falling into a conservatism that confirms the status quo.

Behind legal principles are the legal ideals that established them. My interest is not in this game-playing within the framework of a limited legal principle. Rather, my interest is in changes in the historical, ideological paradigms that recreate the legal principles themselves.

For example, in the age of Imperialism there was no international law prohibiting colonial invasion by the colonial powers. In the United States in the slavery era there was not a single law banning slavery. However, American history of the slavery era was re-written for the first time in histories post-dating this era due to a change in awareness concerning the extent to which slavery is a crime against humanity. Slavery and the massacre of the native population have emerged as stains on American history that cannot be erased. Within the Smithsonian Museum group in Washington DC there is the American History Museum. Here, the exhibits have changed with each revision of history. A reality that from the perspective of indigenous peoples amounted to nothing less than massacre, was until very recently accepted as an honourable conquest among Anglo-Saxon Americans. With the challenge of a counter-reality from the side of minority groups, for the first time American history could be re-written from a pluralistic perspective.[14]

The same can be said of the history of the compulsory internment of Japanese-Americans. One corner of the American History Museum has been allotted to this, and on display is this inexcusable injustice carried out by the American government against its own citizens simply because they were of Japanese ancestry. However, it is doubtful whether such a display would have been realised if Japanese-Americans had not over many years demanded reparation.[15] Of course, what was on display here was the legitimisation of national (citizens') history.[16] However, a history museum is not a repository of dead things. It is a living contemporary site where each revision of history brings about a change of exhibits and the re-telling of history.

It is we who are living today who are re-writing history. In the case of Japan, we can offer as an example the New Ainu legislation.[17] It is we who are living today who re-write acts that formerly were regarded as honourable conquest as being those of barbaric plundering.

Oral History and Testimony

Within the endeavour of women's history there has been a massive shift in methodology over the past two to three decades. Historical awareness and methodology is being tied to practical requirements. It is not necessary to pit scholarship and methodology against practice. For feminism theory is another important form of practice, with discourse the site of battle.

Women's history has as its departure point a criticism of the privileging of documentary sources. The reason for this is that women's history had to start from a point of complete and utter absence in written history. In *The History of Women in the West* Vol. 3 (Duby and Perrot eds, 1995) Michelle Perrot, who is a medieval French historian, laments the absence of source materials to use in the study of women in the middle ages. Of course, documents and icons about women remain. However, these are nothing more than images of women created by men. What facts about women are we given in these images of women created by men? From today's standards of historical research, a naïve view of history that mixes image with fact is no longer viable. While we might equally ask what facts about women are not told in these images of women created by men, these images do speak volumes concerning male ideas, what they think about women and the illusions they have about them.[18] Finally shared among those doing historical research (particularly in the study of imagery) is an awareness that discourses about women, produced by men, are male fantasies of women rather than depicting the reality of women.

The greatest challenge facing women's history is finding ways to allow silenced voices to speak. This is why women's history turned to oral history (history told by spoken words, writing down what is heard, and interviewing). For women's history, oral testimony is extremely valuable. To be sure, in oral history there are a number of problems concerning the value of oral sources. Firstly, there is the problem of lapses of memory and mis-remembering of events. Secondly, there is the problem of inconsistency. With spoken words there is frequently an inconsistency between earlier and later accounts. The third problem is selective memory. Some events are remembered while other events are forgotten, either intentionally or unintentionally. The fourth problem is that recollections are always memories of the past in the present. We assign meaning from the present to our recollections, including self-legitimating ones. For example, whereas those leading a happy life have a tendency to positively reconstruct their past, others who feel their life is miserable will probably look back and seek the cause of their wretchedness. It is because oral testimony has these four special features that those who privilege documentary sources take the position that oral testimony is untrustworthy.

Nevertheless, feminist historians present the counter-argument to this, saying, that it is precisely because of this that there is reality in oral testimony. Turning the criticism of unreliability and ideological products on its head, they throw back the question: just what is written history? Who are the authors of written history? For example, whom is official history written for, and who is entitled to write it? Is it not the case that a historian who writes about a past that he or she was not alive to see must reconstruct this past selectively? When official history is regarded as public memory, who is included in this public 'we', and who is excluded? In a single stroke, the feminist counter-response has raised to the surface a whole range of questions concerning written history.

Problems inherent in oral history are also present in official history legitimated by authority. Firstly, let us take lapses of memory and mistakes. There are many official histories that treat things that happened as if they did not, as in claims that there was no Nanking Massacre. More things are forgotten than remembered in written history. In addition, it is also necessary to ask questions about the censorship that documentary sources go through before being left for us to access or read today. We can only see before our eyes today those documents that have been allowed by history.

Secondly, there is the issue of inconsistency. There are inconsistencies in written history, too. Conversely, it is equally possible to pose the question, 'what is consistent history'? For many years, the study of history for the purpose of finding the laws of historical change called for scientific history, namely historical materialism. Events of the past were located within a coherent linkage of cause and effect, and the mission of history was thought to be predicting the future on the basis of an extension of this. As a result, a deterministic variable was mobilised as, what Louis Althusser referred to as the 'ultimate class' (*dernière instance*), with every event reduced to this. However, the principles of cause and effect (that is scientific history's materialist conception of history), have lost their powers of persuasion. Today, when historical predictions have been disproved, have we not come to look upon this kind of 'consistent history' with scepticism? Is it not too consistent? What is more, this criticism is not limited to the materialist view of history. History that has been written so that it appears consistent has been written in accordance with certain teleological constructions and to give the impression that there is only one scenario in history. From the standpoint that any alternative interpretations are not tolerated, consistent history is extremely dangerous.

The third issue is selective memory. Again, selective remembering in written history is also plentiful. Why are only the acts of the powerful selected and the experiences of those whom they oppress ignored? Why are political events conferred with privileged status while changes in daily life are deemed unworthy of consideration? Why is it that among documentary sources, the highest value is placed on official sources? Is it not the case that social history, popular history and women's history emerged as forms of protest to this kind of selectivity? The issue of what is given priority within documentary sources is nothing more than the selection of a perspective. The important task that Yoshimi Yoshiaki undertook to search for documentary sources relating to the comfort women is something that occurred after the comfort women issue was problematised, and not the other way round. Yoshimi took the testimony of the former comfort women as a challenge to history, and responded to this with integrity.

Finally, written history, like oral history, can only ever be recollections of the past in the present. It is not the case that once definitive versions of the history of the French Revolution or the Meiji Restoration were written that we stopped there. As the era and interpretations change, these histories are forever placed in a position where they are being re-written from the perspective of the present. History is a continuous revision.

Gender history has come under fire from mainstream historians for being too political and ideological, and the reply of feminists in response to this is, that is exactly right, all history is political, then throwing back at them the question: 'Is there any history that is not political?' Joan Scott, the author of *Gender and the Politics of History*, when discussing the importance of gender analysis in history states, 'I am aware of the necessarily partial results such an approach will produce' (Scott, 1988, 1999:10). This acknowledgement that gender history is also 'partial', is an act akin to throwing down the gauntlet, and pronounces that all history that has been presumed to be official history is nothing more than male history and reveals the partiality of this.

> Such an admission of partiality, it seems to me, does not acknowledge defeat in the search for universal explanation: rather it suggests that universal explanation is not, and never has been, possible (Scott, 1998, 1999:10).

This is a bold challenge to totalising history and nomothetical scientific history. Positivist history is not an exception here. Despite calling for objectivity and neutrality in the name of empiricism, a questioning of what is available to us as empirical sources and the political significance of privileging these historical sources has not taken place.

By arguing that all history is partial, including gender history, Scott's position is not tied to a fruitless ideological thesis or indicative of a nihilistic attitude towards scholarship. Scott announces that, just as we have been unable to position a single historical truth, reality is composed of multiple categories and that the mission of social scientists, including historians, is to become more sensitive to this multiplicity and these differences.

Narrating History

If, rather than viewing history as an objective restoring of the past, we see it as a reconstruction in the present, then the issue of historical narrative arises.

The testimony of the former comfort women was shocking not only because of the fact of what happened, but also because 50 years after the war the way in which the story was narrated changed. Until very recently, most former comfort women perceived their past experiences as their personal shame, and allowed them to sink to the depths of their memories. These women put a lid on their past, not even revealing it to their closest family members. Yet through their testimony, they made their victimization public and redefined it. Here we had a drastic change in historical awareness and a shift in paradigm.

It was the Korean democracy and women's movements that brought about this shift. Furthermore, the background to the Korean women's movement was the growing impact of the grass roots women's movement internationally. It was precisely because this paradigm shift had already occurred that a narrative responding to this appeared before our eyes (see Part Two). The testimony of the comfort women would not have been possible without the existence of the women's movement. Even if the court battles have only symbolic significance, the testimony of the comfort women has had profound meaning for the women themselves.[19] A tremendous change occurred in that the women themselves were able to recover this blank past and their suppressed memories. However painful these memories may be, it can be said that by positioning their past as something with meaning, they recovered their integrity in life. Numerous victims have testified how much their past tormented them. If we accept that the women who were former comfort women have dignity, then it was in the very act of giving testimony that they acquired this dignity. The act of denying this testimony is what tramples on the dignity of these women.

If we ask the question, what kept these women silent for half a century, the answer is that the crime continued in the present tense for the whole of this time. In response to those who ask – why are you covering old ground, isn't the comfort women problem something that happened in the past? – my reply is that it is not a crime of the past, but something being perpetrated today. When you think that there are undoubtedly still many women who have not come forward, this is nothing less than the damage continuing to live on in the present. Among those who have not spoken out, the silence of the Japanese comfort women bears heavily on us as our crime. It hardly needs to be said, that the biggest perpetrators here are the patriarchal societies of Japan and Korea.

We can see some interesting parallels with the history of the Holocaust. The Holocaust victims did not exist objectively as victims for everyone to see. There were many post-war twists and turns before the history of the Holocaust took its present form. The greatest change occurred in 1961 with the Eichmann Trial that took place in Israel, when survivors were called up into the witness stand and, for the first time, opened their sealed lips about their experiences; experiences moreover that almost defy expression. Up until then, victims and survivors of the Holocaust were generally regarded as cowardly, even within Israel, for having simply followed orders and going meekly to the gas chambers without so much as a rebellion or an uprising. A view held implicitly among the Israeli people was that they were powerless Jews idling their time away in Europe until they were led away like lambs going to slaughter. As a result of words spoken up in the witness stand at the Eichmann Trial, a past that it had not even been possible to talk about, memories that could not be put into words, surfaced as a huge shock. The recollections of the victims, which were painful for them to even think about, surfaced as reality for the first time through narratives and the existence of those willing to listen to these. Thus, even in the case of the Holocaust it is clear that we are not talking about undisputable facts suddenly surfacing unchanged.

The assumption that I make is that when a victim finally takes the plunge and speaks out, this itself is nothing less than a departure from that victim's oppressive reality. What I am calling reality here is not the same as fact. When there is such a gap between the reality of the assailants and the victims of rape, can we really say that there is a single fact? Instead, what we have here is the existence of two totally different realities, with not even one shared reality between the parties involved. The reason I use the term comfort women with hesitation, despite accepting the historical fact of the existence of the comfort women, is to indicate the reverse side of the fact. If rather than a single reality we think in terms of the existence of multiple 'realities', then two realities co-exist here: the reality of the comfort women system according to the military and the reality of rape for the victims. When there is such a tremendous gap between the reality of former Japanese soldiers (who still today speak nostalgically of their interaction with comfort women) and the reality of the comfort women themselves, the soldiers, who took for granted the shared nature of their experiences, must have been thrown into confusion when suddenly a quite different and unimagined aspect of this experience was thrust before them.

Even though there is such a huge gap between two realities, this does not mean that one is correct and the other is mistaken. However, where power relations are asymmetrical the reality of the powerful becomes the dominant reality and this is forced on the minority party as a definition of the situation.[20] In contrast to this, the act of bringing forth another reality that overturns the dominant reality is for the weak the battle itself; it is the practice of reclaiming a part of oneself that has been denied by the dominant reality.

If the weak do this, then the next issue to emerge is how has the reality of the victims been created. The reality of the victims is constructed for the first time through the process of narration. Put the other way around, we can say that it is through the process of narration that the narrator's subject formation as a victim takes place. The term victim may not be appropriate in this context. On the basis of what we have learned from other cases of sexual violence, it may be better to speak of them as survivors. This is because these women are not simply victims, but as survivors (*ikinobita mono*[21]) of great suffering they are weaving narratives as part of the work of confirming their continued existence today.

The question of narration has a dual aspect. There is the issue of the narrator, *Who narrates?* But there is also that of the addressee, *To whom is it narrated?* Who will hear the testimony of the victims? If there is no one to hear the story, then nobody is going to narrate. When raising the question of to whom is it narrated, it is clear that a narrative is the joint production of the narrator and the audience. The narrator is not a 'talking book' producing the same narrative again and again like a tape recorder.[22]

On the contrary, as oral history research to date has made clear, people placed in a position of weakness tend to tell the story that the audience (as the more powerful party) wants to hear. The site of producing narratives is a clinical site for the exercise of power. The narrative of the weak is multi-vocal and intertwined with complexity. Frequently, a narrative that back-ups or compliments the dominant narrative is produced, and the audience takes for granted that reality is a monolith. This other reality comes out in fragmentary bits and pieces from within the midst of ambivalences, contradictions and inconsistencies. For women's history, it is precisely because of oral history's inconsistencies that it is a decisive factor in indicating cracks in the dominant reality. Moreover, this is exactly why sensitivity is required of a listener at the site of producing complex narratives. If the narrative is sewn up into a consistent story, then again the listener ends up cooperating at this clinical site.

At such a clinical site of producing narrative there is even the creation of a model victim. The story of the model victim, told as the audience wants to hear it, could look like this: One day a naïve and innocent maiden, without warning, is suddenly forcefully abducted, kidnapped, or deceptively recruited, whisked away, gang raped and then made to labour as a comfort woman. Although she tried to escape her plans were obstructed and she managed to survive this living hell. While this is the story of the model victim, in fact there are a diverse variety of scenarios of how women became comfort women. It is difficult to generalise, but for example, by a contract entered into due to poverty or through parents; forced by a local authorities; or by the seduction of pimps and their fraudulent modes of operation. The '*bona fide* authority' of the support groups has the tendency of inventing an image of the 'immaculate victim' by emphasising the innocence of the victims. We need to view with suspicion this way of forming the narrative, as it is quite possible that the unintentional result will be an effective silencing of those who fall even slightly outside the formulation of the narrative. This is very similar to discourses that emphasise the purity of victims of sexual violence, with the unintentional effect that they reinforce patriarchy.

Let me offer a typical example here. Korean-American documentary filmmaker Dai Sil Kim-Gibson visited Nanumu House[23] and made a documentary showing the daily lives of the 'harmony' women.[24] Kim-Gibson noticed that after hearing the stories of the women many times, the narrative formula changed depending on the occasion. The details that one woman gave in her first testimony about how she became a comfort woman told of an unhappy marriage forced on her by her parents, being abused by her husband and then, in order to escape this abuse, being taken in by the sweet words of a pimp and running away from married life. In an interview by, and public testimony for, the Japanese media this changed with no mention of her married life. It is likely that Kim-Gibson's example will be instantly seized on and misused by opposition factions. This example could be used to support those who devalue oral testimony on the basis that it shows how unreliable it is. However, we can look at the same affair from a completely different angle. The audience, in other words the Japanese media and well-intentioned interviewers, exercise their power to transform the narrative formula at the very site where they are engaging in the practice of listening in order to extract the story that they themselves want to hear. In response to the question, in what way is the reality of the victim created by and a consequence of the narrative?, both positivist historians, who at first sight appear neutral, and even well-intentioned support groups may conspire with the perpetrators without even noticing it.

Even today, power relations come into play at each site of narration. This is a familiar experience for those who are knowledgeable about the narratives of the victims of sexual violence or court testimony. Court testimony forces people to speak at the most overpowering and authoritarian of sites. Narratives of the weaker party will certainly not be told in a situation where the narrator lacks a sense of security and trust that the audience will empathise with his or her story. This is something that we should have learned from studying women's history.

Reflexive Women's History

So far I have made a distinction between the terms *gender history* and *women's history*. Due to the seeming neutrality of the concept of gender, there is a tendency for it to be used by those who dislike the terms *feminism* and *women's studies* because of their exclusivity and challenging nature. However, an understanding of the concept of gender as described by Scott makes abundantly clear the political and challenging nature of this term as well. The idea that gender is more moderate and neutral than feminism is quite simply a mistake or a misunderstanding.

There are two reasons for my adoption of the term gender history. Firstly, before the establishment of gender history in Japan there was a long tradition of women's history. Secondly, in contrast to women's history, which is restricted by name to the study of the female arena, gender history brings with it the possibility of using the gender as an analytical category in all domains regardless of sex.

If we speak in terms of the first point, women's history in Japan has had a somewhat contorted relationship with feminism. This is because it was established before the emergence of second wave feminism under the influence of historical materialism and already had a long accumulation of results. The reaction of many women historians to the appearance of women's liberation was a barely concealed bewilderment and animosity (Ueno, 1995a). In addition, amidst the rise of the women's liberation movement in the 1970s and 1980s, women's history in Japan accumulated many important results. For example restoring grass roots local women's history. Yet this occurred without a baptism in the various feminist theories developed contemporaneously and, moreover, in an interdisciplinary manner (Ogino, 1993).[25] To make it clear, when I refer to women's history in this book I am speaking of women's history as it was before a concept of gender was introduced as an analytical category.

With regards to the second point, when women's history was established, scholars in the field thought of it as specialising in research into the female domain, and an area passed over by orthodox history. As a result, it can be called a supplementary history to orthodox history; 'picking up the scraps' of history. Before long, scholars of women's history realised that by simply saying 'women were also there' their effect on orthodox (men's) history was negligible, and they grew increasingly more irritated.[26] In contrast to the sexual division of labour within historical research where women's history deals with the gendered private sphere and orthodox history with the 'gender-indifferent' public sphere, there is gender history which announces that gender is also operating in the public sphere and engenders the very concept of gender neutrality (or what is regarded as gender neutrality). Orthodox history is also engendered as 'men's history'. For example, if female actors are absent from the political and economic domains, we must explain from a gender perspective the phenomenon of women's absence. Therefore, theoretically there is not a domain that gender history cannot intervene in. This is because if we look at the gender effect of constructing a domain so that it appears gender neutral it is clear that hidden behind the appearance of gender neutrality is a male-centeredness. From this kind of analysis, for example, we can see that the soldier and the citizen are constructed in a male mould. By another name, the reality of gender neutrality is male exclusivity and female exclusion.

The paradigm shift in gender history occurred as a result of the move to restore women's agency in history. This occurred in conjunction with the move in feminism generally to restore women's agency, however the restoration of women's agency in history was inevitably accompanied by a questioning of women's responsibility with regards to history. The view that women are not simply passive victims of history, but subjects actively creating history, is tied in with a questioning of the responsibility of women as perpetrators in relation to history. Ironically, this has resulted in feminist historians casting a much harsher eye at women in history than they did in previous times.[27]

Where gender history points to the kind of self-referential and self-reflexive approach common to the cross-currents of post-structuralism, I have attached the name reflexive history. The meaning of reflexive (*hansei*) here is used in the sense of self-reflexive while simultaneously self-referential, and self-critical. For this reason, the connotations are the same as for reflexive sociology and reflexive philosophy.[28]

Rooted in the impact of feminism, reflexive women's history was established as a result of the shift in historical viewpoint where women moved from their conventional position as passive victims of history to being perceived as active agents in the historical process. Then, this reflexive re-examination of modern and contemporary women's history in Japan led directly to a questioning of women's subject complicity and role as perpetrators in the imperialistic aggression in the perpetrator view of history (*kagaisha shikan*).

However, when we talk about reflexivity we are faced with three questions: who should be reflexive; what qualifies them for this role; and what is the object of this reflexivity? Japan is an idiosyncratic state, so perhaps it is in terms of the unprecedented damage that it caused that should be the object of our reflexivity? Alternatively, perhaps it is for war crimes unpardonable in international law or from a humanitarian standpoint that we should be reflexive? Going hand-in hand with this, should we be reflexive about the evil character of what is called that 'war of aggression'?

It is not only Japan where reflexive women's history has emerged and moved towards an indictment of women's wartime collaboration. A similar process born of similar circumstances can also be seen in Germany and Italy. All three countries share the distinction of being former fascist states. However, the trend towards reflexive women's history in Japan and Germany differ remarkably. In Japan, home produced historians are taking the lead in reflexive women's history, while in Germany the task of problematising women's collaboration with the Nazi's has been taken up by American historian Claudia Koonz (1987). German scholars of women's history showed bewilderment and anger at this sudden attack from outside. The reason for the difference in the trend in reflexive women's history is that, even prior to this, there was a huge contrast between Germany and Japan in the national recognitions surrounding war responsibility. In Japan, a national identity was established as *victims of war*, regardless of gender, and as symbolised in the tragedies of Hiroshima and Nagasaki. It was into this that scholars of reflexive women's history 'smuggled' the new perspective of women as perpetrators. In contrast, Germany's national identity was formed on the basis of being perpetrators of a crime with no room for vindication, the Holocaust, and again this paid no attention to gender. It is for this reason that Germany, if anything, repressed the engendering of the perpetrators of war crimes. Koonz, who brought a gender perspective to this, reconstructed German women's collaboration with the Nazis as *collaboration as women.*

On the other hand, in post-cold war reunited Germany, a gender perspective has been brought to the problematization of rape of German women by the 'liberation forces' during the occupation (Sander u. Johr, 1992). From the backlash to the Koonz-type perspective, the taboo image of German women as sufferers was constructed. The rape of German women in the Russian occupied zone was something that had already been discussed. Against the background of the post-Cold War era and the women's movement, this rape, which had been taken as a symbol of German national suffering, was reconstructed as a sexual crime of violence against women by men. Behind this, however, sits a racist discourse that has crept in with stealth purveying the idea that the rapes represented civilization being overrun by Russian barbarism. In addition, the construction of German women as victims also conceals hidden desires concerning national identity (Grossmann, 1995).

In the cases of both Japan and Germany, it would appear that there is no lack of subject matter to be reflexive about. In both cases, however, as long as gender history stays within the framework of national history it will not produce a composition in terms of the 'crimes of the state' that women played a part in. From beginning to end, women are subdominant to the state. Then, in the words of Maruyama Masao, women as 'second-class citizens' are as war criminals only 'second-class criminals'.

Wakakuwa Midori states that during the war, Japanese women played a role of 'war cheerleaders'. Accepting this description, does that mean that women in the Allied countries of the United States and Britain, who similarly functioned as cheerleaders, have no need to be reflexive about their wartime cooperation? Whichever country you look at, the process of nationalising women was surprisingly similar. As long as reflexive history fails to transcend national history, the war responsibility of the victor countries and the cooperation of women in relation to this will not be problematised. So why should it be the case that the fascist states must reflect on their war responsibility while such reflection is not required of the Alliance countries that fought a 'just war' for democracy? While the war crimes of the defeated countries have been adjudicated, is it the case that the war crimes of the victor nations will neither be judged or emerge as targets of reflection?

The United States, as a victor country, used freedom and democracy as tools of world domination in Pax Americana; exempted the Emperor, a key person responsible for the war, from all responsibility for the purpose of its Occupation policy; took exclusive possession of the results of the experiments carried out by Unit 731 on living bodies; and legitimised Hiroshima and Nagasaki. By bringing cross-sectional variables from the gender domain, reflexive history makes comparative history possible. Yet, unless we can question the war responsibility of the victor nations, then reflexive history ends up nothing more than a masochistic exercise. Without such a questioning, women citizens subdominant in the nation will probably end up lining up behind the men of the other side cheering them on – 'you all fought hard for your home countries' – whitewashing the past in a similar way to French President Mitterand and German Chancellor Kohl at the 50th Anniversary of the Normandy Landing operation.

By defining the scope of the subjects who need to be reflexive and the targets of reflection, we are also deciding the limits of reflexive history. The purpose of establishing gender as an analytical category in reflexive history is to allow us to transcend national history.

Going Beyond the Nation-State

I would like to add to our discussion of methodology questions surrounding the subject. In this narrative we call history there are a number of questions we must address. Who narrates and to whom is it addressed? Who is the *I* or *we* that a narrator speaks of? When history brings with it responsibility, who should bear this responsibility?

One of the arguments of the Orthodox History Group is that national pride must be restored. They demand a history that we can take pride in. This desire to seek an official history is equivalent to wanting to frame a collective identity for the people. Here, the identification of oneself with the nation-state both involves seduction and coercion to become an *I* or a *we* who is a national subject. This can include an identity as an *I* who is a person from an aggressor nation. However, this too is based on an identification of oneself with a nation-state. This identification of the individual with the nation-state is called nationalism.

The etymology of the word *nation* is the Latin *nati*, meaning 'to be born'. The English word nationalism can be translated as either *minzoku shugi* [in the sense of patriotism] or *kokka shugi* [in the sense of statism] in Japanese. While there is one more possible translation, *kokumin shugi* [literally, nationalism], *minzoku shugi* and *kokka shugi* are fairly similar, at least within the political system of the nation state where sovereignty rests with the people. Nationalism before a state is established can be translated as *minzoku shugi,* whereas nationalism once a state has been formed is *kokka shugi.* Yet, in European languages there is just the one word to describe these two forms of nationalism.

The word *patriotism*, which is often identified with nationalism, has mistakenly been translated as *aikokushin* or *aikoku shugi* in Japanese [both meaning to love one's country] even though the word originally did not convey the sense of a love of one's nation (*kokumin shugi).* Originally *patri* referred to one's native province or birth place, with the term patriotism simply referring to a love of one's homeland.[29] To look upon the love of the state as an extension of the love of one's birth place, in the manner of a concentric circle, is simply the product of a desire (put more bluntly, a conspiracy) to force a link between a person's birth place and the state. There is a discontinuity between the artificially created state (all states are artificially created) and the native province or homeland. For example, the patriotism of an Italian is a complete and utter love for his or her region, and bears no relationship to [the Japanese translation] *aikoku shugi* (love of one's country). Indeed, it is questionable whether Italian people even share a national identity. This is exactly why the state has been so eager to mobilise any means to create a circuit link running from patriotism to nationalism.

Even within this notion of nationalism, is it the case that *minzoku shugi* or patriotism is right, whereas *kokka shugi* or statism is wrong? Or then again, maybe it is only *minzoku shugi* that we find acceptable? Is it possible to say that the nationalism of the oppressor is bad, while nationalism of the oppressed is legitimate? Is it the case that the nationalism of an imperialist state is oppressive, but the struggle of the colonised people seeking independence is justified? Is nationalism liberating during the period of nation building, but then turns to something oppressive after the state has been founded? Up until what point is nationalism 'wholesome', and at what point does it change to something bad?

When East and West Germany were reunified, cries of 'we are a single people' (*Wir sind ein Volk*) performed a powerful role as a banner of national reunification. It is difficult to make a distinction between 'a people' (of the same ethnos) and 'the people' of a nation. Indeed, as Anderson makes clear, the nation-state itself depends on the imagined community of 'the people' (Anderson, 1985).

One nation-state is very similar to another. The reason for this is that a nation-state in the process of being constructed as a nation-state models itself on other contemporaneous nation-states (Nishikawa, 1995). This being the case, then within the nationalism of the oppressed there is a concealed desire to take on the nation-state form of the oppressor. In other words, there is a desire for a collective identity in the form of the people equal national subjects.

The problem here is the same as that debated by Katō Norihiro, a literary and social critic and Takahashi Tetsuya, a Tokyo University philosopher, in the so-called historical subject dispute.

In *Haisengo-ron* (On the post-war era) 1977, Katō has taken pains not to identify the individual subject with the national subject. He has struggled to build a bridge between the collective subject and the individual subject in the form of the public. Yet, when he carelessly uses the pronoun *we* I cannot suppress the question who is this *we* that he is referring to? Likewise, when borrowing from psychologist Kishida Shū's popularised Freudian influenced *Nihonjinron,* (theories about the Japanese), Katō speaks of 'the character fragmentation of we the post-war Japanese' (Katō, 1997:60). The questions that arises in response to this are, since when did *the Japanese* have a collective identity based on a single character, who is able to make such an assumption and on what basis?[30]

Compared to the complexity of Katō's arguments, civil society theorist sociologist Hashizume Daisaburō's style of writing for the purpose of enlightenment is clear to a degree in that it is too easy to understand. He turns the problem of war responsibility into an issue of continuity between the wartime, imperialist Japan and post-war Japan. Without question, there is a continuity in the legal subject as the current Japanese constitution took the form of a revision of the constitution of Imperial Japan. Similar to the situation of a merger between two companies where any debts must be carried over, debts from Imperial Japan and the occupation after its colonies were relinquished and transferred to post-war Japan. In terms of legal principle, it is correct for Japan to take responsibility for crimes committed by Imperial Japan. Resulting from this legal or logical assumption is the conclusion that it is correct for citizens who have sovereignty to take responsibility as citizens.

However, when he draws the following conclusion from the same argument, I cannot follow what he calls his 'logic':

> Imagine that you or I are living in the period 1935 to 1945, and one day we are called up for national service. This is based on the legal procedure of the state and a duty of citizens fixed in the constitution. Given that this is the case, then being called up and proceeding to the front is entirely correct (Takeda, Kobayashi, and Hashizume, 1997:281).

If Katō's condolences for the 3 million Japanese killed in action is based on a warped sympathy with the agency of the soldiers who went to the war front despite acknowledging that it was a meaningless war, then Hashizume's civil society thesis has the clarity of game of logic. Here, any doubts about the fact that the nation-state has an exclusivity and transcendence so great that it can demand the death of its citizens – the coercive force of this kind of collective identity – are neatly and tidily swept away. Takahashi Tetsuya states that we must 'take responsibility' as 'Japanese' (Takahashi, 1995). If Takahashi's meaning here is that the Japanese have responsibility as members of a political community that we call the nation-state, then his position ends up being not very much different from that of civil society theorist Hashizume. However, Takahashi conceptualises from the standpoint of a much more transcendental logic than Hashizume. Even though, a crime is a crime even if no apparent victim exists (or no accusation has been made). What he has made into an issue here is the 'original sin' of the imperialist state. From this standpoint, Takahashi is making a distinction between the nationalism of imperialists and the nationalism of oppressed peoples, declaring his allegiance with the latter.

I cannot bring myself to say that the nationalism of oppressed ethnic groups is righteous. For example, counter-institutional and unorganised heroic terrorism in independence movements has been made the target of feminist criticism due to the structure of sexual discrimination inherent within them. Likewise, Mahatma Gandhi, whose non-violent, civil disobedience movement has generally been regarded as a model among national-liberation movements, has emerged as a target of criticism in post-colonial analysis for his sexual discrimination in cleverly deploying femininity as a resource (Basu, 1993). Within nationalism we create an *us* and a *them* by identifying ourselves with an ethnic group, but this collective identification awaits us as trap in both the nationalisms of the oppressor and the oppressed. If a concept of the people – the same can be said for culture and tradition – includes the oppression of women and other minorities, than I cannot accept it. This is not a matter of which movement gets priority in terms of the tactics of activists. If this were the issue, have we not already been thoroughly exploited by the logic of the socialist women's liberation movement where the liberation of the working classes was given priority over women's liberation? If in reply to this it is countered that this is because class was subsumed by the nation and the ethnic group, then I would like to know what difference this makes?[31]

Now I would like to turn again to the comfort women issue. Kim-Gibson visited *Nanumu* House and experienced a strong emotional identification as a Korean-American with the *harmony* (grandma) women there. According to Kim-Gibson, it is not possible to make an objective and neutral documentary, and by extension neither is it possible to have an objective and neutral history. Indeed she sat on a panel at a history conference not as a *bona fide* historian, but because she wanted to declare that she intended to stop using a historical type narrative in her work. During her panel speech, Kim-Gibson spoke with emotion about how she got angry and cried along with the *harmony* women. Kim-Gibson remarked that it was as though it was a violence inflicted on her own flesh. Nevertheless, the *we* she constructed in this speech was as a Korean and rooted in a privileging of ethnicity. A Korean-American is American and not Korean. Despite this, it was as a Korean that she identified with the *harmony* women. Faced with Kim-Gibson's narrative, how am I to respond as a Japanese woman belonging to the perpetrator nation? Am I forbidden from speaking the words, I was angry, I cried? What about the case of a woman who is neither Korean nor Japanese, let us say an American woman, what happens then? In any event, surely the reason that the comfort women issue has resonated so widely internationally is that, transcending nationality, large numbers of women have shared the pain as if the violence had been inflicted on their own flesh. The issue here is how this collective identity *we* has been constructed.

In December 1996 at the Department of Education, the University of Tokyo (where Fujioka Nobukatsu is affiliated), an event was organised largely by the students to hear the testimony of the former comfort women. A report of the meeting was put together in a pamphlet entitled *Nanumu no Ie kara Wakamono tachi e – Kankoku moto 'ianfu' no ima* (From *Nanumu* House to young people: former Korean comfort women today). Within this, the following sentiments were expressed by a woman in her twenties:

Until now I personally had run away from the issues, clinging to Professor Ueno Chizuko's words 'you must not confuse the individual and the state; the individual and the Japanese government'. Professor Ueno said that 'it is a frightening nationalism when the Japanese government suddenly starts apologising over the comfort women and its young people take on the government's burden and weep and start apologising, too'. In other words, this means that we must admit and be aware of what the Japanese government did, but take care not to confuse the individual and the state...On the basis of this, I thought 'yeah, that is right, there is no point taking on a grovelling stance'...and that was the end of it. I did not want to get involved. In fact, that was just running away, wasn't it? I have become keenly aware that it is necessary to study history and start acting on your own.

Encountering this kind of sentiment, it is possible that some people may think that my argument that individuals should not identify themselves with the state can be taken as proof that the citizens of an aggressor nation can be exonerated of any responsibility.

Let me explain the instance the woman in her twenties refers to in the above statement. A group of young people went on a visit to Korea and as part of their schedule, an event was arranged for them to listen to the stories of men who had been forcibly recruited and women who had been made to become comfort women during the war. I saw the event broadcast on television, but at the venue a sturdily built young man stood up and suddenly started weeping saying 'I didn't know such things happened. Please forgive us'. This 'moving episode' surrounding this young person's naïve reaction, which undoubtedly came from innocent intentions, instilled in me a terror that in his naivety this young man could so easily identify himself with the state. We need to find a way, other than identification with the state, to express the pain that this young man no doubt felt.

I would like to introduce one more episode. When a social studies teacher at a high school raised the comfort women issue in a class discussion he turned to a girl student, a Korean permanent resident in Japan (*zainichi Kankokujin*), and demanded of the rest of the class, 'all of you, apologise to her'. The Korean student herself reported that this was a bewildering experience. Her matter-of-fact reaction was, 'I don't think that was a proper thing to do'. Undoubtedly this was a 'conscientious teacher'. This demonstrates the trap of the individual identifying with the nation-state, for both right and left.

Can Feminism Transcend Nationalism?

In the Fourth World Conference on Women held in Beijing in 1995 (hereafter, Beijing Conference) Kim Pu-ja, a Korean resident in Japan, and myself organised a workshop on the comfort women issue.[32] Starting out with reservations that the comfort women issue might be used as a bargaining tool over the national interests of both Korea and Japan, I stated that both Korean and Japanese feminism must transcend national boundaries, incurring as a result the most ferocious rebuttal. I will cite from Kim's writing:

> Concerning the question of whether feminism can transcend nationalism [spoken about in Ueno's speech]...a Korean-American offered the following counter-argument. 'My country's borders were invaded by soldiers from your country. You should not be so quick to say that we should forget national borders. Stating that feminism has nothing to do with nationalism is surely no different from the ethnocentric thinking of Western feminism....Nationalism is a an extremely important issue for feminism in Asia (Kim P 1996:285).

Kim's argument here is that a Japanese feminist demanding that feminism transcend the state from women, including those from countries invaded by Japan, may end up nullifying aggression of Japan and the Japanese people. As I argued in Part One of this book, Japanese feminism does not have a history of transcending the state, but is this the same as saying that as a *logical consequence* feminism cannot transcend the state? This is precisely the question I have raised and pursued in this book. The argument I have developed in this book concerns the trap of nationalisation even when trying to mobilise 'second-class' and 'third-class' citizens, and the difficulty of escaping this trap. However, just as with the case of gender, the fact that escaping the trap of nationalisation is difficult is not the same as saying that it is fate.

If feminism is a product of the modern era, then it will not be able to transcend the range of the modern and, as a consequence, has to throw its fate in with it. In the language of nation-state theory, feminism was moulded within the framework of the nation-state, and at most this amounts to little more than an idea demanding a gender-indifferent 'distribution justice' within the nation-state (one-state feminism). In the tone of this retrospective debate about modern feminism, feminism itself is reduced to nothing more than bourgeois liberal feminism in civil society and with the historical limits of this being made clear, it has the appearance of something akin to *wara ningyō tataki* (attacking a straw or caricaturalised figure of the enemy). However, what I have attempted to demonstrate in this book is the paradox of modern feminism, namely that feminism is a contradiction created by modernity itself and inevitably, as a result, the only way it can survive is by breaking through modernity itself.

If based on feminism's history of not being able to transcend the state we pass judgement that it cannot transcend the state, we once again end up being divided by our various nationalities. While it is no longer possible for anybody to erect the kind of optimistic universalism of *Sisterhood is Global* (Morgan, 1984), the reason for bringing the gender category to history is surely not to use this as a basis to conceal differences of class, race, ethnicity and nationality, but to add one more difference; a difference, moreover, that has been naturalized to such an extent that it is not even recognised as a difference, in other words, it is the ultimate and definitive difference. It is said that under post-modern feminism such categories as class and race have been added to that of gender, but if anything feminism should lay the charge that the categories of class and race have until now concealed the gender category.[33] It is not that the categories of class and race have been newly discovered, but that the gender category was the trigger for them to be rediscovered as multiple categories.

The objective of feminism is not to replace one exclusive category with another. The objective is not to construct an essentialist community called *women*. Just as *I* cannot be reduced to the category 'woman', do not reduce *me* to the category 'national subject'. The intention is to relativise these categories.

Terms such as *global citizen*, the *individual* and *human being* invoked to transcend the exclusivity of group identities such as national subject are abstract and universalistic principles. Yet, a concept of the cosmopolitan, universal global citizen who transcends all nationalities is itself fraught with dangerous attractions. It carries with it the illusion of individuals freed from all burdens and constraints, encouraging people to act as though any historical debt did not exist. The *I* is neither national subject nor mere cosmopolitan. What constitutes the *I* is the aggregate of a variety of relationships such as gender, nationality, occupation, social status, race, culture, ethnicity and sexuality. This *I* cannot escape from any one of these, but neither can it be reduced to any one of them. This *I* denies the privileging or essentialising of unitary categories. For this unique *I* – who is definitely not an individual who can be reduced to universalities – something that is absolutely impossible to accept is the logic of representation which equals being spoken for by proxy.

In the way that feminism attempts to transcend boundaries undoubtedly, as Kim Pu-ja fears, we may see the imposition of universalism in the form of imperialist feminism. While this merits due caution, it is also true that feminism cannot remain within national borders. Feminism should cross national borders, and indeed it needs to do so.

The logic of individual claims within the comfort women lawsuits has significance for this transcending of boarders. Standing up to the government's line that the matter of post-war compensation was settled with the bilateral treaty, the fact of taking on the state as an individual and questioning its responsibility is significant as it announces that *my* interests are not represented by the state, *my* body does not belong to and my rights do not reside with the state. The fight of the former comfort women – the idea that *I* want my dignity restored – has the character of not only a stand against the Japanese state, but a rejection of the Korean state's approach where representation of *my* human rights equals being spoken for by proxy.

What if it is the intention of the state to violate *me*? Then *I* have the right and qualifications to reject this. What if the state intends to violate *you*? Then *I* have the right and qualifications to reject this. *My* responsibility is derived from this standing up to and relativisation of the state. This is different from accepting responsibility as a national subject.

My body does not belong to the state and neither do my rights reside with the state. So women (and men) can speak out. If the comfort women issue can be constructed discursively as a human rights violation, then it is also possible to argue that being made to become a murderer for the state as a soldier is a human rights violation for men. Is this within the scope of human rights theory? The question that the comfort women issue has thrust upon us is not simply that of war crimes. *War itself is the crime.*

Ideas that transcend the nation-state lead us by logical necessity to this conclusion. The position of women, in indicating the logical paradox of a female citizen, exposes the cracks in the nation-state. Yet, does that mean we need to accept the essentialist premise that woman equals pacifist. The arrival point for a gender history that has deconstructed an engendering of the nation-state is this de-naturalization and de-essentialization of the category nation-state as well as that of women.

Part IV

Hiroshima from a Feminist Perspective: Between War Crimes and the Crime of War

Feminism, Peace Studies and Military Studies

Until recently, peace studies had no relationship with feminism, and feminism only a remote relationship with peace studies. Now the flip side of peace studies is military research/military studies, and the same can be said about the relationship (or apparent lack of it) between feminism and military studies. Given this background, the theme I have been handed for today's talk, Hiroshima from a feminist perspective,[1] is an incredibly difficult and challenging one as the Hiroshima experience has seldom been gendered.

I took up this challenge mainly because this was a task handed to me by Kanō Mikiyo,[2] an independent scholar of women's history, who herself is a survivor of the atomic bombing. It was Kanō who came up with the phrase 'history of the home front'[3] at a time when no such term existed and women's history was centred on the victim school of history.[4] She has spent the last 30 years digging away at the issue of women's war responsibility and has organized grass roots study groups to explore women's history. She has recognised the complex multiplicity of women's responses to the military regime, not only as victims. She was a real pioneer in this field, founding the history of women on the 'home front', the domain where women were mobilized during the Asia-Pacific War, long before the feminist approach restored women's agency to history. Ever since I first met Kanō when I was in my 20s, I have continued to respect Kanō Mikiyo's work over the past 30 years. When Kanō throws a ball at me, I have no choice but to catch it, whatever direction it goes.

How am I to respond to this difficult task today; a task few feminists have approached before? In this final Part, I would like to try to construct a theoretical framework for looking at this issue from the perspectives of feminist theory and gender studies.

By so doing I would like to take arguments outlined in *Nationalism and Gender* a step further.

Hiroshima as a Symbol

The construction of post-war Japan as a victim

What I mean by the phrase *Hiroshima as a symbol* is of course, Hiroshima as a symbol of war defeat. While to speak about Hiroshima as a symbol may leave some people feeling uncomfortable, especially those who view Hiroshima as a unique experience. But let us ask ourselves, is there anything comparable that serves as a symbol of defeat in Germany? By comparison, the differences between Japan and Germany emerge with a sharp contrast. Without a doubt, the symbol of defeat in Germany is Auschwitz. As a result, post-war Germany's only departure point was as a perpetrator, whereas Japan, in contrast, was able to take as its departure point Hiroshima as a symbol of its suffering and in so doing construct itself as a victim rather than a perpetrator.

Ichioku sōzange (the collective repentance of one hundred million people): a system with no accountability

Behind this self-construction of the Japanese nation as a victim is an unaccountable system symbolised by the phrase *ichioku sōzange*[5] (the collective repentance of 100 million people, or the entire population of the time). Of course, when speaking of war responsibility, there is no reason to treat as the same the war responsibility of the Emperor and that of the common people; the war responsibility of A, B and C class war criminals and the lowest ranked soldiers; or the war responsibility of women, who were denied the right to vote before the war, and that of men. For citizens, suffrage is 'the right of rights', in other words, the right to rights. In short, it is the right to determine one's own fate. Taking this to the extreme, it could be argued that women, having not enjoyed this right, bear no responsibility for the war. While this may be the case, post-war Japan took as its departure point 'the collective repentance of 100 million people'. The fact that everybody has to repent can also mean that nobody has to take

151

responsibility. In a manner of speaking, we can say that, starting with the Emperor, all the people were exonerated of any war responsibility and that the Tokyo War Crimes Tribunal gave the rubber stamp to this approach.[6]

The shock of a 'new type of bomb'

It is historically absurd to insist that the atomic bombing of Hiroshima stopped the war. In the final stages of the war, both the Emperor and the military authorities were fully aware of the fact that a new type of bomb had been dropped on Hiroshima with its disastrous effect. As to the shock that this new type of bomb gave to the Imperial Headquarters, one thing is clear, neither the Emperor nor the Imperial Headquarters made the decision to end the war based on it. Even after another bomb was dropped on Nagasaki, no decision was made to end the war. As historical fact, it is clear that the Emperor and the Imperial Headquarters only accepted unconditional surrender after the Soviet Union entered the war. Therefore, historically speaking it is a mistake to say that the Emperor made the decision to end the war due to this new type of bomb.

Justification for the aerial bombing

While the cruelty of this 'new type of bomb', in other words the A-Bomb, is frequently spoken of, one might ask what about the aerial bombardment of Tokyo? Tokyo residents may feel that it is all very well talking about Hiroshima all the time, but what about the victims of the Tokyo air raids? In terms of civilian casualties, the Okinawa ground battle[7] resulted in a total of 200,000 victims including soldiers. There were initially 100,000 casualties as a result of the bomb being dropped on Hiroshima plus another 100,000 that emerged later, making a total of over 200,000. It is said that the Tokyo air raids produced over 100,000 casualties, thus somewhat more than the 100,000 initial victims of the bomb being dropped on Hiroshima. Carpet-bombing, unlike the so-called pinpoint bombing employed in the Gulf War[8], does more than simply destroy military installations. It is undeniably a direct attack on civilians aimed at destroying the lifelines and livelihood of citizens. In emphasising the casualties of this new-type bomb, there has been a tendency to overlook the barbarity of non-nuclear aerial attacks.[9]

I might add here that political dynamics are at work in these figures of 100,000 or 200,000 casualties. For example, the writer Iris Chang (1997) claims that there were 300,000 casualties in the 'Rape of Nanking'[10] (the Nanking massacre). Iris Chang has good reason for standing by this figure as it surpasses the figure of 200,000 for Hiroshima. Thus, the Nanking Massacre emerges here is a tragedy that surpasses Hiroshima. This competition over suffering can be called a 'pyramid of victimhood', and Iris Chang's intent here is to knock Hiroshima from the top of the apex.

Attacking non-combatants was a war crime under international law even at that time. While it is said by opposition voices that an atomic bomb cannot distinguish between combatants and non-combatants, can it really be said that an attack aimed at non-combatants is unjust? The problem we encounter here is that modern wars are total wars accompanied by a total mobilisation regime. Civilians are responsible for cooperating with the execution of war, the largest undertaking of a nation-state. As a result, there is every reason to attack non-combatants during periods of total war.

Hiroshima as seen from an American Perspective

With Hiroshima being the post-war point of departure for Japan, it is all too evident that even 50 years after the war there is a huge chasm that cannot be bridged between Japan's perspective of Hiroshima as a symbol of its victimhood and the way in which Hiroshima is perceived in the United States. Nothing demonstrates this more than the Smithsonian dispute of the mid-1990s. There was a major controversy over plans by the Smithsonian Museum group to display the Enola Gay, the warplane that dropped the nuclear bomb, in its Air and Space Museum. In the end, the liberal side [which wanted to see artefacts from aftermath of the bombing of Hiroshima put on display, and thus show something of the human suffering] was defeated.

It is said that Truman's 'decision'[11] to drop atomic bombs on Hiroshima and Nagasaki hastened the end of the war, and that by dropping the bombs a ground war was avoided, which helped to reduce the number of American casualties. Nevertheless, this so-called *decision* is not fact but a myth fabricated after the event to legitimise dropping the bombs. As already stated above, it was not the dropping of the two atomic bombs that led to the Japanese military authorities and the Emperor accepting defeat, but the Soviet Union's entry into the war. Furthermore, it is said that the reason that two bombs were dropped rather than just one (which would have been enough to fulfil any intention towards experimentation), was that Truman had within his sight a post-war strategy aimed at the Soviet Union.

The Smithsonian controversy

I personally visited the Enola Gay exhibition in the American Air and Space Museum. A 14-minute spooled videotape of an interview with the captain of the Enola Gay was playing on a huge screen. I listened to this very carefully. The captain was saying that:

> We dropped an atomic bomb on Hiroshima. Even then Japan did not
> accept unconditional surrender. As a result, we had no choice but to
> drop another bomb on Nagasaki. Even after this, Japan did not accept
> unconditional surrender. We feel that dropping the bombs on Hiroshima
> and Nagasaki was the right thing to do.

After the captain says this, a picture of the 14 crew appears on
the screen. The narration that accompanies this is, 'Look, they
are patriots'. Young American men and women and other
tourists watched this intently. For me, it was truly a sickening
experience.

The initial scenario for the Enola Gay exhibition at the
Smithsonian – a scenario that was fiercely opposed by the
American Veterans' Association and quashed, one that even
brought about the resignation of the curator – included a plan to
borrow and display relics from the Hiroshima Peace Memorial
Museum. It was this plan that got shot down. At the time, when
I heard that America was going to borrow relics from Hiroshima
for the Enola Gay exhibition my first reaction was 'what
arrogance!' and I felt extremely angry. I argued that not a single
item should be moved from Hiroshima to the U.S. Around the
same time, Ōe Kenzaburō[12] argued in favour of these relics being
lent out. Looking back on this from where I am today, I realise
that I was being completely narrow-minded. It was my visit to
the Smithsonian that led to this change in my thinking.

What appeared on the screen at the Smithsonian were images
viewed from the same angle as the pinpoint bombing that took
place during the Gulf War. Hiroshima seen from above, the
mushroom cloud seen from afar, but with almost no information
covering the experiences of people who had been living down
below or the devastation that occurred. In other words, the
perspective was extremely one-sided. My own thinking changed
and I realised that for people to understand what happened below
that mushroom cloud it was necessary to display the personal
effects of the bomb victims. Fortunately the current Hiroshima
City mayor, Akiba Tadatoshi,[13] is an advocate of friendly
relations between Japan and the U.S. So, if in return for the
Dogwood trees given by America, he made a gift of some personal
effects of the survivors, even in replica, and had the Smithsonian
create a special display room, then I think this would have an
extremely positive effect on the two countries relations.

Just wars and unjust wars

This one-sided perspective of America towards Hiroshima has continued largely unchallenged for over half a century. A rhetoric justifying the dropping of the atomic bombs is predominant even today. Behind it is the belief that it was a war to defend freedom and democracy against fascism, and that it was a 'just war'. Even now, few Americans question the use of military force if it is in the name of justice. They believe that there are two types of wars, just wars and unjust wars.

This begs the question, what exactly is a just war and how does it differ from an unjust war? With the subjugation of the native-American Indians during the era of nation-building made into an exception, there is only one blemish on U.S. history where it waged an unjust war and that was the Vietnam War. Yet, I am unable to suppress the thought, what if America had won the Vietnam War? In other words, there is a correspondence here with outcome, in that a war goes down as a just war in history if it was won, and as an unjust war if it was lost. Testimony of this is not only the complete lack of any reflection by the Americans on their unilateral invasions of Nicaragua[14] and Grenada[15], but also the fact that the U.S. did not emerge as a target of United Nations sanctions either. In a similar vein, the Tokyo Trials are widely said to have been a trial of the losers by the winners.

The Hague International Court of Justice and the De-Criminalization of Nuclear Weapons

The diplomatic stance of the Japanese government

America is not entirely to blame for generating this gap between the U.S. and Japan concerning the dropping of the atomic bombs. The post-war Japanese government has supported and reinforced this. You will perhaps remember the response of the Japanese government as recently as the 1990s when an inquiry was held into inhumane weapons at the International Court of Justice in The Hague. The delegate sent by the Foreign Ministry testified that 'it cannot be said that the atomic bomb is an inhumane weapon'. At the same venue, the Mayors of Hiroshima and Nagasaki gave testimonies that were in direct contradiction to that of the Foreign Ministry. Biological and chemical weapons and poisonous gas munitions all come within the category 'inhumane weapons'. Yet despite the fact that biological and chemical weapons and poisonous gas munitions have been designated inhumane weapons by the International Court of Justice, it is the official position of the Japanese government that nuclear bombs cannot be called an inhumane weapon. It is the citizens of this country, myself included, who have supported this kind of government and it is my feeling that we should all feel ashamed of this. Japanese diplomacy has continually nestled up to the United States and given unwavering support to American attempts to legitimate the dropping of the atomic bombs.

Conspiracy and the Nuclear Non-Proliferation Treaty (NPT)

Although the Nuclear Non-Proliferation Treaty (NPT)[16]came into being under American leadership, it is quite clear that it was a conspiracy of international politics. The NPT does not allow countries other than those superpowers that have already become major nuclear powers to possess nuclear weapons and so obviously protects vested interests. Therefore, it is not surprising that there has been opposition from late-comers with the ambition of becoming the next nuclear powers. Among the superpowers, France in particular has behaved with extreme arrogance. Under President Chirac, France carried out a series of nuclear tests. These were carried out in the Mururoa Atoll, a colony which, as yet, France has refused to give up, and one feels like saying that 'if you are going to do it, you can at least do it in France!' In reaction to this, India and Pakistan carried out nuclear testing in succession in a kind of violent outrage, yet the nuclear superpowers are hardly in a position to berate such acts.

The Split in the Peace Movement

International politics during the Cold War

In contrast, in Japan the anti-nuclear movement has continued unwavering throughout the post-war years. A moving illustration of this is a housewife in Suginami Ward in Tokyo who started an anti-nuclear petition in the 1950s at the time of the Lucky Dragon the Fifth Incident[17] and collected one million signatures. Although the peace movement has been supported by this kind of grass roots anti-nuclear sentiment, it also has a history[18] of division on the basis of party interests among the leftists under the pressure of Cold War international politics. Recently, after almost forty years since the peace movement against nuclear bomb testing was split, we are at last seeing a shift towards patching up this divide. What has happened here is a small domestic version of what has been happening in international politics; the splintering of reformist groups during the Cold War era and their re-grouping in the post-Cold War era. When the Soviet Union and China began conducting nuclear testing under the Cold War regime, peace activists fell into a dispute over 'good nukes and bad nukes' between those referred to as the Soviet-Chinese faction and those against them. People from Hiroshima might wonder how there can be good and bad nuclear weapons, nevertheless, it was the grotesque logic that there could be good and bad nukes that brought a political split in the Japanese peace movement. The Japanese peace movement got caught up in the polarised Cold War confrontation between the U.S. and the Soviet Union with the end result being the birth of the logic that, the communist countries have good nukes as they are there to stop the capitalist international strategy.

Has there been a national consensus formed around the elimination of nuclear weapons?

When it comes to the question of whether a national consensus has truly been formed in post-war Japan on the issue of the elimination of nuclear weapons, in actual fact, through to today, no such consensus has been formed. This is evident from the split in the peace movement. Clearly, looking at the Japanese government's nuclear power program, the use of nuclear power for peaceful purposes has been promoted as a national policy and even the so-called 'allergy' of the Japanese people to anything nuclear has in reality been undermined. The fact that the Three Non-Nuclear Principles,[19] which may have been created as a result of the earnest wishes of post-war Japan (even by a conservative Liberal Democratic Party) government, lost any substance a long time ago is something that we have sadly been aware of for some time.

The undermining of the three non-nuclear principles

It is hardly necessary to remind the people of Hiroshima that the Three Non-Nuclear Principles are the daring three principles that Japan, will not possess, produce or bring nuclear weapons into the country, regardless of national capability or technical expertise. Before its reversion to Japanese administration in 1972, Okinawa was an exception to the application of the Three Non-Nuclear Principles, as it was not a part of Japanese territory. However, when Japan regained sovereignty over Okinawa, attention focused on whether the Principles should apply there or not. The Satō government in power at the time officially said that the Three Principles would apply, but in reality behind-the-scenes bargaining with the U.S. took place. This has recently been exposed with the release of documents from the time. Concerning the question of whether or not Okinawa reverted to Japanese administration nuclear-free, in reality it did not. It is also common knowledge that since then we have not seen Okinawa falling into line with mainland Japan, but the reverse. According to the agreement between the two countries, whenever an American nuclear submarine enters a Japanese port, the U.S. government is responsible to answer questions concerning whether it is equipped with nuclear warheads or not, yet never once has there been an on-board inspection. With Japan taking America at its word as a matter of principle, the 'Okinawa-ization' of mainland Japan has long been underway. This again is a matter of fact. Furthermore, it is us who have continued to give our support to this shameful government.

The De-Criminalization of State Violence

The disarmament and the criminalization of murder and violence in civil society

When we make an issue out of the premise that citizens are disarmed, and that murder and violence are criminal acts, then we come up with the following questions: What actually is this military power that states employ and what is the basis for justifying state violence, in other words the use of military power? Here I would like to respond to these questions.

It can be said that the basis of military power is the de-criminalization of state violence. After all, an act of violence committed under any other circumstances is a criminal act. In civil society it is a crime to hit somebody on the street. In civil society murder and violence are also criminal acts, yet these same acts are not regarded as criminal when carried out by the state. How can we make sense of this? Following this line of thought confronts us with the issue of the formation of the modern civil society and the nation-state, and the distribution of violence within these. Inside civil society citizens are disarmed, and murder and violence are established as crimes.[20] If this is the case, then we can only conclude that the state does not constitute a part of civil society.

Civil society and beyond: the state and the private sphere

In actual fact, there is another sphere that does not constitute a part of civil society. This is what is referred to as the private sphere. At the time that civil society was established it produced two spheres external to it; the state sphere and the private sphere. It is not simply a surprising coincidence that two types of violence that do not belong to civil society – violence carried out by the state on the one hand, which we can call public violence, and violence that occurs in the private sphere, which we can call private violence or more recently domestic violence, on the other – have quite evidently not been criminalized. It has long been realised among civil society theorists that society is differentiated from the state. In other words, civil society is different from the public sphere and, in addition, the family, or the private sphere, is set aside from the rest of society, where civic rules do not apply.

The criminalization of public and private violence

It was through the work of Linda Kerber (1998) an American scholar of women's history, that I came to realise that the de-criminalization of public and private violence occurred simultaneously with the criminalization of violence in civil society. Instead of asking general theoretical questions such as 'Is violence a crime or not?' or 'Is the state inherently violent?', I would like to re-frame these questions and ask, 'Under what conditions does violence become a crime and under what conditions does it not emerge as a crime?' By so doing, we find that to systematically commit murder or acts of violence as a member of a national army can turn you into a hero, whereas punching someone in a bar can brand you as a criminal. By re-framing the question in this way, we can inquire further by asking, 'What is the difference here?'

Kerber, as a scholar of American history, has conducted empirical research into the reciprocal relationship between military service and civil rights in the U.S. since the War of Independence (1775–1783). Her work was so inspiring to me that I would like to take her findings a step further by asking the question, What might we learn if we treat violence in the public and private spheres and civil society as paired? Asking such a question has led me to the following development.

Two Lawless Zones

Civil society comes under the law. Yet it has become clear that there are quite evidently two lawless zones external to civil society. One of these lawless zones is international society. Nation-states are constituent members of international society. This international society is in a lawless zone. Gradually rules in the form of international law have been introduced into this lawless zone. Rules have been created such as: 'If we are going to have a war, let's do it in a gentlemanly fashion'; 'Let's not use inhumane weapons'; It's okay to have a war, but let's go about it in a fair way'; or 'Let's have a war without committing any war crimes'.[21] These rules are totally unrealistic and send a shiver down my spine just to repeat them. However, international law serves to justify the use of armed force as a means of settling disputes between nations.

The rhetoric of peace-keeping operations

Now we have what are called the United Nations Peace-Keeping Operations (PKO), yet there is a clear through-line between peacekeeping operations and military operations. The word *operation* comes from a military term. Let us explore the etymology of the word *peace*. The word *peace* has its origins in the verb *to pacify*. From the verb peace we also derive the noun *pacification*. Pacification is the suppression of an inferior force by a superior force. It was Hasegawa Michiko,[22] a female new-right intellectual, who imparted the wisdom to me. Hasegawa is a real smart old fox and, while she may be an adversary, I have something to learn from her. She obviously came out with this to emphasise the violent character of peace-keeping, but according to Hasegawa peace-keeping without recourse to violence is not possible. She hit the nail well and truly on the head when she said that a peace-keeping operation is the act of suppressing the use of force locally by a superior, overwhelming military force. Consequently, it is clear that peace-keeping operations are, above all else, military action and are being continually carried out in the name of human rights in order to justify military intervention. The aerial bombardment of Kosovo[23] is one example.

The site where decision-making of this nature takes place is where the United Nations (UN) convenes. That the bi-polar domination of the U.S. and Soviet Union has in the post-Cold War era given way to the monocratic domination of the U.S. is also common-knowledge in international politics. America holds on to the international hegemony within the UN. If it was necessary for UN forces to intervene in Kosovo in the name of human rights diplomacy, then why has it not intervened in the Palestinian conflict?[24] Prior to this, when the U.S. carried out military interventions unilaterally during the invasion of Grenada, the UN took absolutely no action at all. Likewise, in the current Palestinian conflict the UN has made no attempt to intervene. This is because Israel is America's Achilles heel. America's opportunism is all too apparent. When a country other than the U.S. breaks the rules of international society the UN intervenes in the name of 'justice', but when America itself breaks the rules it is a case of 'you can do whatever you like'. This is the reality of the US, which plays the role of the world's policeman with no request from anyone else. The reason that I say that international society is a lawless zone is because the logic of 'might is right' still operates within it.[25]

On the other hand, in the private sphere domestic violence (DV) in the name of patriarchy is rampant. Given that this is the case, then the question that arises is whether there is any logical consistency or thread between these two lawless zones in civil society.

Who is a Citizen?

The right to be a first-class citizen and the obligation of military conscription

When we ask ourselves, who has the right to exercise violence?, the answer is citizens. But let us consider here whom we are talking about when we use the word *citizen*. We are talking about those people who are first-class citizens. Historically this meant male heads-of-household who were married, owned private property, had an obligation to pay taxes, and were eligible for military service. Those who fit into this category have come to be referred to as first-class citizens. If first-class citizens engage in systematic violence in the name of the state it is de-criminalized. Likewise, within the scope of private property rights – and a wife falls within the range of being private property – if one of these first-class citizens is violent towards his wife, this too is de-criminalized. For example, when you consider that the legal principle upon which the crime of adultery[26] is founded is the right to claim compensation for a violation of propriety rights, it becomes clear that a wife is regarded as one part of a husband's private property. While before the war, this right was one-sided and now the obligation is bilateral, the legal principle that a spouse has exclusive rights of ownership on the (sexual) use of the partner's body has been preserved even if this is now reciprocal.

These two forms of violence – public and private – are two poles, and when an individual citizen, meaning first-class citizen, uses violence, civil society de-criminalises it on both sides. In contrast, it is only violence between more than two citizens that ends up being criminalized. From this perspective we are able to see this surprising sleight of hand.

The theory of the war origins of the welfare state

Here I would like us to consider the inseparable relationship between first-class citizens and military conscription since the early stage of the founding of the nation-state. Recently, welfare-state theory has been all the rage, and it has become clear from historical research that the welfare state has its origins in war.

According to Linda Kerber (1998), the welfare system in America was first established as the privilege of soldiers who were injured or became sick during the War of Independence. It was then extended as a perk enjoyed by retired servicemen. In concrete terms, this meant being able to enjoy civic privileges throughout one's life as result of military service, including priority recruitment for civil service jobs, lifelong pension rights, and priority enrolment into public universities.

Public Violence and Gender

Military (meaning state) violence as a male monopoly

As military conscription was an obligation that only males fulfilled it resulted in structural gender bias in the allocation of these lifelong civic privileges. Women in the mainstream feminist organisation such as National Organisation for Women (NOW)[27] in the U.S. spoke out saying that this was unfair. During the period of the Vietnam War, NOW actually filed lawsuits again and again to have women included in military conscription and for women to be able to register for the draft. It would appear then that the goal of feminism at that time was equality as first-class citizens and, sitting behind this, gender equality in military service.

Should women also have the right to become 'spirits of dead war heroes'?

What happens if we introduce the category *gender* into an analysis of public violence? The military represents the systematisation of state violence, and as such the demand for gender equality in the military comes down to the assertion that, it is outrageous for men to have a monopoly over violence, give women a slice, too! I once wrote an essay, somewhat tongue-in-cheek, entitled *Should Women also be Given the Right to become 'Spirits of Dead War Heroes*, ('*Eirei' ni naru kenri o onna nimo?*) (Ueno, 1999a). A 'spirit of the war dead' (*eirei*) refers to someone who has made the noble self-sacrifice of giving one's life for the state. Nevertheless, the other side of this is a much cruder reality. 'Dying for one's country' in fact also means 'killing for one's country', in other words exercising the right to kill in the name of the state. The military is a place where people are trained to kill efficiently. Is feminism really seeking gender equality in terms of this kind of right, too?

Do women seek an equal right to commit acts of folly?

No matter which way you look at it, it is a whole lot better not to kill than to kill, and among all the various deeds that human beings engage in, it must surely be called the 'folly of follies'. A male scholar of ethics, Katō Hisatake[28] presents the simplistic notion that if feminism demands equality between men and women in every sphere, then it should also demand equal rights to commit acts of folly. This kind of cheap understanding of feminism or macho misconception of feminism, which advocates that 'if men commit acts of folly we want a go too' or 'we want equal rights to commit acts of folly,' is currently in circulation. Such a misunderstanding of feminism demonstrates nothing less than the 'poverty' of imagination of male intellectuals. That such men can only conceive of gender equality by taking themselves as a standard reveals their limitations.

The symbolism of the Pieta

If we look at history, the path that led to women supporting the war effort during the last World War was not through female military service, that is to say participation in the military. The self-sacrifice of women that was meant to rival that of being a spirit of a dead war hero was that of being the mother of the military hero who becomes a war god, or a guardian spirit of the state after his death. For women this meant offering to the state their most valuable, most precious possession. This was the life of their sons. This ties in with the symbolism of the Pieta. The Pieta is the image of Christ and his lamenting mother. Wakakuwa Midori (1995)[29] indicates in *Sensō ga tsukuru josei zō* (Images of Women Created by War) that the symbolism of the spirit of the dead war hero and his mother appeared repeatedly in wartime propaganda. During total war it was thought that despite the fact that women could not themselves become spirits of dead war heroes, they could contribute to the state in a way to rival that of men simply by becoming the mothers of war gods or the mothers of spirits of dead war heroes.

Motherhood and pacifism – A de-essentialised relationship

If we look at the history of motherhood being mobilised for military purposes, then we find that the essentialist idea of women as pacifists being contradicted. Motherhood may have become a symbol of peace in peacetime, but during the war it was mobilised as a symbol in the execution of the war. Here we can discard the question, Is motherhood pacifistic? This is because it is the same as asking: 'Is motherhood essentially pacifistic? and within feminist theory terms like *essential* and *natural* no longer make sense. This was the theoretical point of arrival for feminism in the 1990s. In its place we are able to re-frame the question as follows: Under what conditions is motherhood mobilized for the purposes of peace, and under what conditions is it mobilized for military purposes? It is clear from history that motherhood can be mobilized for different purposes depending on the context.

This shift in the way that the question is framed is one of the theoretical achievements of feminism. For example, we can re-frame the question: Is motherhood a handicap for women? to now read: Under what conditions does motherhood become a handicap for women and under what conditions is it not a handicap? In so doing, it becomes evident that it was industrialisation in modern society that made motherhood a handicap for women. Motherhood does not emerge as a handicap in agricultural societies, and neither is it a handicap among elite women, in fact the reverse is the case. As another example, let us consider the question: Is sex, labour? This is rather an odious question as I am sure no-one would want to think of an act of love in terms of labour. The problem here is that the question has been framed in the wrong way. Discarding the question, What in essence is sex?, we can ask in its place the following question: Under what kind of conditions does sex become a form of labour and under what kind of conditions does it not? By contextualizing the question in this way, we sever the essentialist relationship between motherhood and pacifism.

Women's Participation in the Military

The feminisation of the military or the militarization of women?

The assumption that participation of women in the military is unnatural is no longer sustainable. Women's participation in the military in the name of equal participation of men and women in all fields and the enhancement of women's professionalism and access to employment is entirely feasible. But what is likely to happen as a result of this? Will it lead to the feminisation of the military? Or would it cause the militarization of women? Which of these will occur first?

The answer is already there for us to see in the historical experience of the U.S.. Based on the fact that women have already entered the military in America, we can give the following answers to a number of questions. Can women kill? The answer is yes. Can women undergo training to kill at the same level of efficiency as men? The answer is yes. Do women have the physical abilities necessary to handle combat duty? The answer is yes. Have women been accepted into the front line platoons and the marines? The answer is yes[30]. These are the answers that have been brought forth from the militarization of women in the U.S..

The Nationalisation of Women

Assimilation and the completion of the nation-state

Let us consider here once again what we mean by the idea of women becoming first-class citizens or first-class national subjects. The end result of women arguing that they too can be fully-fledged members of society just like men is that the nationalisation of women becomes the goal. Within nation-state theory we have seen an increase in research concerned with the nationalisation of women. This has been aided by the new theory of what is referred to as post-colonialism.[31]

Let us consider, for example, assimilation policy as a part of colonial rule. Assimilation policy aims at complete national unification, including colonial subjects. This year [2000] Arakawa Akira,[32] an intellectual who opposed the return of Okinawa to mainland Japan in 1972, had his book *Okinawa – tōgō to hangyaku* (Okinawa: integration and resistance) published by Chikuma Shobō. Arakawa states that this year's Okinawa Summit and the printing of the 2,000 yen note with a picture of *Shurenomon* Gate are a 'symbol of the final completion of the national integration of Okinawa'. The path of resisting national integration is tied in with the rejection of assimilation.

The gendered nature of the model of the national subject

The act of rejecting assimilation amounts to a questioning of who is a national subject and who is a first-class national subject at the time that nationalisation takes place. When the model of the first-class national subject has already been cast in a male mould, then we must say no to this and refuse to assimilate, as to be like men or to resemble men is not a feminist goal. Within post-structuralist[33] gender theory, Christine Delphy formulated the idea that gender does not consist of two items, but is the practice of differentiation to create two asymmetrical arenas. She says the following about the significance of gender:

> To become like men is to become the ruler, but to be the ruler requires somebody to be ruled...For this reason it is not possible to conceive of a society where everybody is a ruler (1989).[34]

In other words, as it is not possible in either theoretical or practical terms for women to be treated the same as men or for women to be like men, it is clear that the goal of gender equality can only be to dismantle these gender differences themselves.

Citizens, individuals and human beings

Post-colonialist intellectuals theorize in a very similar way in relation to assimilation policies. In an essay by Nomura Kōya (1997), an Okinawan scholar, I came upon a passage arguing the following, and was surprised at how closely it tallies with gender theory. He states that for Okinawans 'to resemble the Japanese is for them to become an oppressor. To become an oppressor will not bring liberation to the Okinawan people' (Nomura, 1997).

Women, Okinawans and colonized people are all second-class national subjects, and Nomura describes exactly the trap of national integration that awaits second and third-class citizens who attempt to be nationalised as first-class citizens. Looking at this from the perspective of where nation-state theory, gender theory and post-colonialism are at the moment, it is clear that we are now in an era where questions are being asked about what exactly we mean when we use terms such as citizen or the individual. This process demands that we also question the gender, ethnic and class bias of these concepts.

Gender justice and distribution justice

What exactly is this *gender justice* that feminism is demanding? One way of understanding this is that it means demanding justice in the distribution of all resources in civil society. It means justice in the distribution of all rights and obligations that reside in civil society. Yet, is this kind of distribution justice the goal of feminism? Among the various rights enjoyed by national subjects is the right to become a spirit of a dead war hero, meaning distribution justice in the execution of the state's violence, or the right to kill. Consequently, it includes distribution justice in the right to commit acts of folly. This being the case, the question that we are forced to confront is whether this really is the goal of feminism?

The trap of seeking equality on a par with men

If we think of gender justice as justice in the distribution of various clustered groups of rights and obligations that take men as their model, then we find that there is a history of the expansion of women's rights being achieved within the confines of a specific group and with specific limitations. For example, among middle-class whites in the U.S. the gender wage gap has been significantly reduced over the past 20 years. Some women would probably say that this is the same as an elimination of discrimination against women. However, others are paying the price of this elsewhere. During the same period, the wage gap between whites and other ethnic groups actually widened. In other words, a structure has been created where white middle-class women can hire childminders from other ethnic groups, for example Hispanic, and carve out their own careers.

Is state feminism possible?

This kind of equality within the confines of a group and with specific limitations I call a 'members-only club'. As long as you become a part of this members-only club you can attain a specific level of equality within it, and without a doubt some women have obtained the fruits of this. This again is a fact. If we take it that one-state feminism is possible, then it is probably possible to establish it within specific boundaries. In the countries of Northern Europe we have even seen the birth of a concept of state feminism. However, we are still left with the question of whether this is our goal. If women are nationalised in this way it means that women must play a role in total war, the largest project that a state undertakes, but should women support or take part in the execution of public violence carried out by the state? Mainstream American feminists, for example NOW, would probably answer yes to this question. I wonder what Japanese feminist might answer in response to this question.

Between War Crimes and the Crime of War

Women's history of defeated nations and women's history of victor nations

Taking a rather roundabout route, I would like to consider the next question: 'What is a war crime?' If we consider the difference between victor nations and loser nations, although this may sound a little odd, it becomes clear that within women's history we also find that there is a women's history of victor nations and women's history of loser nations. Since the 1980s, there has been a trend in women's history towards reflexive history, but this has only taken hold in Japan, Germany and Italy. This is something more than coincidence. The women's history of Japan, Germany and Italy is also the women's history of the former Axis countries. At the same time, it is also the women's history of the former fascist nations and, moreover, the women's history of the countries defeated in the war. If we look at this on a world scale we need to ask the following: Has a movement towards reflexive women's history also materialised in the women's history of the former Allied nations, or the victor nations? The answer is no. Within British women's history and American women's history there has been a trend to reflect on colonial rule and the oppression of indigenous peoples in the form of Imperialist feminism. However, in the women's history of the Allied countries, in other words those on the winning side, there has been little reflection on either the First or Second World Wars; 'wars of freedom and democracy' against 20th century fascism. A reflexive history concerning World War II has arisen in France, but it is self-critical of the Vichy government, in other words co-operation with Nazi Germany, whereas the fight against fascism is consistently defended. It is reasonable to say that a movement similar to the kind of reflexive history as seen in Japan is hardly present in France, with few exceptions.

Those women of the victor nations who do not question state violence

In *Images of Women Created by War,* Wakakuwa comes out with the wonderful expression: 'As one would expect, women did not go to the front line, however they fulfilled the role of war cheerleaders' (Wakakuwa, 1995). In their role as cheerleaders, did women of all the nation-states contribute in the same way to their respective countries? American women must have taken on the role of cheerleaders, and so too must have German women. Why do you think it is that despite having fulfilled the same cheerleader role, women from the defeated nations must reflect on this whereas those from the victor nations can get away without any reflection?

It is because women in the victor nations do not question the execution of public violence in the name of justice. This is still the case today. American women support the use of military force if it is in the name of the United Nations, such as PKO and PKF[35] activities, or in the name of 'freedom and democracy' even without U.N. agreement. We are even seeing a movement among German women to support the participation of German troops in a PKF in the name of NATO. Given this, the move to avoid military force in Japan is extremely exceptional when we look at the international situation, which we can interpret to mean that what is commonsense for Japan would be viewed as nonsensical by the rest of the world. But truly, which of the two is nonsensical? The Japanese Constitution, though imposed by the Occupation Forces led by the U.S., prohibits Japan to use the military power to solve any kind of international conflicts, and the majority of citizens have given their earnest support to this decision reflecting sincere regret and the painful memory of the war. We are facing the cost of neglecting to make the Japanese view of state violence the commonsense view of the world over the last 50 years.

The Women's International War Crimes Tribunal and a definition of war crimes

In December 2000, the landmark Women's International War Crimes Tribunal was held under the leadership of Japanese women and with Matsui Yayori[36] playing a pivotal role.

Behind the act of judging war crimes lies, what in reality, are some truly frightful questions. The flip side of defining what is a war crime is the simultaneous act of defining what is *not* a war crime. This is because in criminalizing some kinds of violence you are also excusing all forms of violence that fall outside these parameters. This being the case, feminism must provide an answer to the question: What kind of violence is excusable and under what kind of circumstances? I was very keen to see how far the organisers of the Women's International War Crimes Tribunal were ready to go to give an answer to this question. In reality, the Tribunal adopted the principle of judging war crimes of that time according to the international law of that time, and did not delve into defining what is a war crime. Clearly, this demonstrates the limits of the Tribunal. Yet within these limits, the organisers exerted themselves to the utmost, and out of this we saw the restoration of justice to the victims, which was an enormous achievement.

That fact that defining what is a war crime simultaneously involves legitimating non-criminalized acts of war is a real problem for me. I feel that it is akin to being caught in a trap to discuss war crimes without asking whether or not war itself is a crime.

Is violence excusable?

The question: What kind of violence is excusable and under what kind of circumstances? is tied in with the answer to the question, Is there such a thing as justified violence? There is only one answer feminism can give to this question and that is to say that there is no justified form of violence, which leads to the criminalization of all forms of violence.

Here I am fully aware that women can also exercise violence. American feminists have carried out a campaign to 'fight back the night', as a response to the ever-present dangers of rape and muggings in their society. Some feminists have urged women to take courses in self-defense training. Other women insist that it leaves women in a less defensive position if they partake in state violence. Yet I would ask: is feminism an idea that seeks to catch up with men on all terms; socially, mentally, physically, and so on?' Some women may be able to 'catch up', but we should not forget that others cannot. Suppose you are aged or handicapped and incapable of fighting back, what happens then? Even the exercise of violence in the name of self-defense is a right that can be enjoyed by only those who are capable of it, those who are equal to this task. Victims of DV who do not dare to run away, demonstrate the lesson that you risk being beaten up even more severely if you try to fight back.[37] You can also think of the case of prisoners in concentration camps. Are any of us in the position to ask: Why do you not stand up and fight back? The case of DV tells us that the private sphere functions no better than a concentration camp for victims. If feminism does not stand for the weak, by which I mean those who are incapable of counter-attack, it has no meaning for me.

The contribution of feminism equals the criminalizing of war

The criminalization of all forms of violence is the only answer that feminism can give. Yet if we answer in this way we will almost certainly be faced immediately with protests of 'but that is not realistic'. I can easily imagine the barrage of questions. Who will protect you from violence? Will you refuse police control as well? Would you not retaliate when a dictator like Saddam Hussein invades Kuwait? Would you just sit by and watch when a 17 year-old youth hijacks a bus?[38]

When the police use violence in the name of justice employed for the good of the community, the concept is then extended to the use of military force employed by the state for self-defence. However, here again, history shows us that societal violence employed by the community or state in the name of justice ends up being exercised only on behalf of its own citizens rather than for those perceived as enemies. The lesson we must learn from history is this: it is almost impossible to prevent the abuse of violence, once the use of violence is justified. No military dictatorship can be maintained simply with the use of force and violence, as it also needs to establish authority, namely the agreement of the ruled. Might without authority will not last long. Here then, my proposal is simple, though difficult: to never authorise the exercise of any form of violence.

To say no to all forms of violence includes the criminalization of both public and private forms of violence. Recently, domestic violence has at last been problematised. It was feminism that pushed forward to criminalize violence in the private sphere, which traditionally has been de-criminalized. We are now at the stage of criminalizing acts of violence in the private sphere. If feminism has even the slightest hope of preventing men from engaging in acts of violence in the private sphere, of building relationships with men who have no intention of using violence against women, and of raising sons to be this kind of non-violent male, then instead of using essentialist language such as *masculinity is violent by nature*, we must say that *masculinity is also constructed* and as a result it can be transformed.

A minority idea

In my understanding, feminism is not an idea about distribution justice, of being on a par with men concerning rights and obligations. While feminism is frequently received this way, it is not an idea advocating that whatever men can do, women can do too.

In my view, feminism is from first to last an idea of, for and by the minority. By minority, I mean those people who are oppressed, handicapped and/or discriminated against, and those who are weak and vulnerable. Feminism is not an idea that advocates that women should become powerful on a par with men, an idea I call a 'catching-up strategy', but should be an idea that respects the dignity of minorities just as they are. I may be no match for a man in terms of muscular strength. I may not be able to make it through life single-handedly. But why simply because of this, should I be forced to obey somebody else? It is feminism that has argued for this kind of respect for the weak. This being so, my answer is that there is only one possible solution for feminism and that is to aim in the direction of criminalizing all kinds of violence, regardless of whether it is public or private. It goes without saying, that this also includes the criminalization of war.

Epilogue

A quick glance at this book may give the impression that it is only concerned with events that happened in the past. Be that as it may, my intention has been to discuss current issues. My reasoning here is that firstly, the construction of the past is always a current project and secondly, there has never been a period when the revision of history has been more controversial than today in this post-Cold War era.

While I feel I have done my best to fully express myself concerning the arguments in this book, even so I would like to respond here to criticisms and questions that I expect will be thrown at me. These I predict will be from the standpoint of how in reality we should respond to questions put by those who have survived being comfort women and who demand an apology and compensation. Indeed, they may extend to the question of how we should respond to the unresolved problem of post-war compensation generally. Yet, this book was not written to discuss ideas about activism. At the same time, there is a strong resistance on the activist side to the reality of the comfort women becoming a target of academic speculation concerning what may or may not have happened, or the comfort women issue being made into a tool for interpreting history. Moreover, due to the creation of the Asian Women's Fund by the Japanese government in 1995, the movement to compensate the victims is currently in deadlock and a more effective policy solution to replace this has yet to be found. Given this situation, it is perhaps necessary for me to express my own position here.

Firstly, as a member of the nation-state that exists in reality as Japan, I feel that in political terms a piece of special legislation on post-war compensation is required. Transcending various political interpretations and the constraints of the Bilateral Treaty between Japan and Korea, it is possible to seek a transformation of the rules through special legislation by reflecting on the passing of half a century where post-war compensation has been consistently disregarded. It goes without saying, that the logic of individual claims must be incorporated within this. Even if the current reality is that this kind of standpoint is politically a minority view, the setting of such a goal is of itself significant. Moreover, while it is the case that two-thirds of those with Japanese nationality were born after the war, this fact actually accounts for the increase in those who are of the opinion that Japan must apologise and offer compensation. The task for post-war generations changes from one of passing down personal memories and experiences, to that of questioning how we should reconstruct the past. Our discursive battle is taking place in order to get more people to sympathise with this point of view [that individual claims should be recognised]. It is noteworthy that many of those who have been responsible for bringing about an actual paradigm change surrounding the comfort women are Japanese and Koreans born after the war.

As indicated by Hashizume Daizaburō,[1] the post-war Japanese constitution was legally formulated on the basis of a revision of the constitution of the Japanese Empire. It is not the case that we are living under a revolutionary government that denied and overturned the former administration. Given this situation, it is self-evident that we must accept that the nation-state has the status of a legal entity meaning that the post-war Japanese state must take over the debts and liabilities of the state of the Japanese Empire. On this point, I am in agreement with the opinion of modern rationalist Hashizume.

Nevertheless, can we say that under a democratic system of political representation that this kind of political choice requires only that we exercise our rights as a citizen by voting in elections for individuals or parties whose policies we support? Clearly this is not the case, as the issue does not end there.

Secondly, we have a responsibility as citizens. Just as the state and the people are not the same, the government and citizens are not one. On the premise that the nation equals the voters, can we say that the matter is settled just because the government entrusts the tasks of making a state apology and paying compensation to policy-makers? Here in the world of representative democracy we see the logic that representation equals being spoken for by proxy. Standing in opposition to this is the logic of participatory democracy and individual activism that we see in Non-Government Organisations (NGOs). NGOs do not speak for the government and neither do they allow the government to speak for them. For example, even if you have a government that supports nuclear testing, an NGO can carry out action that is against this. Moreover, citizens have a responsibility to be involved in the kind of activities carried out by NGOs. In terms of the comfort women issue, the groups that immediately formed to support the law suit and the meetings held in many local areas by non-government, civic groups to hear the testimony of former comfort women and to consider the issue of post-war compensation represent the kind of direct action I am referring to here. In contrast, when every prefectural assembly and every city, town and village assembly took the decision to call for the deletion of all descriptions of the comfort women from history textbooks, the activities of citizens can also attempt to confront this backlash.

However, the logic of representation inherent in policy-making and court trials has its limits, as both must proceed according to pre-existing political and legal procedure. Although I do not deny the significance of court battles, at the same it is necessary to acknowledge their limitations as well.

It is then possible to make a case for raising funds to support the lives of survivors from within the above kind of citizens' activism. At the same time, it goes without saying that the Asian Women's Fund is a distortion that will do little to unravel the comfort women issue. It was established by the government and, as the Japanese name reveals, despite its private guise it is a national *(kokumin)* fund *(kikin)*.[2] On the one hand the Japanese government repeats insistently that it cannot compensate individuals, yet on the other 'atonement money' is paid out in the name of the government, which has employed a double logic to suit itself. This inconsistency has already been widely criticised. Firstly, as the public character of the Asian Women's Fund is ambiguous the issue of who is taking responsibility is also unclear. Secondly, and as a direct consequence of this, there is real concern that the Asian Women's Fund is being used to cover up the fact that the state is not paying out any compensation. Thirdly, with the turn of phrase that all the people should take responsibility we are once again reproducing a system that has no accountability in the manner seen in 'the collective repentance of 100 million people' *ichioku sōzange*).[3] More importantly, the Asian Women's Fund was established by riding roughshod over the opposition of the survivors and their support groups. Despite many survivors expressing the view that they would not accept such an 'illogical payment of money' or that this was 'not the kind of money that they had been seeking', the fund was created without their consent (Yun 1997, Yi et al., 1995). Furthermore, once the Asian Women's Fund was up and running the concerns of the people involved quickly became reality. For a start, it gave the anti-comfort women lobby a pretext to campaign that the women were only after money. Another, is that it brought a division among the survivors and among the support groups on the question whether they should accept the money or not. The Fund has served as a testing ground (*fumi-e*) and the divisions that this has brought have caused deep trauma and undermined relationships among survivors and support groups.

In the spring of 1997, only seven women had accepted any atonement money from the Asian Women's Fund. After that it was reported that by early 1998, 50 women had accepted the money.[4] Payment is carried out in secret, and even those who appealed for the setting up of the Asian Women's Fund and its board members have expressed concern that it has brought with it a rift among survivors and their support groups. Nevertheless, it was the side for the Asian Women's Fund that created the situation of 'the buttons being put in the wrong button hole'. Two-and-half years have passed since the Asian Women's Fund was set up. Even though the Fund may have been created with good intentions – if the policy is assessed not on the basis of the logic of intentions but by the logic of results – those who appealed for the Fund to be established and its board members are responsible for the political stalemate and the escalation of mistrust in the Japanese government. Miki Mutsuko, political leader and the widow of late Liberal Democratic Party prime minister Miki Takeo, although previously among those who appealed for the Fund to be established, later resigned her position expressing criticism of it. It would not be that strange if we saw board members resigning in order to take responsibility for the political turmoil caused today by the Asian Women's Fund; a turmoil that nobody predicted when it was first established.

What is incomprehensible is that post-war liberal intellectuals are among the names of those who have enthusiastically supported the Asian Women's Fund. Behind their motivation to support the Fund lie two factors. Firstly, they shared the political realism that given current political conditions, the chance of individual compensation being paid out is close to zero. Secondly, they also share feelings of sympathy and goodwill, presumably genuine, towards the survivors. One often hears the rhetorical question: What is wrong with the Fund?' However, instead of complying with the appeal made by the government, why do they not start NGO fund raising-activities in the name of citizens?

In fact, it is my opinion that there is nothing wrong with fund-raising itself. The problem here is that it is not being carried out by an NGO, but by the government. A few years before the Asian Women's Fund was set up, my colleagues in feminist activism and I conceived an idea to carry out fund raising in an organised way through an NGO to support survivors in their every day life, and made preparations in secret. Due to numerous difficulties and obstacles, ultimately this idea never came to be realised. But because preparations for the fund-raising coincided time-wise with the announcement about the Asian Women's Fund, some feminist activists made the distorted interpretation that we were fulfilling the will of the government.

Nevertheless, the idea of fund-raising activity existed from early on within the support group movement. Even today, there is the NGO *Sengo Hoshō Jitsugen Shimin Kikin* (The citizens fund for realising post-war compensation) represented by Kawada Fumiko, which is opposed to the Asian Women's Fund. Inside Korea, the Korean Council carried out independent fund-raising activities, which was later taken over by the Korean government paying out livelihood support to the survivors. Perhaps one reason that fund-raising has not emerged as a core task for activists [in Japan] is that it was feared that a fund raising campaign would serve to atone and pardon through money those citizens who responded to it. There has been a tendency for fund-raising to be a 'prohibited strategy' within movements due to a concern that it would further promote a climate in Japan where money can buy anything and, moreover, that it would cast a damper on the demand for the state to pay compensation. On the Korean side, support groups have gone as far as to express the notion that the provision of livelihood support should be 'with our own hands'. So instead, a demand for state compensation has been the core strategy within support movements to the last.

NGO fund-raising is for livelihood support, and does not take the form of an apology or compensation. This is because citizens cannot emerge as subjects responsible for offering an apology nor providing compensation for crimes committed by the state. The responsibilities of the state can only be fulfilled by the state. Nevertheless, we feel that citizens as citizens have their own way of showing solidarity and sympathy. It is fine to object to the Asian Women's Fund, nevertheless, our inability to effectively organise a civil movement as an alternative to this is regretful evidence of our own incapability. I feel in my bones that there is widespread sentiment among the Japanese people who feel that they would like to do something for the victims, but we cannot find the way ahead, and that the Asian Women's Fund has plugged up the entrance point for people who think this way.

In outlining my own position on the comfort women issue, a key point is the responsibility of the contextualised *I*. Personally for me, gender studies is both a profession and a vocation. The comfort women issue has tested my own gender theory and become the site of the most fervent struggle. Put another way, I took the questioning of the existence of the former comfort women as a questioning of my own positionality. A feminist friend who is a Korean resident in Japan stated the following: 'The comfort women problem is a Japanese problem so let the Japanese think about it'. I completely agree with her. In 1991, when Kim Hak-sun made her testimony I was staying in Germany. Seven years have passed since I was confronted with important questions surrounding differences in the way that Germany and Japan have atoned for the atrocities of the last war. This book is the result of my attempt to respond to these questions to the best of my limited ability.

* * * *

Parts I and II of this book are based on revised versions of a paper given at the Second International Symposium of the Japan Society for the Promotion of Science, Grants-in-Aid for Scientific Research General Project on 'Wartime Mobilisation and Structural Change' (representative Yamanouchi Yasushi). The theme of the second symposium was 'Women and the Wartime Mobilisation System' and held on July 9th 1997, Tokyo University of Foreign Studies. I am extremely grateful to Yamanouchi Yasushi, Narita Ryūichi and Nakano Toshio for organising the symposium that day. In addition to myself, Ute Frevert also presented a paper that day, and Nishikawa Yūko and Himeoka Toshiko were kind enough to act as commentators.

Part III is based on a revision of a lecture sponsored by the *Ajia Josei Kaigi Nettowāku* (Asian women's conference network) for the panel 'Contemporary Japan Seen from a Gender Perspective' on

April 29th 1997 at the Bunkyōku Josei Sentā (Women's Centre in Bunkyoku, Tokyo). I am grateful to Funabashi Kuniko and Tachi Kaoru for providing me with the opportunity to make such an important presentation just after I had returned from a year's leave in the United States and Mexico. Kim Pu-ja and Han Myong-suk were on the same panel. The symposium 'Nationalism and the Comfort Women Issue' sponsored by The Centre for Research and Documentation on Japan's War Responsibility (September 28th 1997, Surugadai Kaikan, Tokyo) gave me opportunity to explore these arguments further. I greatly appreciate the effort made by the Yoshimura Mariko from the executive office. Yoshimi Yoshiaki, Soh Kyong-shik and Takahashi Tetsuya were on the same panel, and Kim Pu-ja and Nishino Rumiko kindly took on the job of co-ordinators.

At a symposium sponsored by the Institute of Social Sciences, University of Tokyo (1 October 1997), I acted as commentator for reports given by Wada Haruki, Korean studies specialist, and one of the executive committee members of the Asian Women's Fund, and Ilse Lenz, a German scholar of women's studies. Ōsawa Mari, a feminist scholar in social policy, was kind enough to take on the job of co-ordinator.

The questions I raised concerning historical methodology were taken up, and led me to a number of dialogues with historians. At the symposium 'How should History be Narrated?' sponsored by The International Institute of Language and Cultural Studies, Ritsumeikan University (July 5th 1997, Ritsudai Matsukawa Kaikan, Kyoto), I was one of the speakers along with Narita Ryūichi and Sasada Kyōji, with Iwasaki Minoru and Watanabe Kōzō taking on the role of co-ordinators. I am extremely grateful to Nishikawa Nagao for organising the symposium. The *Sōgō Joseishi Kenkyūkai* (Association of Integrated Women's History) held a seminar on 'The Methodology of Women's History' with myself as a speaker (November 29th 1997, Kyodai Kaikan). Nishikawa Yūko who had been involved in the planning of the seminar acted as Chair that day. Wakita Haruko, Nakatani Ayami, Furukubo Sakura offered stimulating feedback as commentators.

On March 14th 1997, I was able to have my own panel on 'Nationalism and Women' at the Association of Asian Studies annual conference in Chicago, and had an opportunity to discover the reaction of American researchers. Ikeda Keiko co-ordinated the panel with me, and also chaired it on the day. Nishikawa Yūko,

Ogino Miho, and Beth Katzoff travelled all the way from Japan especially to take part in the presentations. Claudia Koonz played the part of an extremely stimulating discussant. The incumbent President of the Association of Asian Studies, Carol Gluck, worked as an intermediary to welcome Claudia Koonz as the discussant and exerted considerable energy behind the scenes to ensure her participation in the Asian Studies Conference though she was not a member of the association nor a regional specialist.

In the same year, on 24 March, the same speakers were welcomed at a symposium that was held by the Department of East Asian Studies, Columbia University. As would be expected, Atina Grossmann developed a stimulating discussion.

Next, I am extremely grateful to the following people who provided me with opportunities to present my ideas on related themes in the form of public lectures, and, moreover, to those writers who involved me in discussions: Miyoshi Masao, Fujitani Takashi, Yoneyama Lisa, Soon-Suk Moon, Richard Okada, Don Roden, Dorothy Koh, Bonnie Smith, and Choi Kyon-Hi (all titles omitted).

I would like to express my thanks to Ikegami Yoshihiko from the editorial department of *Gendai Shisō* (contemporary ideas) and Fukada Taku from the editorial department of *Impaction* for providing me with an opportunity to present my arguments for the first time in their publications. In particular, the editor of *Gendai Shisō* took the decisive step of publishing in one go, all 140 pages of my original manuscript.

After the first article was published, I received feedback from a variety of people both for and against, and my response to this is incorporated into this book. In this process I owe much to discussions with the following people: all those who enrolled in the class I taught on 'Japanese Feminist Thought' at Barnard College, Colombia University in the autumn term of 1996; all those who took the 'Ueno Seminars' in the Graduate School of Humanities and Sociology, University of Tokyo, in particular the special seminar course on 'Nationalism and Women' in the academic year 1997–1998.

 · · · ·

Part IV has been added to this English version as an update of the original Japanese edition, as I wished to include further developments in my thinking. I am extremely grateful to my translator, Beverley Yamamoto, and my publisher, Yoshio Sugimoto, who supported me in this idea. I cannot find words to express my gratitude to both of them, for discovering some importance in sharing my ideas with English-speaking academic communities, and who took painstaking trouble and patience throughout the entire process. I am also grateful for the financial support of the Japanese Council for the Promotion of Social Sciences, without which this project would not have been realized.

Ueno Chizuko
24 November 2003

• • • •

Postscript

As an up-date, I would like to add the latest information regarding the Asia Women's Fund. The Fund, set up in 1995, completed its brief this year. Over the eight years since it was established, the Fund has delivered atonement money accompanied by a formal letter of apology from the current Prime Minister of Japan to up to 285 women survivors from Korea, Taiwan, and the Philippines. In addition 79 Dutch women received government money for health care. In total, 364 survivors have been recipients of money from the Asian Women's Fund. The distribution in numbers of recipients by country is not available. This is because the Fund has tried to keep from public view the number of Korean recipients due to concern that those receiving funds may be stigmatised. At the very least, it can be said that more than half of the recognised survivors in Korea refused to accept the money. The historical evaluation of the Fund as 'better than nothing' is still open to question.

15 December 2003

Chronology of Related Events

1890
- Enactment of the Public Meetings and Political Association Act (*Shūkai oyobi Seisha Hō*). This law banned women from public meetings and political associations.

1900
- Enactment of the Police Security Law (*Chian Keisatsu Hō*) banning women's political activity.

1925
- Enactment of the Universal (Manhood) Suffrage Law (*Futsū Senkyohō*).

1927
- October 10: Inauguration of the Greater Japan Federation of Young Women's Associations (*Dai-Nippon Rengō Joshi Seinen Dan*).

1928
- May 13: The establishment of Mother's Day.
- July 1: Enlargement nationwide of the Special Higher Police Force ('Thought Police') (*Tokubetsu Kōtō Keisatsu*, abbreviated to *Tokkō*).

1930
- May 10: Passing of the Women's Civil Rights Act (*Fujin Kōminken Hō*) in the House of Representatives. Ran out of time in the House of Peers.

1931
- February 28: Passing of the Women's Civil Rights Act (*Fujin Kōminken Hō*) in the House of Representatives. Rejected in the House of Peers.

- March 6: Founding of the Greater Japan Federated Women's Association (*Dai-Nippon Rengō Fujinkai*). Celebration of the Empresse's Birthday (the Empress's birthday becomes Mother's Day).
- September 18: The Manchurian Incident.

1932
- January 28: The Shanghai Incident.
- March 1: Founding of the puppet state of Manchuria (*Manshūkoku*).
- March 18: Inauguration of the Osaka Women's Association for National Defence (*Ōsaka Kokubō Fujinkai*)
- October 24: Inauguration of the Greater Japan Women's Association for National Defence (*Dai-Nippon Kokubō Fujinkai*). In the ten years after its inauguration the Greater Japan Women's Association for National Defence has a membership of 10 million.

1933
- March 27: Japan withdraws from the League of Nations.

1934
- November 20: Discovery of a plot for a planned coup by commissioned officers from the Imperial Way faction.

1935
- Two prominent socialist women writers, Chūjo Yuriko and Kubokawa Ineko, are arrested.

1937
- July 7: The Marco Polo Bridge Incident. Beginning of the Sino-Japanese War.
- August 24: Publication of the Outline for the Implementation of National Spiritual Mobilisation (*Kokumin Seishin Sōdōin Yōkō*).
- September 28: Founding of the Japanese Federation of Women's Groups (*Nihon Fujin Dantai Renmei*).
- October 12: Founding of the Central League for National Spiritual Mobilisation (*Kokumin Seishin Sōdōin Chūō Renmei*). Councillors include Yoshioka Yayoi, President of the Greater Japan Federation of Young Women's Groups, and Sanjonishi Nobuko, President of the Greater Japan Federated Women's Association.

- November 20: Establishment of the Imperial Headquarters.
- December 13: The occupation of Nanking. The massacre starts. Following the massacre, comfort stations are established systematically throughout China.

1938
- January 1: The Mother and Child Protection Law (*Boshi Hogo Hō*) comes into effect.
- January 11: The Ministry of Welfare is established to promote population policy and improvement of physique.

1939
- February 18: Founding of the Research Centre for Contemporary Women's Issues (*Fujin Jikyoku Kenkyūkai*) with Ichikawa Fusae as president.
- May 12: The Nomonhan Incident
- December 26: Korean's forced to use Japanese family names.

1940
- May 1: Enactment of the National Eugenics Law (*Kokumin Yūsei Hō*). Establishment of Eugenic Marriage Counselling Centres (*Yūsei Kekkon Sōdansho*).
- July 10: Women's groups mobilised to purge the use of unnecessary luxuries.
- July 19: Establishment of the Institute for Population Problems (*Jinkō Mondai Kenkyūsho*). An Outline on Population Policy (*Jinkō Seisaku Taikō*) is agreed on.
- September 12: Dissolution of the Women's Suffrage League (*Fujin Sanseiken Dōmei*).
- September 21: Dissolution of the League for the Acquisition of Women's Suffrage) (*Fusen Kakutoku Dōmei*), which is integrated into the Research Centre for Contemporary Women's Issues.
- October 12: Inauguration of the Imperial Rule Assistance Association (*Taisei Yokusankai*).
- November 3: Ministry of Welfare chooses families with ten children or more for the Rewarding of Excellent Families with Many Children (*Yūryō Tashi Katei no Hyōshō*) awards.

1941
- January 22: The Outline for Establishing Population Growth (*Jinkō seisaku Kakuritsu Yōkō*) is agreed on.

- November 22: Issuing of the National Labour Patriotic Cooperation Ordinance (*Kokumin Kinrō Hōkoku Kyōryoku Rei*).
- December 8: Attack on Pearl Harbour. War between Japan and the United States begins.
  The name the 'Great East Asian War' (*Dai-tōa sensō*) agreed on at a cabinet meeting to describe the war against the United States and Britain.

1942

- February 2: Founding of the Greater Japan Women's Association (*Dai-Nippon Fujinkai*) combining The Women's Association for National Defence (*Kokubō Fujinkai*), membership nine million, The Women's Patriotic Association (*Aikoku Fujinkai*), member-ship one million, and The Greater Japan Federated Women's Association (*Dai-Nippon Rengō Fujinkai*).
- February 15: The Japanese army occupies Singapore.
- April 18: The first air raid attack on the Japanese mainland by U.S. jetfighters.
- November 5: Maternity passbooks start to be issued.

1943

- February 1: Japanese army retreat from Guadalcanal (more than 25 thousand die in battle or from starvation).
- June 25: Outline for the Establishment of a Wartime System of Student Mobilisation (*Gakuto Senji Dōin Taisei Kakuritsu yōkō*) is agreed on.
- July 12: Women's Total Action Central Rally (*Fujin Sōkekki Taikai*).
- September 22: Decision made to move ahead with the mobil-isation of women.

1944

- January 19: 143 Women's Volunteer Corps enter Harima Shipbuilding Company.
- March 8: The Imphal strategy is put into action (30,000 dead and 45,000 war wounded or sick).
- July 7: Total defeat in the Battle of Saipan followed by U.S. air raids of the Japanese mainland.
- August 23: Student Mobilisation Ordinance (*Gakuto Kinrō rei*). Women's Voluntary Labour Ordinance (*Joshi Teishin Kinrō rei*).

1945

- February 1: Recruitment of women for aircraft maintenance work.
- March: The Air Force recruits 600 female medical orderlies.
- March 6: National Labour Mobilization Ordinance (*Kokumin Kinrō Dōin Rei*).
- March 10: Air raids on Tokyo.
- March 18: Outline on Educational Measures for the Final Battle (*Kessen Kyōiku Sochi Yōkō*) decided on (With the exception of elementary level, all school classes cancelled, and general mobilisation for production of munitions and food).
- March 25: Organised evacuation of pregnant women and infants.
- April 1: Training of female medical orderlies.
- April 7: Sinking of the battleship Yamato by the U.S. in air attack in the waters off the coast of Kyushu (24,988 crew died). The Yamato was on route to Okinawa.
- June 13: The Greater Japan Women's Association is dissolved in order to form the National Volunteer Combat Corps (*Kokumin Giyū Sentōtai*).
- June 23: Voluntary Military Service Law (*Giyū Heiyeki Hō*) (men aged 15 to 60 years, women aged 17 to 40 years organised as National Volunteer Combat Corps).
  Annihilation of the Okinawa defence force (190,000 dead).
- August 6: Dropping of the atom bomb on Hiroshima.
- August 9: Dropping of the atom bomb on Nagasaki.
- August 15: Japan accepts unconditional surrender with the Potsdam Declaration. War defeat.
- August 18: The Home Ministry gives instructions for the establishment of sexual comfort stations for the occupation forces.
- August 25: Ichikawa Fusae recommences the Women's Suffrage League.
- August 26: Recreation and Amusement Associations (RAA) (*Tokushu Ian Shisetsu Kyōkai*) established.
- December 17: Revision of the voting law (granting of women's suffrage).

1946

- January 19: International Military Tribunal for the Far East Ordinance.

1946–1948
- Trials of medical and military personnel held throughout Asia Pacific region (trials for B- and C-class war criminals).

1948
- The Batavia Trial (trying those accused of involvement in the use of 35 Dutch women as comfort women).

1951
- San Francisco Peace Treaty.

1956
- Authorisation of Japan's admission to the United Nations.

1965
- Treaty on Basic Relations between Japan and the Republic of Korea. The Korean government gives up the right to further compensation in return for economic aid from Japan.

1973
- Restoration of Japanese sovereignty over Okinawa.
- Korean women's campaign against sex tourism by Japanese men in Korea.

1988
- Korean women's groups carry out an investigation of comfort stations established by the Japanese military.

1990
- May–June: Korean President Roh Tae Woo's visits Japan. A demand made in the Diet for an investigation of the comfort women issue. The Japanese government denies the state's involvement, stating that civilian operators ran comfort stations.
- October 17: The Federation of Korean Women's Groups sends an open letter to the Japanese government demanding an apology and an investigation.
- November: Formation of The Korean Council for Women Drafted for Military Sexual Slavery.

1991

- August: Kim Hak-Sun (aged 68) is first former comfort woman to come forward as a victim.
- November 26: The inauguration in Tokyo of the Yuri Yoson Network on the Comfort Women Issue.
- December 6: Thirty-two former soldiers, civilian personnel and surviving families, including Kim Hak Sun and two other former comfort women, file suit in the Tokyo District Court (Asia-Pacific Korean victims' demand for compensation suit).

1992

- January 13: Japanese government acknowledges for the first time its involvement in the establishment of comfort stations.
- February: Comfort women issue is taken up by the UN Commission on Human Rights.
- July: Publication of documents by the Japanese government showing official military involvement in the comfort stations.

1993

- The comfort women issue presented to the UN Sub-Commission on the Prevention of Discrimination and Protection of Minorities. The comfort women issue re-presented to the UN Commission on Human Rights. The comfort women issue presented to the Working Group on Contemporary Forms of Slavery.
- May: The Japanese government repeats that all claims were settled with the bi-lateral treaty between Japan and Korea, and that it has no legal obligation concerning individual compensation.
- August 4: The Japanese government acknowledges and apologises for the forced recruitment of comfort women.

1995

- August 15: The Japanese government inaugurates the Asian Women's Fund (*Josei no tame no Ajia Heiwa Kokumin Kikin*).
- September: The comfort women is one area of focus during the NGO forum at the UN Fourth World Conference on Women in Beijing.

1996
- April 19: The UN adopts Coomaraswamy's *Report on the Mission to the Democratic People's Republic of Korea, the Republic of Korea and Japan on the Issue of Military Sexual Slavery in Wartime.*
- August: The Asian Women's Fund moves ahead with paying out 'atonement money', which 50 Filipino women accept but other women reject.
- December: The inauguration of the Japanese Group for Orthodox History Education (*Atarashii Kyōkasyo o Tsukuru Kai*). The group demands that references to the comfort women be deleted from school history books authorised for use in the academic year 1997–1998 by the Ministry of Education.

1997
- January 1: Seven Korean women receive payments of atonement money from the Asian Women's Fund.
- December 6: A report by the Asian Women's Fund is featured in Korean newspapers. The Korean government states that this is 'undesirable'.
- December 16: Kim Hak-Sun dies aged 73.

1998
- January 1: Announcement by the Asian Women's Fund that more than 50 women have received atonement money, which serves to create conflict among the survivors.
- August 14: Opening of the memorial museum on the comfort women attached to the House of Sharing (*Nanumu*).

2000
- December 7–12: Women's International War Crimes Tribunal 2000 for the Trial of Japanese Military Sexual Slavery held in Tokyo as a citizens tribunal by the Violence Against Women in War Network International (VAWW-NET International).

2001
- December 4: A final judgement is issued by the judges of the Women's Tribunal. This finds the late Emperor Hirohito guilty for the practice of military sexual slavery.

2002
- September: The Asian Women's Fund finishes its project and announces that a total of 364 women of 4 nationalities have received atonement money to date.

Notes

Translator's Introduction

1 The term World War II is Euro-centric and fails to take account of the fact that Japan's military expansionism started with the Manchuria Incident in 1931 and continued through until surrender in 1945. Japan moved into a phase of total war with China in 1937, following the China Incident, and continued to push further into Asia until the Pacific War began with the invasion of Pearl Harbour in 1941, bringing the United States into the conflict. John Dower notes that 'At the peak of its expansion in 1942, Japan bestrode Asia like a colossus, one foot planted in the mid-Pacific, the other deep in the interior of China, its ambitious grasp reaching north to the Aleutian Islands and south to the Western colonial enclaves of Southeast Asia' (Dower, 1999:21). Some writers speak in terms of the Fifteen-year War, but I prefer the geographical explicitness of the term Asia-Pacific War.

2 Yoshimi Yoshiaki is Professor of History at Chūō University in Tokyo. He is a founding member of the Centre for Research and Documentation on Japan's War Responsibility (Nihon no sensō sekinin shiryō sentaa), and has been actively involved in unearthing documents and coordinating scholarly research concerning Japanese war crimes. It was the publication of documents discovered by Yoshimi in the Japanese Self-defence Agency archives that led to the government finally admitting military involvement in the operation of the comfort women system and offering an apology to the survivors. His book the *Comfort Women* (both Japanese and English editions) is considered essential reading on the subject. In his Pulitizer Prize winning book *Embracing Defeat*, John Dower notes that 'exceptional research and analysis' on war crimes has been carried out by Yoshimi Yoshiaki and acknowledges that he is indebted to his scholarship (Dower, 2000:17).

3 After the war the comfort women issue was raised as a war crime in the case of the comfort stations that had been set up in Semarang on the island of Java. Those involved in operation of the comfort stations were tried for war crimes in a case brought to the Dutch military court in Batavia in 1948. There were 13 defendants of which 11 were found guilty (seven officers and four civilian comfort station operators). Sentences ranged from 2 years penal servitude to the death penalty. What is notable about this trial is that the Dutch Government excluded all cases where the women acknowledged that they had more or less 'volunteered' to work in the comfort stations (see Yoshimi, 1995: 171–175).

4 At the Tokyo Trials, 'Crimes against Humanity' were defined as 'murder, extermination, *enslavement*, deportation, and other inhumane acts committed before, or during the war, or persecution on political or racial grounds in execution of or in connection with any crime within the jurisdiction of the Tribunal, whether or not in violation of the domestic law of the country where perpetrated. Leaders, organizers, instigators, and accomplices participating in the formulation or execution of a common plan or conspiracy to commit any of the foregoing crimes are responsible for all acts performed by any person in execution of such a plan' (Dower, 2000,456; emphasis added). Clearly, there was ample room within this definition for the comfort women system to have been treated as a Crime against Humanity at the Tokyo Trials.

5 It is interesting to note that initially the group had called themselves the Korean Council for Women Drafted for Military Sexual Service. The fact that today they only use the phrase 'sexual slavery' is indicative of the paradigm shift that occurred in how the comfort women issue has been understood. I am grateful to one of my post-graduate dissertation students, Elisabeth Frischknecht Kind, for this insight.

6 In fact, the content of this TV debate and the content of what Yoshimi 'admitted' to has been the focus of a heated debate between Yoshimi and Ueno. Yoshimi has reacted strongly to Ueno's accusation of 'privileging of documentary sources'. For a record of this debate see Yoshimi, 2003 and Ueno, 2003).

7 In keeping with recent trends, it was re-named the Kitakyushu Municipal Gender Equality Centre MOVE in 2002.

Introduction to the English Edition

1 [Translator's note] The *historikersteit* refers to the near explosion of historical debate in Germany in the mid-1980s fought out in professional journals as well as the media concerning how World War II should be remembered.

Part I: Engendering the Nation

1 In response to claims made by German historian Ernst Nolte in the 1980s, German intellectuals including Jürgen Habermas and Jürgen Kocka have been engaged in an explosive debate over how to understand Nazi war crimes. Should they be viewed as typical of the kind of atrocities carried out by totalitarian regimes and therefore ranked alongside crimes committed in Russia under Stalin's dictatorship or in Indochina under the Pol Pot regime? Alternatively, does what happened in Germany have no parallel in history? A review of this debate can be found in Habermas et al., 1987.

2 Through structuralism to the current trend of thought known as post-structuralism, the development of linguistics (semiotics) since Saussure has led to a broad area of shared epistemological ground. A change in

epistemological paradigm occurred with the realisation that things and meanings do not exist as givens to which linguistic signs are conferred, but instead the sign is the preceding factor and constructs meaning and content. A central core of post-modernism is that the subject is completely self-referencing, nothing more than the effect of linguistic practices.

3 [Translator's note] Michel Foucault (1926–1984) has been a controversial figure in the social sciences since the 1970s. A French post-structuralist philosopher, Foucault is best known for his four studies: *Madness and Civilization* (1961), *The Birth of the Clinic* (1963), *Discipline and Punishment* (1975) and *The History of Sexuality* (vol.1 1976). Through these case studies of madness, medicine, prisons and sexuality, Foucault was able to demonstrate that across time and space major shifts have occurred in the discursive formations (structures of knowledge) used to order our knowledge of the world. Such shifts force a change in the systems we use to categorize knowledge, which impacts our everyday beliefs and practices. Foucault argued that discursive formations have the power to both shape and exert power over social objects, from large institutions to individual human bodies. Thus, structures of knowledge are inherently political structures.

4 Both of these phrases were cited in the prefaces of Suzuki 1996a and 1996b.

5 [Translator's note] Immanuel Kant (1724–1804). Kant is considered to be one of the greatest of all modern philosophers. He attempted to synthesize the dominant rival epistemological traditions of his day: empiricism and rationalism. Kant rejected the central doctrine of empiricism that substantive human knowledge is limited to that which can be tested by empirical observation. Yet, he also rejected the rationalist claim that knowledge comes from reason alone. Kant argued that there are forms of human knowledge that are not mere tautologies despite being based on reason rather than derived from experience. Yet knowledge gained from an understanding of 'things-in-themselves' could only be legitimately applied within the realm of experience. As such, he tried to resolve the tension between acknowledging a world beyond what is immediately observable, and accepting what he considered to be the bogus claims to knowledge of theology and metaphysics based on faith, intuition of 'pure reason'.

6 For example, in the case of problems that people are reluctant to discuss in public such as domestic violence and child sex abuse, even if those involved do come forward and testify, it is frequently the case that their testimony is denied on the basis that it is not 'fact'. In extreme cases the testimony is thought to be false memory or a lie and the victim is deemed to be in need of medical treatment.

7 [Translator's note] In the original Japanese the author used the equivalent of quotation marks around the phrase comfort women throughout to emphasise the fact that it is a highly contentious term. In the English translation, while acknowledging the contentious nature of the phrase, I will omit the quotations marks hereafter in the interests of the publisher's house style, where a minimalist approach is taken to punctuation. I will follow the same approach with other contentious terms, inserting quotation marks only on the first occasion that they appear.

8 In Part II there is an in-depth discussion of the comfort women issue.
9 [Translator's note] Recent scholarship, particularly within the field of post-colonial studies, has pointed to the created rather than inherently authentic nature of much of what we call tradition. The invention of tradition is considered to be a key part of the process of nation building; a tool employed for creating and unifying national identity.
10 Speaking from the perspective of post-colonial analysis, Oguma's argument is incomplete. By accepting the concepts of 'people' and 'nation' as givens, he is led into the trap of taking the heterogeneous or multicultural nation for granted (see Tomiyama, 1997).
11 [Translator's note] The *Kojiki* (The record of ancient matters) was compiled in 712 and is Japan's earliest surviving 'historical' narrative. It covers the period from the mythical creation of Japan to the reign of Emperor Suiko (AD544–628). The *Nihon Shoki* (The chronicles of Japan) was compiled in 720 and is a mythological narrative of the founding of the Japanese state focusing on the Imperial Household line. It traces the imperial line from the 'descent from heaven of the descendants of the gods' (tenson kōrin) to the reign of the Jito Emperor (690–697).
12 Yamanouchi suggests that Mitani Taichirō's *Shinpan Taishō Demokurashi-* (New edition Taishō democracy), published by University of Tokyo Press in 1995, and Mitani Taichirō's *Taishō Demokurashi-* (Taishō democracy), published by Iwanami Shoten in 1974 and then again in 1994, are representative of accepted theory here.
13 For example, we can find the classical argument in this area within the field of family history. The discontinuity view of history's overestimation of post-war democratisation contributes to the creation of the phantom of the pre-war family system as a 'relic of the feudal system'. As a result, the 'modern' characteristics of the pre-war family and the oppressive characteristics of the post-war family end up being disregarded by the official paradigm even in much of the empirical research. In contrast, the continuity school of history underscores the commonalities between the pre- and post-war family in terms of structure and character, but offers two versions of this. One viewpoint emphasises the discontinuities between the pre-modern and modern family, the other stresses anew the continuities. The former viewpoint can be seen in the importance placed on modern family characteristics of the Japanese *ie* (household) in Ueno 1994a, which later produced the 'Modern Family Controversy' (Tabata, Ueno and Fukutō, 1997). From the latter viewpoint, the modern characteristics of the family (characteristics that fit in with the modernisation project) are traced back to the pre-modern era to verify there immanence and spontaneity, and in so doing the continuity and superiority of Japanese cultural identity ends up being emphasized (Hirayama, 1995; Yamazaki 1990). Proponents of the latter viewpoint, who can only be described as the ultra-continuity school of history, clear the way for a new cultural nationalism and frequently end up contributing to the theory of Japan's uniqueness.
14 Narita Ryūichi coined the name 'neo-continuity theory' (Yamanouchi, Narita, Ōuchi, 1996b:10).
15 Yamanouchi's argument contains one more innovation, namely the total mobilisation system. He embraces Systems Theory here to argue that with

the introduction of total mobilisation the modern nation-state entered a new stage of being a so-called 'system society'. I do not hold with this part of Yamanouchi's thesis for three reasons. First, a 'system' as Systems Theory terminology is a generic concept that is open to being applied to any system. The fact that any social system can be described as a 'system society' renders it a virtually indefinable concept. Second, the implication of the system society is that, as a system of interdependence lacking a centre, it is an irresponsible system with no subject, which is one of the clichés of the post-war *Nihonjinron*. As such, it cannot be said that this is a unique concept that requires the creation of new terminology. Third, if the 'system society' implies that there is a bureaucratic leadership model of an irresponsible system with no centre, it is because through the attribution of personified agency to the system it has become linked with political conservatism that supports the status quo. Yamanouchi's idea of a system society needs greater theoretical elaboration and until the implications of it are clarified I would like to reserve judgement on this part of his thesis. Here I think that with the nation-state as a key concept the term nationalisation is more than adequate. On this point, I am greatly indebted to Nishikawa Nagao, 1994.

16 See Ueno 1995b for a discussion of the concept gender. There is a misunderstanding that gender studies takes a more neutral and objective position than feminism or women's studies (so this fits in with calls for the current governmental policy of a gender-equal society!) and there are those who, based on this misunderstanding, are repelled by or critical of the concept. However, I can only say that both positions are mistaken. The aforementioned study considers the political and militantly critical nature of the concept gender. Moreover, as will become clear later, a concept of gender works to demolish the myth of gender neutrality.

17 In retrospect, I must confess that a hidden motive behind my underestimation of the state was my reluctance to enlarge the role of the state. When *Capitalism and Domestic Labour* (1985) was published by Kaimeisha, which formed the basis for *Patriarchy and Capitalism* (1990), I was criticised by Takenaka Emiko, a leading feminist economist, and various reviewers for underestimating the welfare state model as a solution in my analysis of unpaid labour. While this criticism was absolutely appropriate, prior to this I had already regarded the welfare state as a version of the control state, and indicated my scepticism about its role. According to recent news reports (*Asahi Shinbun*, 26 August 1997), it has become clear that between 1935 and 1976 the Swedish government carried out compulsory sterilisations on 60,000 people under the Sterilisation Law, including those deemed to be 'inferior persons', single women who had borne many children, 'abnormal persons' and 'gypsies'. The reason for this was an economic one (if the people become healthier there would be fewer people needing social security) and can be said to demonstrate more clearly than anything else that a welfare state is a reproductive control state. While the Sterilisation Law was abolished in 1976, Sweden's generous maternal protection policies and family policies in the 1970s were triggered directly by a decrease in the birth rate (the reproduction rate fell below population replacement level) and can be considered a continuation of population policy.

It is not difficult to imagine that a state that adopts generous pronatalist policies in response to a decline in the birth rate will implement population control policies in the case of overpopulation. For those who regarded the Swedish model of the welfare state as ideal, the above reports must have come as a shock. Yet, for somebody who views the welfare state as a version of the control state it came as no surprise.

18 The word *citoyen* (citizen) comes from the Latin word *civitas*, and 'human rights' actually mean 'civil rights'. These civilized citizens then go on to create civilisation. Along with the universal idea that anybody who has been civilized or enlightened can become a citizen, the notion of human rights that came out of the French Revolution also brought with it the imperialist logic of exclusion and hierarchy (see Nishikawa, 1992).

19 A classic example of this was the women's suffrage movement that grew up after the American Civil War. After slavery was abolished women in the movement argued over who should get the vote next, the freed black man or the white woman.

20 Even after formal education was made compulsory many parents were unenthusiastic about their children attending school as it meant having precious labour power snatched away from them. The Conscription Ordinance, which snatched up able-bodied young men, also met with considerable resistance. Wild rumours circulated that one's life blood was taken away if one went into the army, and opposition movements sprang up in areas where military service was referred to as 'blood tax' (tax paid in blood). While it is said that school and the military are two great agencies for disciplining the nation, it is not the case that these two systems were established without any objections.

21 Tachi notes: 'In terms of a legal understanding, as both countries were Japanese colonies at the time, males from Korea and Taiwan were also included in the category 'male Japanese imperial subjects' and were among those who possessed Japanese nationality... What is more, as it was made a principal that voters had to be resident in mainland Japan, the voting rights of Japanese, Koreans and Taiwanese living in the colonies went wholly unrecognised' (Tachi, 1994:126).

22 With regards to the paradigm change in women's history, see Ueno, 1995a.

23 The 23 June 1945, the day that the Volunteer Military Service Law was promulgated was 'ironically also the day that the Okinawa garrison was completely wiped out' (Katō, 1996:257).

24 For a discussion of Germany see Koonz, 1987 and Himeoka, 1993. At a symposium where I gave a paper that formed the basis of this book, Ute Frevert, a German scholar of women's history, suggested that in Germany the mobilisation system was the integration model, but I suspect there is room for debate on this point.

25 Katō Yōko points out that, 'there is doubt about whether the National Volunteer Corps actually functioned in real terms because they were not formed until after Japan had been defeated' (Katō, 1996:258).

26 The contribution made by military nurses was forgotten for a long time after the war. It was not until the 1960s, and as a result of demands made by the Japan Nursing Association, that the government agreed to pay

military nurses and the family of the deceased compensation equivalent to a military pension. Those who died on active service came to be enshrined together at the Yasukuni shrine. This indicates the extent to which the war was considered a man's war, and even the existence of those women who served at the front was ignored.

27 [Translator's note] The pre-war motherhood protection debate (*bosei hogo ronsō*) referred to here took place between 1915 and 1919. The main protagonists in the debate were Hiratuska Raichō, Yosano Akiko, Yamakawa Kikue and Yamada Waka. It can be analysed in terms of the classic equality versus difference conundrum that has dogged feminism over the years. Thus, while Yosano Akiko, for example, argued for women's economic independence from men and the state through paid employment, Hiratsuka Raichō took the position that it was impossible to properly care for the house and any children while holding a job, and demanded state protection of motherhood in the form of paid maternity.

28 Suzuki frequently claims that the individual characteristics of these women activists – their 'elitism' and/or 'a burning sense of mission' – account for their support and participation in the war. She confesses a kind of idealism along the lines that if the division between the leader and the follower was eliminated and everybody became 'autonomous individuals', we would be able to avoid making such a mistake. However, surely we should not reduce causes to the individual characteristics of these women, but seek them in their social positioning?

29 While studying at university, Hiratsuka took up meditation and in 1906 was given permission to take the special Zen Buddhist name Ekun by Shaku Sōkatsu, a senior Buddhist priest supervising her at the Ryōbō – a temple in Nippori. Again in 1907, she was given another special Zen name, Zenmei, by Nakahara Zenchū a senior priest at the Kaiseiji temple in Nishinomiya city. For further details, see Ueno 1997b.

30 This was a debate that took place between Yosano Akiko, Hiratsuka Raichō, Yamada Waka and Yamakawa Kikue, among others. See Kōuchi 1984.

31 [Translator's Note] Ellen Karolina Maria Key (1849–1926) was a Swedish thinker and writer who, like Hiratuska Raichō, viewed women's role in the home, especially their role as mothers, as something akin to a sacred mission. The importance of this mission meant that it was necessary for women to sacrifice the outside world in favour of focusing their creativity on producing the next generation. As with many maternalists, this fervour for motherhood incorporated eugenic ideas about improving the physical qualities of the 'race' through reformed practices of parenthood. Her ideas became popular in Japan around the same time that Ibsen's theatrical work generated attention with the staging of *A Doll's House* by many university drama circles in 1911–12. Again, like Hiratsuka, Key was a commentator on Ibsen's work. Hiratuska acquired an English copy of Key's *Love and Marriage* (1911) and translated sections for two editions of *Bluestocking*.

32 Jang Jing's (1995) *Kindai Chūgoku to 'Ren'ai' no Hakken* (Modern China and the discovery of 'love') splendidly illustrates the argument that

translation is the selective reception of culture. Jang discusses from the perspective of comparative literature the circumstances on the Chinese side that dictated what would be adopted or rejected when modern China imported a concept of 'love' via Japan.

33 [Translator's Note] Charlotte Perkins Gilman (1860–1935) was a prolific American writer of fiction, social commentary and feminist criticism, although much of her work is not widely known or accessible. Among feminists, Gilman is best remembered for *Herland,* originally published in 1915. In *Herland* Gilman creates a feminist utopian society made up entirely of women with its own distinct social and cultural arrangement, and its own political system. The roots of radical feminism are often traced back to this amusingly satirical book.

34 [Translator's Note] Olive Schreiner (1855–1920) was born in South Africa where she spent her childhood. Her English mother and German fathers, strict Calvinists, had been sponsored by the London Missionary Society to do missionary work in South Africa. Her father's financial insolvency resulted in Olive Schreiner being separated from her parents at the age of 12. In 1881, Schreiner paid her own passage to England having worked as a governess for 11 years. The publication of her novel *The Story of an African Farm* in 1883 brought her acceptance as a novelist and social activist. In her writing and activism, Schreiner was anti-imperialist and a stalwart pacifist. Her political activism included participation in the women's suffrage movement in England.

35 Miyake's thesis rode upon the current of new women's history in the 1980s, and was written with the intention of raising the question of the war responsibility of Japanese feminism. In her summary of the 'motherhood protection debate', Miyake argues that the maternalistic tendency within Japanese feminism, from Hiratsuka to Takamure, encouraged war participation. In other words, the cause of wartime cooperation was the incompleteness of individualism within Japanese feminism. However, the problem of individualism in Japanese feminism should be dealt with separately. The reason for saying this is that the view that feminism equals the women's version of modern individualism is itself a reflection of a modern bourgeois liberal feminist viewpoint, and the limits of modern individualism have already been made clear.

36 Furthermore, in the same debate Hiratsuka stated that the reason that Yosano was opposed to the idea of motherhood protection was that she was shackled to the old fashioned view that one's child is one's own private property and that the job of motherhood is a private activity. However, the view that motherhood is a private activity is definitely not an old fashioned idea, but rather the product of the birth of the private sphere as a result of modernisation, namely the privatisation of reproduction. What is more, Yosano did not even view motherhood as a private activity.

37 On this point, we cannot ignore the different backgrounds of the two women: Hiratsuka the daughter of a bureaucrat in the new capital Tokyo and Yosano born into the world of a merchant family in a local city.

38 For publications that supplement the deleted text in *Takamure Itsue's Collected Works* see Kōno, 1997 and Akiyama, 1973.

39 For two consecutive years, 1994 and 1995, the Society of Comparative Family History decided upon the theme *The Current Situation of and Themes in Women's History and Women's Studies* as its focus, and in the second year, 1995, held a symposium on *Transcending the State and Motherhood: What Can we Learn from Takamure's Women's History?* The speakers were Ishimure Michiko, Kurihara Hiroshi and Nishikawa Yūko, with Ueno Chizuko as the chair. A record of the content of the reports and discussion can be found in *Jendā to josei* (Women and gender), edited by Tabata, Ueno and Fukutō 1997.

40 [Translator's note] John Langshaw Austin (1911–1960). The 'illocutionary speech act', or 'performative speech act' as it is generally described today, is a key term in Austin's speech act theory introduced in *How Do Things Work with Words* published by Oxford University Press in 1962. Austin distinguishes between 'performatives' which through their utterance linguistically perform the act to which they are referring and 'constatives' which are concerned with the truth or falsity of a statement (see Andermahr, Lovell and Wolkowitz eds 2000). In the case of the former, for a person performing a marriage ceremony, saying the words 'I now pronounce you man and wife' is itself the act of marrying two people. So what Ueno appears to be suggesting is that for Takamure to state that women had played a more significant and active role in history than had previously thought was a 'performative speech act' in that the words themselves contributed to the liberation or encouragement of women by providing a vision to aspire to, even if the sources themselves had been falsified (I am grateful to Graham Healey, University of Sheffield, for his input on the above point).

41 These criteria are relevant to the debate over how to evaluate the women's movements of the 1950s within feminism, such as the peace movement *Haha-oya Taikai* (Mother's Convention) and the campaigning of *Shufuren* (National Housewives Organisation).

42 In [Japanese] society at that time, the economic independence advocated by Yosano could only be achieved by women like Yosano who had a privileged work situation. Yet the protection of motherhood advocated by Hiratsuka was not something that the state aspired to in its social policy at that time. On these points, both arguments have been criticised as unrealistic. However, forced to make a choice between workers' rights or the right to an existence, Yamakawa's argument should have been to sublate workers rights and the right to live, but instead she offered as the only possibility transforming contemporary economic relations. In other words, a socialist revolution, a policy which at the time looked exceedingly unlikely. On this point, Yamakawa's argument was also unrealistic.

43 Taken and abridged from Yamakawa's memoirs (Yamakawa, 1979:66).

44 Yamakawa was also scathing of women's activists stating that, 'It was business as usual, these women displayed the virtues of Japanese women and changed direction in accordance with male demands...' (Yamakawa, 1979:81).

45 During the period when the communist party was illegal, [male] activists and female supporters lived in the guise of married couples, and the term

'housekeeping' refers to the housework services, and in some cases these included sexual services, that the former received from the latter. Although it was legitimised as 'for the party', it emerged as an issue after the war (Yamashita C., 1985).

46 The conclusion reached in studies of women's voting behaviour since they gained the right to vote after the war is that women's suffrage did not change Japanese politics. On the contrary, it functioned to support the long period of one-party conservative rule. It was not until 1989 that there were indications of a trend towards women's voting behaviour becoming independent of the household vote.

47 This does not only apply to Yamakawa. Even Takamure, who was supposed to be confined to the house in the aloof lifestyle of a scholar, wrote numerous essays and other manuscripts. Unable to get by living off their gardens at their places of evacuation or through farming, these female intellectuals felt that any road to making a living other than through writing would be a difficult one. Through the benevolence of those around them they were supplied with opportunities to write, and the end result is that during the war these women left behind an unexpectedly large amount documentation giving their opinion.

48 There were seven participants at this meeting. In alphabetical order: Hiratsuka Akiko [Raichō], Katayama Tetsu, Okuda Yoshiko, Tatewaki Sadayo, Tatsuno Takashi and Yamakawa Kikue.

49 The interpretation that the dissolution of Ichikawa's Association for the Promotion of Women's Suffrage was an unavoidable choice made in order to protect the women's suffrage movement is denied by this self-managed dissolution.

50 Working conditions and the reality of motherhood protection at the places where women were drafted were even cruder than in peacetime. In reality, even the Women's Volunteer Labour Association (*Joshi Teishin Kinrōkai*) in 1944 while demanding the mobilisation of women aged 12 to 40, set as a condition the exemption of persons who are pivotal in the home. It is clear that the government did not view work and motherhood as compatible.

51 Ironically, targets set during the war were actually achieved post-war despite a change by the government to a policy of suppressing population growth.

52 The term venereal disease, *karyūbyō*, literally 'red light district disease' in Japanese, refers to sexually transmitted diseases. In Japanese it is called *karyūbyō* because it was in the red light districts, *karyūkai*, that these diseases spread.

53 In fact, when an Aryan race child was discovered in an occupied territory as a result of the Cranium Measurement Law they were abducted and brought up [by the Nazis] (Yonemoto, 1989).

54 The participation of female soldiers in combat did not arise as an issue until after the American invasion of Panama in 1989.

55 Davin's pioneering results teach us two things about the relationship between imperialistic aggression and motherhood: 1) it is not something limited to the Axis powers, but something shared with the Allies; 2) it is

not limited to the exceptional times of total war, but accompanies the forming of the modern imperialist states.

56 In Sweden policy makers use the term state feminism openly, and there are feminists in Japan who take the Swedish form as a model. However, as seen in the sterilisation of people with disabilities, even in the Swedish Welfare State, only suitably qualified citizens share the benefits of equality.

57 After being released from the purge from public office, Ichikawa ran for a seat in the 1953 elections for the House of Counsellors as a candidate for the Tokyo constituency, and was duly elected. Following this, she continued as a Diet member for 18 years until she was defeated in the 1971 elections. In 1974, she once again stood as a candidate for the national constituency in the House of Counsellors elections, and after being elected in first place went on to hold office for another seven years until she passed away in 1981 at the age of 81.

58 According to persons concerned, there are still a considerable number of documents in safekeeping at the Ichikawa Fusae Memorial Hall that have not yet been sorted or released to the public, and it is felt that if they were all made public it would have a considerable impact on the study of Ichikawa.

59 In a recent study *Hiratsuka Raichō no hikari to kage* (The light and shade of Hiratsuka Raichō) (1977), Ōmori Kahoru wrote the following. 'It is precisely because Raichō had deep in her heart the bitter experience of the wartime regime while she was young that she strove single-mindedly for world peace after the war, became a symbol of the movement and, despite her delicate constitution, continued to be involved in a large number of campaigns' Ōmori, 1997:222). However, there is no speculation about expressions that might suggest that Hiratsuka underwent a post-war conversion. Moreover, there is presumption of discontinuity between pre- and post-war.

60 Inoue Kiyoshi's *The History of Japanese Women* was published in 1948. Along with Takamure's *The History of the Women of Greater Japan*, it is ranked as one of the classics in post-war women's history. Although their historical viewpoints are different, these two classics share in common their understanding of surrender and occupation as women's liberation. Following this, in the revised editions of 1953 and 1962 Inoue does an about turn and criticises his own mistaken view that occupation policies represented liberation (see Ueno, 1995a).

61 As already outlined, the person who deleted wartime statements from Takamure's Collected Works was her husband, Hashimoto Kenzō. At the very least, this shows that for Hishimoto, Takamure's wartime activities were a 'blemish' on her career, but in her autobiographical recollections written after the war *Hi no kuni no onna no nikki* (A Diary of a women from the country of fire) there are no passages suggestive of self-criticism.

62 Moreover, it cannot really be said that the self-apparent nature of this historical perspective is shared by the majority of citizens through to today.

63 [Translator's Notes] Comintern is an abbreviation of Communist International. The Comintern was created in 1920 and consisted of a single

(Russian centred) communist party with braches in countries around the world, rather than a series of national communist parties, as had previously been the case.

64 Mizuta Tamae in her recent book *Nihon ni okeru Feminizumu shisō no juyō* (The acceptance of feminist ideas in Japan) developed the argument that maternalism is the characteristic acceptance of feminism in 'backward countries' like Japan. She argued that in Japan as well as in Germany it induced women's wartime cooperation (Mizuta, 1997). In addition to having doubts about whether this book, as suggested by the title, amounts to anything more than the acceptance of Western feminism by modern Japanese feminism, it is problematic to have positioned Japan as a 'backward' country. As with Miyake's (1994) thesis, the result of making 'weak individualism' a characteristic of Japanese feminism is, firstly, that it is impossible to escape the drawbacks of the existing modernisation theory that takes the West as its model. Secondly, as a result of this, it constructs the West into a monolithic model. Thirdly, in idealising individualism, the roles that individualism has created within modernity are beyond criticism. If we demand from capitalism or the nation-state the integration of women 'as men' within an individualism based on the logic of equal opportunity, then female soldiers are also being endorsed. I wonder what Mizuta's response would be to this.

Part II: The Military Comfort Women Issue

1 Numerous claims have already been made concerning the terminology *jyūgun ianfu* (military comfort women). There is the view that the term *jyūgun* (going with the military) brings to mind the voluntariness of war correspondents or military nurses and, as a result, it is more appropriate to use terms such as 'Imperial Army comfort women', 'Japanese army comfort women' or 'army comfort women'. Another argument is that the term *ianfu* (comfort women) is an army euphemism and the reality was that the women were nothing less than sexual slaves, therefore we should not adopt the language of the oppressors. It is further argued that, while it may have been comfort for the soldiers, for the victims it amounted to nothing less than rape and, as a result, the term comfort women serves to conceal reality. We have even seen the appearance of a book entitled *Watashi wa 'ianfu' dewanai* (I am not a comfort woman) by the *Sensō Giseisha o Kokoro ni Kizamukai* (The Association to Take the Victims of War into One's Heart) (1977). We have also had the appearance of the so-called Liberal School of History's argument that the term *jyūgun* refers to civilians and conclude from this that the term *jyūgun ianfu* is not a historical term. If *jyūgun ianfu* is not a historical term, they continue, then there was no such historical reality. However, the argument that because no such terminology existed the historical reality similarly did not exist is plainly a leap in logic. Fujioka Nobukatsu claims that Senda Kakō coined the term. However, the word *ianfu* appeared in the Kōjien Dictionary before Senda's book *Jyūgun ianfu* (military comfort women) was published (Senda, 1973). The term

jyūgun means nothing more and nothing less than following the army to the war front (Senda, 1977). The question of what terminology is used is itself political. Here I will use the term *ianfu* (comfort women) as a historical term. Now there are various ways of referring to comfort women from the Korean peninsula such as *Chōsenjin ianfu* (Korean comfort women) and *Chōsen/Kankokujin Ianfu* (North Korean and South Korean comfort women), but to-date little is known about comfort women from North Korea. The data I have is largely limited to the activities of women with South Korean nationality, so I will adopt the term South Korean here. This convention does not hold when I am citing the work of another person.

2 Kim Hak-sun passed away 16 December, 1997 aged 73. She died six years after filing the suit without hearing the conclusion of the court hearing and without receiving a response suggesting sincere intentions from the Japanese government. Nevertheless, after coming forward she, among other things, gave evidence at the United Nations Human Rights Committee and her influence internationally was profound.

3 Recruitment was carried out for female Volunteer Corps on the Korean peninsular just as it was in mainland Japan, but because some women who signed up for the Volunteer Corps were forced to become military comfort women the term *Teishintai* (volunteer corps) has come to be linked with comfort women in the minds of many inside Korea.

4 The comfort women issue had already been problematised within the women's liberation movement in the early 1970s, and it has been pointed out that Japanese women were torn between whether they should view themselves as the oppressed and the oppressors (Ueno, 1994a: 9–10; Inoue et al., 1994:89). This is one of the earliest examples of the problematising of the comfort women in post-war Japanese society, but the women's liberation and feminist movements that followed did not pursue this question.

5 This was a reply to the question: Why is it that the comfort women issue has surfaced 50 years after the war ended? The writer responsible for this item was Matsui Yayori. Yet, she does not touch upon sexual torture within the democratising movement or Kwon In-suk's indictment.

6 Liza Go, a Filipino woman who has campaigned energetically for the *Japayuki*san (women bound for Japan in search of work) argues that sex tours to Asian countries by Japanese men and the sex discrimination directed at Asian women within Japan have the same roots as the comfort women problem under the emperor system. She was the first person to problematise Filipinos resident in Japan as a problem of long-term foreign residents in Japan. Go has indicated the racism in Japanese feminism and has appealed for minority feminism.

7 Haga Tōru, '*Bunka Kaigi*' (Culture Conference), 1992:10. I have simply re-quoted Ehara who notes that: 'However this is taken from Nishio Kanji '*Kutsujoku to zōo no kankei o ippen saseru 'nikkanhishoku' no susume*' (Advice for a 'no-touch Japan-Korea' that will change in a single stroke the relationship of humiliation and hatred). (SAPIO, 12 November 1992). Both Haga Tōru and Nishio Kanji are connected with the *Atarashii Rekishi Kyōkasho o Tsukurukai* [literally, the society for the making of new history

textbooks, but the official English name is The Japanese Institute for Orthodox History Education; hereafter Orthodox History Group] formed at the end of 1996. The Orthodox History Group demanded the erasure of all references to the comfort women from textbooks approved by the Ministry of Education [now Ministry of Education, Culture, Sports, Science and Technology] for use in schools from April 1997.

8 Likewise, in the pre-war period the crime of adultery was constructed on the patriarchal logic of 'an infringement of the husband's property rights'. The wife's sexuality belonged to the husband but, as the husband's did not belong to the wife, there was no reciprocity in the crime of adultery. In the post war Civil Code the obligation of chastity between husband and wife is now reciprocal. However, the fact that the wife of a husband who has been unfaithful can demand compensation from her husband's lover amplifies the logic of an infringement of property rights.

9 Senda explains this situation as follows: 'The society being a male-centred society still tied to the vestiges of feudalistic ideals, means that the Korean people have a strong sense of discrimination towards women. I was told by social critics who talked about the situation during this period that it would not have mattered how the circumstances arose, as women who had once been comfort women and, moreover, as raped women there would have been only one way of looking at them. It did not emerge as a problem because the women's themselves were aware of this attitude and so they hid themselves in obscurity in one corner of society' (Senda, 1997:54). Here the 'one way of looking at them' that Senda refers to is with a patriarchal consciousness rooted in sexual discrimination.

10 'She (Takahashi Kikue) said to me that: "I think that the leaders of the military when they thought up a system like the military comfort women used the system of licensed prostitution within Japan as a basis" ' (Senda, 1997:53).

11 For more about the dismantling of the rape myth see Ogura Chikako (1988) *Sekkusu shinwa kaitai shinsho* (The dismantling of the sex myth) and Beneke, Timothy (1982) *Men on Rape.*

12 Moon's postal savings were not paid as compensation for sexual services. It was money that she had saved in her own name from casual income such as tips from soldiers. She states that she received no wages from the operators of the comfort stations. On the contrary, even if she were to have won the lawsuit, these savings amounted to only a nominal sum of money, pointing to the inappropriateness of saying that she became a comfort woman for the money or that the law suit was only taken up for money. For Moon, the case was of symbolic significance; a demand for justice.

13 According to Sone Hiromi (1998) who has studied prostitution in the Edo period, the etymology of the word for prostitution *baita* [now *baishunfu*] was originally the act of 'selling women' (*onna o uru*). After this it shifted to indicate 'women selling spring' (*baishun*). According to another study by Sone (1990), there were five actors involved in prostitution: 1) the prostitute, 2) her family, 3) the agent 4) the customer 5) and the government. With the exception of the first, the prostitute, the remaining four actors were all central players profiting from prostitution as part of the sex industry.

14 Recent research on women's history points to the prostitution discrimination inherent in the principle of the Anti-prostitution Law and the views of the women Diet members who promoted this piece of legislation.

15 Those in the Orthodox History Group narrowly limit the meaning of 'forced' to 'forcibly taken away'. In terms of continued forced labour under conditions of confinement, the forced nature of the comfort women system is quiet clear. Even if recruitment occurred on the basis of free will, a system of forced labour contravening the free will of the woman concerned was established in the comfort stations.

16 In actual fact, when the comfort women issue was first introduced overseas, the term *'ianjo'* (comfort station) was translated as 'military brothel' and *'ianfu'* (comfort women) as 'prostitutes'.

17 Separate from the standpoint of the continuity of categories, a sharp distinction has frequently been made between the privately run brothels and the military run comfort stations. On the grounds of protection and prevention, not only were military personnel strictly prohibited from entering privately run prostitution facilities, but also private citizens had only restricted entry to the military controlled comfort stations. However, in pointing to the continuity between categories, many theorists (Suzuki, 1997b; Fujime, 1997) have suggested that the military comfort stations were an extension of the system of licensed prostitution. Needless to say, this does not mean that either the system of regulated prostitution or the comfort women system are being pardoned.

18 However, in 1948 in Batavia in Indonesia at a class B and C war crimes trial, a total of 11 members of the military and civilians employed by the military were found guilty of forcing 35 Dutch women to become comfort women, with sentencing including the death penalty.

19 [Translator's note] See Coomaraswamy, Radhika 1996.

20 The United Nations Human Rights Committee established a Human Rights Sub-Committee and within this a working group was set up on Contemporary Sexual Slavery. This working group has dealt with the comfort women issue. The problem-setting of issues, such as international trafficking for the contemporary sex industry, violence against women both inside and outside the family, violence against women (including sexual violence) during armed conflict, was unified through the sexual slavery paradigm.

21 In addition to clearly acknowledging the involvement of the army in the military comfort women model, Kurahashi in an article written in 1989 judged that the treatment of the women in these comfort stations would have been better than in the 'civilian-run' types. The basis for this was firstly, that the comfort women as 'weapons' would have been treated with care, and secondly, due to the standardisation of the military as a bureaucratic system they 'should have received the same handling and treatment' (Kurahashi, 1989:81–2). For a historian, neither of these grounds amount to anything more than inappropriate conjecture. Considering that it was published in 1989, it is possible to appreciate this essay as an early scholarly achievement concerned with the comfort women issue. However, both the grounds outlined by Kurahashi are refuted by the testimony of the former comfort

women. Kurahashi raises the question: 'out of these two situations, which was really the better for these women?' He then concludes that: 'in both cases there was no saving these women'.

22 Prior to the rape of the 12-year old girl in Okinawa, the rapes of two other women, one 22 years old and the other 19 years old, were reported. However, the anger of local citizens rallied around the symbolic innocence of the 12-year old victim. In the cases of the two adult women, where there could be slightest doubt about consent, these reports did not trigger the same level of outrage. However, the power that created the climax of the campaign, a mass meeting of 100,000 local citizens in October of the same year, was a contingent of the Okinawa Movement on Women who had just arrived back from the Fourth World Women's Conference in Beijing. The group's leader, Takasato Suzuyo, is an activist who has been grappling with the problem of military-base prostitution for a long time. Within the women's movement in Okinawa, rape and military-base prostitution are contiguous as both are forms of violence against women.

23 Yamashita states in note 6 of this article: 'As I, along with a number of other people, have pointed to the problematic nature of this section, it was announced that it would be cut in the Japanese edition' (Yamashita, Y., 1996:55). The significance of this kind of high quality piece of work is coming out of the Korean women's movement should not be underestimated. When the Japanese government's answer in relation to Korea was quite clearly ethnocentric, we have to respect and value the self-critical stance taken towards the ethno-centrism that has arisen in response to this on their own side.

24 Originally, gender history was established through the process of confronting the mono-theoretical, materialist historical viewpoint of class domination and by emphasising the independence of gender (sex) as a variable. If we turn Fujime's expression on its head, gender history criticised hitherto views of history that simply put the priority on class by neglecting a gender perspective. It can be said that criticism from gender history has done a full circuit in that the importance of variables such as class, nation and ethnicity has once again surfaced. In my own words, contemporary gender studies has reached a point where 'a problem cannot be analysed solely by gender, but there is not a problem that can be analysed without gender' (Ueno, 1995b).

25 That Taiwanese women were not sent to the front line in China is not unrelated to the fact that one of the aims of the comfort women system was the prevention of espionage. There were fears that troop movement and other military information would be leaked to the enemy via the comfort women. Taiwanese women could understand Chinese. On this point, Korean women were ideal targets as they could understand Japanese, but could not speak Chinese.

26 Kurahashi Masanao introduces documents from 1933 after the establishment of Manchuria as the prehistory of the military comfort women. 'The '*jōshi gun*' (Amazonian troops, namely troops made of maidens) were definitely not prostitutes (*inbai*). When fighting suddenly broke out they would lay down their lives to dodge artillery fire to carry army provisions to the troops.

Therefore, to the injured soldiers they were like wives and nurses. In what way were they prostitutes, I am forced to exclaim. Rather than selfishly indulge in meaningless sexual play like the modern girl and modern boy, they accompanied the troops and were truly Amazonian troops. Why do those modern girls not serve the army with their sexual service?' Nakayama Tadanao *Tōyō*, November, 1993:419; Kurahashi, 1989:143). It is indicated that within this 'sexual comfort' was one way of offering oneself for the nation.

27 The work of historian Tanaka Toshiyuki (1993) and a film maker, Sekiguchi Noriko with the film *Senjō no Mura* (The village battleground) have revealed that after the victory of the Allied Forces, comfort stations in the southern battlefields were then used as comfort stations by the soldiers of the Allied Forces and that the women become targets of rape by these soldiers.

28 Kawabata Tomoko (1995) develops a precise argument concerning the sexual double standard and prostitute discrimination. According to Kawabata, the 'prostitute label' is nothing more than an expression of social sanction towards women who deviate from the role patriarchy expects of them.

Part III: the Politics of Memory

1 In October of the same year at a symposium on Japanese Modern History held at the University of Colombia in New York, Narita Ryūichi predicted that in the Japanese version of revisionism the comfort woman issue would probably perform the role that the Holocaust has in German Revisionism, and his prediction has turned out to be true. Moreover, this prediction became reality at a faster pace than we had expected.

2 It is revealing that popular women writer and essayist, Hayashi Mariko and Agawa Sawako, who appear on the list of names of those who made the appeal to start the Group, have maintained a continuous silence, not even appearing once at a news conferences and turning down all requests for a meeting (Tsukurukai sandōin intabyū [An interview with supporters of the Orthodox History Group], *Ronza*, May 1997, Asahi Shinbun Company).

3 Nakano wrote 'I decline putting my name to anything that functions to use my notoriety as a writer as a means of influence'. She also commented that she did not want to make statements as an expert, and stated that 'with this in mind I declined giving my signature, but…perhaps you would call this is rather a negligent stance…I do not have much confidence in my judgement'. If she is unaware of the very fact that her writing was published in the print media supported by her notoriety then her irresponsibility and cowardice cannot be covered up. Nakano Midori '*Rensai essei 14,2 Mangetsu Zakkichō*' (Serialised essay, 14,2 Fullmoon Essays), Sundē Mainichi Shinbun, 15 December, 1996.

4 A similar inconsistency is evident in the fact that most of the Japanese media voluntarily refrain from using the word *rape*. The official reason is that it is 'too offensive', but at the same time the term murder is used quite

indifferently. Yet surely it is clear what is concealed when terms like teasing (*itazura*) and assault are used instead, and who benefits from this (Ueno, 1996).

5 The study of Japanese post-war history cannot necessarily be reduced to naïve positivist history. Both scientific history based on a materialist interpretation of history and the perspective of total history are heavy with ideological overtones. It seems to be only with this issue that, rather than being a debate over historical paradigms, it is a dispute at a level of true or false questions concerning facts? If validity is being adopted as popular persuasion technique, then this is, firstly, extending the life of naïve positivist history by placing off-limits questions from a historical perspective and, secondly, it is underestimating the audience (Ueno, 1996).

6 In response to this, historian Yoshimi Yoshiaki and non-fiction writer and activist, Nishino Rumiko have already voiced criticism that the presence or absence of coercion has been sneakily switched to a problem falling within the scope of [the women] being intentionally hauled away. However, the parameters of the problematizing here, no matter how they are set up, leave unchanged the fact that everything has to be fought out on the basis of positivism.

7 [Translator's note] Yoshimi had first come across the relevant documents before a two-year sabbatical to the US in the later 1980s, but had not made them public. As Ueno points out, they only became significant after the paradigm shift occurred (see Yoshimi, 1995:35).

8 Yoshimi himself testifies to this situation: 'In August 1991 in Korea, Kim Hak-sun came forward for the first time under her real name. In December 1991, Kim Hak-sun along with two other former comfort women, and former soldiers and civilians attached to the military and/or the bereaved families filed a lawsuit at the Tokyo District Court seeking an apology and compensation from the Japanese government. At this point the Japanese government was denying any involvement and no attempt had been made to seek out any documentation. As it happened, I was aware of the existence of relevant data and, as a result, set about investigating the matter anew with the results of this published in the *Asahi Shinbun* newspaper in January 1992. Unable to reject these findings, the government was forced to admit involvement' (Kasahara et al., 1997:154).

9 Two young scholars of folklore studies, Ōtsuki Takahiro and Akasaka Norio (1997) together declared that they agreed with Sakurai Yoshiko. Irokawa Daikichi, a modern historian and militant anti-imperialist, severely criticised them suggesting that surely this amounted to a denial of Folklore Studies: 'Ōtsuki Takahiro is involved in the Orthodox History Group, but where he is pitiable is that while a scholar of folklore studies he forgot that the departure point for folklore studies was a distrust of documents created by the state or the authorities. Is it not the case that folklore studies came about from listening to the stories of ordinary people and creating oral history?' (Irokawa, 1997).

10 Wakakuwa Midori (1997) similarly argues that in court cases involving sexual crimes the burden of proof should shift from the victim to the perpetrator. In the first ruling of the Akita sexual harassment case (January

28th, 1997) the judge passed judgement on a suspected interaction between the man and woman concerned that took place behind closed doors without witnesses, and after having 'impartially' examined the statements of both sides, declared that the reliability of the woman's case was weaker. The reason given for this was that the speech and behaviour of the woman at the scene of sexual harassment, being contrary to the Judge's own common-sense, was deemed unnatural. Again, in the famous sexual harassment dispute between Anita Hill and Clarence Thomas in the United States, the end result of Congress making what was said to be as impartial judgement on the reliability of the testimony was Hill's defeat. Once again, those bringing judgement did not question their own so-called neutrality and objectivity.

11 [Translator's Note] The term historicization refers to the practice of placing the object of study within its own particular historical context.

12 I was criticised by Maeda concerning an article that I wrote (Ueno, 1997a). The following points are partially a response to Maeda's criticisms (Maeda, 1997b).

13 Nothing demonstrates this more blatantly (and with less shame) than the enactment of the Okinawa Special Measures Law (*Okinawa Tokubetsu Sochi Hō*) in April 1997. In the middle of a dispute following legal principles over the rejection of a request for an extension of land-lease rights for the American military base in Okinawa by the land owners and as a result of a change in the legal principles themselves, a new law was created to legalise use of the land by the American military without the consent of the landlords. What is more, under a system of a ruling-party coalition government, the Okinawa Special Measures Law was enacted with 90 percent of Diet members voting in favour. As indicated by many people, this is akin to changing the rules in the middle of a game and is an unreasonable intervention.

14 A current point of contention is the bronze statue of Jefferson in front of the Natural History Museum in New York. It is truly a colonialist symbol with Jefferson on horseback with a black man and a Native American in tow at his feet. Groups representing Native Americans have continued to protest against this statue. Some time in the future this statue of Jefferson will probably be preserved as historical material of the stain of its history of conquest or usurpation and at the same time as an explanation of it.

15 The claim for compensation for Japanese-Americans subject to compulsory internment was finally realised in 1988.

16 Here the framework of national history has not been transcended. Japanese-Americans were 'loyal Americans' just like other citizens, with Japanese-American GIs the symbol of this 'loyalty to country'. Moreover, it was this loyalty that was placed on display along with an exhibition of life in the compulsory internment camps. To the end, the rhetoric of the America's National History Museum is that this was a crime (racial discrimination) committed by the state against its own citizens who are loyal to the state'.

17 [Translator's Note] The New Ainu Law (*Ainu Shinpō*) was passed in May 1997. The New Law nullified the Ainu Protection Act, which had been

enacted in 1899 and revised in 1968, which had essentially institutionalised ideas of Ainu inferiority by representing these indigenous people of Northern Japan as a 'dying race' in need of state protection (Siddle, R., 'Ainu: Japan's Indigenous People' in *Japan's Minorities: The Illusion of Homogeneity* edited by Michael Weiner (1997). In contrast to the Protection Act, the New Law is committed not to the assimilation of the Ainu people, but the preservation of their indigenous culture. It is this shift in official representations of the Ainu people that Ueno is alluding to here.

18 What is more, as far as Perrot is concerned, the main producers of discourses on women in the middle ages were Christian ecclesiastics, in other words, by definition men who were prohibited from having contact with women. This means, ironically, that we are being made to read illusions about women created by men who knew nothing of women.

19 It is taboo for members of the support groups to acknowledge that the chances of winning a court case are slim. To admit this would be considered defeatism. The logic of the support groups is only natural; if you are going to fight, then you have to develop a battle strategy where you have a winning chance, and if you do not envision winning then you will not be visited with victory. However, repeatedly since the end of the war, in cases where post-war compensation has been sought for individuals the claimant has been 'turned down at the door' on the grounds that the claim does not fit domestic law. Where laws are created for the convenience of policy makers, court battles can neither be objective nor neutral. Indeed, with the rules of legal principle forced upon them, the individual must fight from a position of disadvantage on the 'home turf' of his or her adversary. If one daringly takes a case to court fully aware of these disadvantages, it is less for the sake of winning and more due to an expectation of the symbolic impact that a discursive battle in the court will have in a public space.

20 Let me cite a familiar example of this; divorce among middle-aged couples. The reason that it so frequently comes as a shocking 'bolt out of the blue' for a middle-aged husband broached with the subject of divorce is because these men fail to question whether their wife shares the dominant reality that they themselves had defined. Looking at statistical data, among couples aged sixty or over who were asked the question, Is a married couple 'one heart, one mind' (*isshindōtai*), 60 percent of husbands answered 'yes', whereas less than 30 percent of wives did so. There are cases of couples living together with one party continually thinking of divorce, and where this serious discommunication continues over many years. The dominant party's power of imagination is not sufficient to conceive such a huge gap in the two realities. What if we could imagine that the reality we experience in our lives has a very different aspect from the perspective of another party? Acknowledging multiple histories is accepting that there is not a single reality and that for another person a completely different reality exists.

21 Takahashi Tetsuya uses the term '*seikansha*' (survivors; literally those who have returned from the living hell) (Takahashi, 1995).

22 Tonkin refers to the illusion that part of a narrative is repeated unerringly in the same story the 'talking book fallacy' (Tonkin, 1992).

23 Nanumu House is an institution in the suburbs of Seoul where the former comfort women victims can live communally. A Buddhist group administrates it. The word *nanumu* is the Korean word for 'sharing'. Two documentaries about the life of the women have been directed by Byeon Yeong-ju *The House of Nanumu I* and *The House of Nanumu II*.

24 According to a report made at the American History Association conference, comfort women section meeting held at the Sheraton Hotel in New York, 1 January 1997.

25 As a result, one side has criticised the other. Women's history has accused women's studies (representing feminism) of relying on the importation of Western ideas and knowing little about the situation in Japan. From the other side, women's studies has criticised women's history for falling behind important changes in other academic fields. For the complex relationship between women's history and feminism in Japan, see Ueno, 1995a. For a discussion of attempts to bring the two sides closer together, see Tabata, Ueno and Fukutō, *Jendā to josei* 1997.

26 Scott is well informed about these conditions. She remarks that, 'the discrepancy between the high quality of recent work in women's history and its continuing marginal status is the field as a whole (as measured by textbooks, syllabi, and monographic work) points up the limits of descriptive approaches that do not address dominant disciplinary concepts, or at least that do not address these concepts in terms that can shake their power and perhaps transform them. It has not been enough for historians of women to prove either that women had a history or that women participated in the major political upheavals of Western civilization. In the case of women's history, the response of most non-feminist historians has been acknowledgement and then separation or dismissal (women had a history separate from men's, therefore let feminists do women's history, which need not concern us; or women's history is about sex and the family and should be done separately from political and economic history). In the case of women's participation, the response has been minimal interest at best (my understanding of the French Revolution is not changed by knowing that women participated in it) (Scott, 1999:30–31).

27 In British women's history a new research theme under the title Imperial Feminism has emerged investigating the attitude of bourgeois feminists of the time concerning the policies of imperialist invasion under the British Empire. For example, from a thorough re-reading of the text it has been demonstrated that female abolitionists called for the liberation of slaves either from an anti-racist position or argued for the abolition of slavery as a 'noble duty precisely in order to establish the supremacy of the Caucasian race' (Midgley, 1992). Ann Davin's *Imperialism and Motherhood* is a pioneering achievement of this kind of reflexive women's history (Davin, 1978).

28 Ōgoshi Aiko suggests that my concept of reflexive women's history differs little from Fujioka Nobukatsu et al's 'self-hating masochistic view of history' (*jikoaku- gyaku shikan*)? (Ōgoshi and Takahashi, 1997). However, on a number of points she conclusively reveals her ignorance and misunderstanding. Firstly, I had already used the term reflexive women's

history in 1994 in an article entitled *History and Feminism*. At that time, Fujioka's term *self-hating masochistic view of history* had yet to make its appearance, and my concept of reflexive women's history was established completely independently of his movement. Secondly, the term reflexive itself does not have a negative meaning. Her argument does not understand the context within post-structuralism that the term reflexive was established. Thirdly, reflexive women's history is a movement that can be seen all over the world, regardless of nationality. It is not a Japanese trend.

29 To reiterate the point, one's native province is just another 'imagined community'.

30 Naturally, Katō reveals considerable deliberation in his work to the extent that he writes, 'because Japanese society is not a single person it is not possible to explain the construction of the fragmentation of Japanese society without assuming that what is being refered to here is a collective ego' (Katō, 1997:319). Thus, while he starts out with the words 'I understand' and 'I am aware', Katō ends up retreating into a collective subject, a *we* with one character (Katō, 1997:75).

31 Naturally, the same can be said of the category women. Categories where the group equals a *we,* regardless of what kind of category this is, there is a move to highlight differences with the outside and conceal internal differences. In feminism it is no longer acceptable to simply rely on one single category woman.

32 The workshop entitled 'The Japanese Military Comfort Women: From the Perspective of Japanese Women and Women Living in Japan' was held on 6 September, 1995 at the Beijing Conference NGO Forum and was sponsored by the Asian Women's Conference Network (AWCN).

33 The identity of ethnic minority women, for example black women, is first as a black and then as a woman. As a result, it is exceedingly difficult to mobilize women who identify with an ethnic group to participate in the women's movement. At the same time, problematising the gender category within the ethnic group – which needless to say is male dominated – is viewed as a taboo if not an act that serves the interests of the enemy. The indignation that Alice Walker's *Color Purple* generated in black, male society illustrates that identification with the male-centred ethnic group includes the oppression of women. We can add to this the class-centeredness of socialist women's liberation theory that early radical feminism opposed. As here too loyalty to one's class meant loyalty to the men of that class group.

Part IV: Hiroshima from a Feminist Perspective

1 [Translator's Note] In the original Japanese the word Hiroshima was written in *katakana* (the script generally reserved for words of non-Japanese and non-Chinese origin), rather than in *kanji* (ideographs) as would be expected. Ueno has done this to emphasise that the subject is not only the place Hiroshima, but also Hiroshima as an actual and symbolic event that began with the dropping of the nuclear bomb from the Enola Gay

on August 6th, 1945. Other than this first occasion, I will not put any special emphasis around the word.

2 The speech was originally given as part of an event at The Hiroshima Kanō Cram School (*Hiroshima Kanō Juku*), the Hiroshima Women's Studies Course (*Hiroshima Joseigaku Kōza*), sponsored by Kazokusha. Between April and August 2000, Kano held a lecture once a month. Approximately 35 participants attended each lecture. The theme of each session was as follows:

   i) Feminism and Women's History.
   ii) War and Women: the Military Comfort Women and the Women on the Home Front.
   iii) Peace and Women: the Maternal Myth and Peace Campaigning.
   iv) Feminism and War: Focusing on the Issue of Female Combat Troops.
   v) Hiroshima and Feminism: An essay on Hiroshima Women's Peace Studies.

Continuing into 2001, Kazokusha and the Course Planning Committee sponsored lectures on the following themes and with the following speakers:

   i) Hiroshima Women's History: Its Significance and Methodology (Kanō Mikiyo).
   ii) Things We Can Discover from the Approach of Local Women's History (Okayama, Matsue, Shimane and Hiroshima Women's History Group and Kanō Mikiyo).
   iii) A-Bomb Damage and Women (Seki Chieko).
   iv) A Reading From the Perspective of A-Bomb Literature (Esashi Akiko)
   v) An Essay on The Hiroshima Women's Peace Studies: Nukes and Feminism (Kanō Mikiyo).

3 The Fifteen-Year War that began in September 1931, was an aggressive war carried out by Japan with the aim of colonizing Asia. It was a total war fought on the basis of a system of gender segregation with men on the front line and women on the home front. The phrase *history of the home front* was applied to the history of women who supported the war with pride on the home front. In 1967, the Society for Questioning Women Today (*Josei no genzai (ima) o toukai*) was formed to get a clearer picture of why and in what way women supported the war. With Kanō Mikiyo playing a pivotal role, a number of independent researchers of women's history at the grass roots level gathered together and inaugurated the Society's own publication *Jyūgo shi nōto* (A Note on the History of the Home Front). Between 1977 and 1996 a total of 18 volumes were published, including the final issue.

4 Based on a Marxist school of history, which emphasises the establishment of a system of private property in bringing about class and the oppression of women, the victim school of history sees the history of women as one of oppression as a subordinated class. Here women are regarded as passive victims of history and it is, therefore, also a liberationist view of history, a kind of evolutionist history, seeing women as more liberated as history develops. It is the position taken by Takamure Itsue as well as Inoue

Kyoshi, two great authors of bestseller textbooks on women's history after the war, though the former did not share the historical view of the class struggle with the latter.

5 On the August 28th 1945, Prime Minister Higashikuni Naruhiko (Commander-in-Chief of Home Defence during the war), appealed for the 'collective repentance of 100 million people' (*ichioku sō zange*) saying that it would be pitiful for the Emperor to be pursued for war responsibility.

6 The Tokyo Tribunal equals the International Military Tribunal for the Far East. In accordance with the clause in the Potsdam Declaration on 'the punishment of war criminals', following the allied countries' occupation of Japan, war leaders and those who had abused prisoners-of-war were arrested. Among the A-class criminal war leaders, there was Tōjō Hideki (former Prime Minister), 28 military leaders and politicians who were prosecuted, of whom seven were executed by hanging and 18 received life-sentences (commuted after independence). A-class suspects, such as Kishi Shinsuke, did not come to trial. The government accepted the judgements at the San Francisco Peace Treaty and a settlement was achieved diplomatically.

7 In the closing stages of the Fifteen-year War, starting with massed air raids by 355 American military carrier-based aircraft on 23, March 1945 and 30 Japanese and American warships open firing on each other on March 24, the US Military landed in Okinawa on April 1st. This was the beginning of a fierce ground battle between Japan and America stretching over a period of 3 months. During what is referred to as the 'Storm of Steel', a wave of mass suicides took place in every district, beginning in the Kerama Islands. In addition, the Japanese army forced locals to commit suicide. With mass suicides, the Battle of Okinawa resulted in massive casualties. The previous year, as part of the fortification of Okinawa, the Imperial Headquarters had deployed 110,000 preparatory forces, but the US military had injected a force of 550,000 (183,000 went ashore). Most of the Japanese military died an 'honourable death' [carried out suicidal attacks], with 90 percent ended up as war dead. It is said that 100,000 local people and 100,000 military personnel and voluntary military corps were victims of the ground battle. With the annihilation of the Japanese army, organizationally the war in Okinawa ended on the June 23rd.

8 In reaction to the invasion of Kuwait in August 1990 by Iraq, the UN Security Council demanded a withdrawal. A resolution was passed recognising the use of armed force if Iraq did not withdraw by January 15th 1991. Immediately after this deadline had passed, air raids on Iraq were initiated by a multinational force, but with the U.S. as the main power. With the multinational force having overwhelming supremacy, the Iraqi military withdrew at the end of February. Despite war defeat, Saddam Hussein's regime survived, and he went on to repress the Shiite Muslims in the South and Kurd's in the North who had risen up against him. Japan also shouldered part of the financial burden of the war.

9 It is suspected that the Occupation regime prohibited any problematising of the Tokyo aerial bombing. Unlike the case of Hiroshima and Okinawa, it was only in the mid-1980s, when the civic memorial museum was

established for the victims of Tokyo air raid, with no public financial support, that the number of victims even began to be calculated.

10 *The Rape of Nanking: The Forgotten Holocaust of WWII*. Published in America in December 1997, it became a best seller selling over 500,000 copies. It was published in China in Chinese at the same time. Iris Chang is a young journalist who is a Chinese-American.

11 Harry Truman (1884–1972). Thirty-third president of the United States (1945–1953). He became Vice President in 1944, and took office as President upon the death of Roosevelt. It was Truman who took the decisions to drop the atomic bombs on Hiroshima and Nagasaki; to loan money to Western Europe; and to send American troops to the Korean Peninsular. In order to countermine the Communist Bloc, he promoted a policy that provided Western Europe with military and financial aid (Truman's Doctrine).

12 Ōe Kenzaburō (1935–). In 1958, Ōe received the Akutagawa Prize for literature for his book *Shiiku* (feeding). In 1994, he won the Nobel Prize for Literature. He has been a prolific writer and his work includes critical essays such as *Hiroshima Notes* and *Kaku jidai no sōzōryoku* (The power of imagination in the nuclear age).

13 Akiba Tadatoshi (1942–). Current Mayor of Hiroshima (1999–) and mathematician. In 1978 he launched the Akiba Project, inviting overseas news correspondents to Hiroshima and Nagasaki. He has held the post of assistant professor at Hiroshima Shūdō University since 1988. Since 1990 he has been a member of the House of Representatives [the lower House of the Japanese Diet] (Third term, Social Democratic Party).

14 The invasion of Nicaragua. In 1979 the Samosa dictatorship was overthrown and the Sandinista National Liberation Front (FSLN) set up a left-wing government. However, in 1982 civil war broke out between the Sandinista government and the American backed right-wing guerrilla faction, the Contras. In 1984, in the presidential elections, left-winger Ortega [Savedra] was elected with overwhelming support, but as a result of tough sanctions being imposed by the U.S. the country fell into economic crisis and the people started to move away from the left. In the 1990 presidential elections a centrist/right-wing coalition government was set-up under the presidency of [Violeta Barrios de] Chamorro. In 1996 the country transferred to the right-wing Aleman government.

15 The invasion of Grenada.in October 1983. The island kingdom of Grenada (under the umbrella of the British Commonwealth) was invaded by armed forces made up largely of the U.S. military and backed-up by forces from Jamaica and the Organisation of East Caribbean States (OECS). The left-wing government was overthrown and a pro-U.S. government was formed. In 1979, the authoritarian government in Grenada had been overthrown and an anti-colonialist, moderate process of social reform was under way when a pro-Soviet military general seized power in a coup d'etat. It was amidst the ensuing chaos that the invasion took place.

16 This treaty prevents any country other than the U.S., Russia, Britain, France and China becoming nations with nuclear capability. One hundred and eight-seven countries are signatories to this treaty. India, Pakistan,

Israel and Cuba are non-signatories. The treaty was signed in 1968 and was published in 1970. In 1998, India and Pakistan carried out nuclear testing and, along with Israel, became in effect nuclear powers.

17 On March 1st 1954, a Japanese fishing vessel, the Lucky Dragon the Fifth was exposed to radioactive fallout as a result of nuclear testing being carried out at the Bikini Atolls in the Marshall Islands. Although the vessel was outside the danger zone, all 23 crew came upon severe radiological hazards and the captain, Kuboyama Aikichi, died as a result. This incident served to intensify the ban-the-bomb movement throughout Japan. In 1976, a Lucky Dragon the Fifth exhibition hall was opened on Yume Island in Tokyo by the Tokyo Metropolitan government.

18 The split in the ban-the-bomb movement. Behind the attainment of 30 million signatures supporting the banning of the bomb was the first World Convention Against Atomic and Hydrogen Bombs held in Hiroshima on August 6, 1955, with 5,000 delegates from 11 countries. In the same year, the Japanese Council Against Atomic and Hydrogen Bombs (*Gensuibaku kinshi Nihon kyōkai*; abbreviated to *Gensui kyō*) was founded. In 1959, the conservative faction broke away from this over the revision of the Japan-U.S. Security Treaty. In 1961, the Democratic Socialists formed the *Kakuheiki kinshi heiwa kensetsu kokumin kaigi* (People's conference on banning the bomb and constructing peace; abbreviated to *Kakukin kaigi*). Within the Kakukin kaigi there was a deepening of tensions between the Socialist Party of Japan and 13 groups within the General Council of Trade Unions of Japan on one side, who were against any country having nuclear weapons, and the Communist Parties and its allies on the other, who advocated the acceptance of Soviet nukes and the idea of the Soviet Union as a force of peace. In February 1965, the *Gensuibaku kinshi Nihon kokumin kaigi* (Japanese Peoples' Conference Against Atomic and Hydrogen Bombs; abbreviated to *Gensui Kin*) was formed around the axis of the Socialist Party and the General Council of Trade Unions of Japan. While the *Kakukin Kaigi* was short-lived, the two groups held conventions and campaigned on their own terms. In 1977, a unified convention was realised, but splintering occurred again in 1985.

19 In December 1967 during a session of the Lower House Budget Committee, then Prime Minister Satō Eisaku from the LDP stated that not possessing, not producing and not allowing entry of nuclear weapons in to the country was government policy. In November 1971, an agreement was reached in a Lower House plenary session concerning the Agreement between Japan and the United States of America Concerning the Ryūkyū Islands and the Daitō Islands, that along with obeying the three nuclear principles not to possess, produce or bring nuclear weapons into the country, it would be necessary for the government to take steps to demonstrate that there would be no nuclear weapons in Okinawa at the time of the reversion of Okinawa to Japanese administration. On the other hand, as a counterplea the government stated that as an interpretation of the constitution it is not prohibited to possess the minimum level of force for self-defence and that providing it does not exceed this minimum level, it would be constitutional to have nuclear weapons, thus making it just a matter of government policy.

Except that due to the NPT, Japan could not make or possess nuclear weapons.

20 [Translator's note] When I suggested to Ueno Chizuko that citizens in American society were never completely disarmed she came back with the following reply. As a result of the only partial disarming of citizens in the United States, 'violence among citizens has become more serious and fatal than in other societies. Yet, the government would not accept the idea of guns being bought and sold freely. Moreover, individuals are not allowed to own nuclear bombs nor jet fighters even if they could afford buy them'.

21 In a narrow sense, war crimes are acts that are in contravention of the rules of armed conflict (crimes committed during wartime). A broader definition includes Crimes against Peace and Crimes against Humanity. Crimes against Peace include wars of aggression, the act of planning or starting a war that is in violation of international conventions, agreements or covenants, and supporting a conspiracy. Crimes against Humanity are murder, massacre, enslavement, forced migration, and other inhumane acts, as well as political, racial and religious persecution. In 1998, the treaty creating a permanent International Criminal Court was adopted (not yet published).

22 Hasegawa Michiko (1949–). Professor at Saitama University. Received the Watsuji Tetsurō Culture Prize in 1997. Her publications include, *Kara gokoro* (Chinese way of thinking), *Seigi no sōshitsu* (The loss of justice), and *Anata mo konnichi kara Nihonjin* (From today, you too are Japanese), which was written along with [Orthodox History Group member] Nishio Kanji.

23 The aerial bombardment of Kosovo. NATO forces became involved in the conflict between Albanian's seeking the independence of the autonomous region of Kosovo and the Serbian Republic (Kosovo Conflict). In March 1999, in the middle of the peace talks, aerial bombing was initiated. Over 78 days, more than 10,000 air raids were carried out and 1,200 civilians and 5,000 military personnel were killed. The total cost of the damage was 14.5 billion yen. The economies of the neighbouring Balkan countries also took a terrible battering. Peace was established in June, 1999 and an international force (KFOR) of 50,000, made up mainly of NATO troops, was deployed in Kosovo.

24 In June 1992 the Rabin government was established. Peace talks with the Palestine Liberation Organisation (PLO) moved ahead, and a peace consensus was reached. In 1994, a Palestinian Interim Self-Government Authority came into being in the Gaza Strip and Jericho. In 1995, Israeli forces withdrew from cities on the West Bank of the Jordan River (with the exception of Jerusalem and Hebron), however, that same year Rabin was assassinated. In May 1996, Israel was on the brink of a general election when a series of bombing incidents took place at the hands of Islamic extremists. A sharp swing in public opinion led to the opposition party, Likud, coming to power with Benjamin Netanyahu as prime minister. After this, the peace process came to a halt. In 1999, a Labour Government was returned to power with Ehud Barak as prime minister.

In July the peace talks held at Camp David failed. In September the Al Aqsa Intifada (a Palestinian popular uprising) broke out. In February 2001, hardliner Ariel Sharon's government was formed. The peace process broke down completely.

25 Unfortunately enough, this has become clearer in the Iraq War after I wrote this essay.

26 The following were recognised under the Meiji constitution, 1) in criminal law, the crime of adultery (criminal penalty), 2) under civil law, adultery was a reason for requesting a divorce (adulterous behaviour), 3) the right to claim for damages. The above could be immediately applied in the case of the adultery of a wife, but in the case of the husband it only became a problem if the relationship was with a woman who was married and her husband sued and criminal charges were imposed. After the war, equality between men and women under the law was highlighted in the new constitution. In 1947, the crime of adultery was removed from criminal law and provision was made within civil law for adultery to act as a reason for filing for divorce and to claim for compensation for both men and women equally.

27 National Organisation for Women (NOW). NOW is the largest organisation of feminist activists in the United States. It was established in 1966, with Betty Friedan as the first President, and has campaigned for complete equality between men and women, focusing particularly on legal and economic equality. Its headquarters are in Washington D.C., and there are a total of 550 chapters, embracing a membership of 500,000. The organisation wielded immense political power, but was strongly criticised for being a platform for white, middle-class women. Since the 1980s it has aimed at bringing about gender equality by fighting all types of discrimination, including racial and class-based discrimination. Recently it has expanded it campaigning to include such issues as the right to abortion, sexual and reproductive freedom, eradication of gay and lesbian discrimination, and prohibiting violence against women.

28 Katō Hisatake (1937–). President of Shimane Environmental University. Emeritus Professor at Kyoto University. Won the Yamazaki Prize for the Promotion of Philosophy and the Watsuji Tetsurō Culture Prize. His publications include, *Kankyō rinrigaku no susume* (An Introduction to environmental ethics), *Ōyō rinrigaku no susume* (A case for applied ethics). His edited works include *Chikyū kankyō dokuhon* (A Reader on the global environment).

29 Wakakuwa Midori (1935–). Feminist art historian (Italian art history). After working at Tokyo National University of Fine Arts and Music and at Chiba University, she is now Professor in the Department of Literature teaching art history and gender studies at Kawamura Gakuen Women's University. Her publications include, *Bara no iconorojī* (The iconology of the rose), *Imēji o yomu* (Reading the Image), *Gui to shōchō no joseizō* (The hidden meaning and symbolism of the female image), *Shōchō toshite no joseizō* (The female image as a symbol), *Kōgō no Shōzō* (The portrait of the Empress).

30 Rayner, Richard (1997), *Women in the Warrior Culture*, New York Times Magazine, June 22:55.

31 Post-colonialism. A theoretical trend after Orientalism, which de-constructs the binary opposition between the West and the Orient. This new criticism focuses on the cultural imperialism that has continued even after political independence was achieved in former colonies. According to Gayatri Chakravorty Spivak 1990, post colonialism can be defined as 'a child born out of rape.'

32 Arakawa Akira (1931–). A leading intellectual in Okinawa, who pursues Okinawan independence and protested the reversion of Okinawa to Japan. His books include, *Shin nantō fudo ki* (A new geography of the southern islands), Hankokka no kyōku (The counter realm against the state), and *Ryūkyū shobun igo* (Since the disposal of the Ryūkyū).

33 Post-structuralism A new school of thought introduced in response to the reductionist and determinist nature of structuralism. Stressing the undetermined characteristics of the structure and arbitrariness of value in language, post-structuralism opened up the path to restore linguistic agency, however limited it may be. As it is derived from and stands in reaction to structuralism, it therefore inherits the anti-essentialist constructionism stance taken since the linguistic turn. Among the most well-known post-structuralist feminists are Joan Scott and Judith Butler.

34 Delphy, Christine (1941–). Materialist feminist and activist in France. She played a leading role in MLF both in theory and in practice. She has also made an important contribution to the post-structuralist theory of gender. Author of *Main Enemy, Close to Home* and others. Her paper, *Sexe et Genre* (1989), was presented at the International Seminar on Women's Studies, National Women's Education Centre, Saitama, Japan.

35 [Translator's note] PKO and PKF. United Nations Peace Keeping Operations and United Nations Peace Keeping Forces.

36 Matsui Yayori (1934–2003). International Journalist. Formerly a correspondent with the Asahi Newspaper. In 1977 she founded the Asian Women's Association and in 1995 the Asian Women's Document Centre. She was representative for the Violence Against Women and War Network (VAWW-Net Japan). Her books include: *Onnatachi ga tsukuru Ajia* (Asia created by women) and *Gurō-baruka to josei e no bōryoku – Shijyō kara senjyō made* (Violence against women under globalisation: from the market to the battle field).

37 [Translator's note] It is also worth noting that victims of DV are in greater danger at the point that they decide to leave an abusive relation-ship. In other words, any sign of fighting back tends to cause an escalation of the violence.

38 The Hijack of a bus by a 17-year old youth. In May 2000, a 17-year-old youth from Saga City took over a long-distance coach bound for Fukuoka City. He killed a 68-year old female passenger. A note was found in his house and seized containing references to two other incidents involving youths of the same age in Kobe. Among other things, he mentioned that he wanted to experience killing another person. The youth was sent to a juvenile medical treatment facility for a minimum of five years.

Epilogue

1 Hashizume Daizaburo (1948–). Sociologist and conservative nationalist thinker. He is the author of many books such as *Bukkyō no gensetsu senryaku* (Discursive strategy of Buddhism) and *Tennō ron* (Theories on emperorship). He justifies fighting for the nation based on the civil contract and, at the same time, supports compensation [of comfort women] by the state based on the legal continuity of the modern Japanese state.

2 [Translator's Note] The official name of the Asian Women's Fund is *Josei no tame no Ajia Heiwa Kokumin Kikin* (literally, the Asian Peace National Fund for Women), although it is usually abbreviated to '*Kokumin kikin*' (the national fund).

3 [Translator's note] On the 28th August 945, Prime Minister Higashikunie Naruhiko, who had taken office on the 17th August, announced at a cabinet press meeting that the military, government officials and all the people must thoroughly reflect (*hansei*) and repent (*zange*) on what had happened. He stated that the 'collective repentance of 100 million people' (*ichioku sō zange*) was a necessary step in the re-building of the nation.

4 By summer, 2002, a total of 285 women from three countries (Korea, Taiwan, and Philippines) had accepted the money. In addition, 79 Dutch women had received medical welfare.

References

Adachi, Mariko, Akasaka, Norio 1997 'Seijuku e no michiyuki wa kanō ka' (Is a road to maturity possible?), *Asahi Shinbun*, 24 August 1997.

Akiyama, Kiyoshi 1973 *Jiyū onna ronsō* (The women's debate on freedom), Tokyo, Shisō no Kagakusha.

Andermahr, Sonya, Terry Lovell and Carol Wolkowitz eds (2000) *A Glossary of Feminist Theory*, London: Arnold Press.

Anderson, Benedict 1985 *Imagined Communities: Reflections on the Origins and Spread of Nationalism*, New York, Verso.

Aoki, Tamotsu 1990 *Nihon bunka ron no henyō* (The transformation of theories of Japanese culture), Tokyo, Chuokoronsha.

Asahi Shinbun 1997 'Ototta hito Jipushi issō-seyo - 6 man nin ni kyōsei funin shujutsu' (The cleansing of 'inferior persons' and 'gypsies' - 60,000 underwent forced sterilization), *Asahi Shinbun*, 26 August 1997.

Asia-Japan Women's Resource Centre (ed.) 1997 *Ianfu mondai Q&A - Jiyū shugi shikan e onnatach i no hanron* (The 'comfort women' issue; Q&As: the counter-argument of women to the Liberal View of History Group), Tokyo, Akashi Shoten.

Atarashii Rekishi Kyōkasho o Tsukuru Kai no Yobikake Nin 1996 *Atarashii Rekishi Kyōkasho o Tsukuru Kai sōsetsu ni atatte no seimei* (Statement on the establishment of the Japanese Group for Orthodox History Education), Atarashii Rekishi Kyōkasho o Tsukuru Kai, 2 December 1996. For an English translation see:

Jordan Sand 1999 'Statement on the Establishment of the Council for the Creation of New History Textbooks', *History and Memory*, 2(2):127–128, Indiana University Press.

Basu, Aparna 1993 *The Role of Women in the Indian Struggle for Freedom*. Paper presented at the Women in Asia Conference, 3–4 October 1993, Melbourne, Australia.

Beneke, Timothy 1982 *Men on Rape*, New York, St. Martin's Press.

Bhabha, Homi K. 1993 *Nation and Narration*, New York and London, Routledge.

Bock, Gisela 1994 'Nazi Gender Politics and Women's History', in F. Thebaud (ed.) *A History of Women in the West, V. Toward a Cultural Identity in the Twentieth Century*, Cambridge, Harvard University Press.

Buckley, Sandra 2000 *Broken Silence: Voices of Japanese Feminism*, Berkeley, Los Angeles and London, University of California Press.

Chang, Iris 1997 *The Rape of Nanking: The Forgotten Holocaust of WWII*, New York, Basic Books.

Coomaraswamy, Radhika 1996 *Report on the Mission to the Democratic People's Republic, the Republic of Korea and Japan on the Issue of Military Sexual Slavery in Wartime*, Geneva, United Nations Commission on Human Rights.

Davin, Anna 1978 'Imperialism and Motherhood', *History Workshop 5*.

Delphy, Christine 1989 *Sexe et Genre*. Paper presented at the International Seminar on Women's Studies, National Women's Education Center, Tokyo.

Dower, John 1999 *Embracing Defeat: Japan in the Wake of World War II*, New York, W.W. Norton and Company; London, The New Press.

Ehara, Yumiko 1998 *Feminizumu to kenryoku sayō* (Feminism and mechanisms of power), Tokyo, Keisō Shobō.

.... 1992 Jūgun ianfu ni tsuite (The military comfort women), *Shisō no Kagaku,* December 1992.

Enloe, Cynthia 2000 *Bananas, Beaches and Bases: Making Feminist Sense of International Politics*, Berkeley, Los Angeles, London, University of California Press (First edition 1989).

Fraser, Arvonne S. 2001 'Becoming Human: The Origins and Development of Women's Human Rights', in Agosín Marjorie (ed.) *Women, Gender and Human Rights*, New Brunswick, New Jersey and London, Rutgers University Press.

Frevert, Ute 1996 *Nazism and Women's Policy*. Paper presented at the International Symposium on National Mobilization and Women, Tokyo University of Foreign Studies, 19 July 1996.

Fujime, Yuki 1991 'Akasen jūgyōin kumiai to baishun bōshi hō' (The labour union of the red-light district workers and the anti-prostitution law), *Joseishigaku* Vol.1, Joseishi Sōgō Kenkyūkai.

.... 1996 *Sei no rekishigaku* (The history of sexuality), Tokyo, Fuji Shuppan.

.... 1997 'Joseishi kara mita "ianfu" mondai' (The 'comfort woman' issue seen from the perspective of women's history), *Kikan Sensō Sekinin Kenkyū* Vol. 18 Winter 1997, Sensō Sekinin Shiryo Center.

Fujitani, Takashi 1994 'Kindai Nihon ni okeru kenryoku no tekunoroji : guntai "chihō", shintai' (Power and technology in modern Japan: the military, 'regions' and the body) *Shisō* 845, November 1994, Tokyo, Iwanami Shoten.

Furukubo, Sakura 1991 'Raichō no "bosei shugi" o yomu' (Understanding Raichō's maternalism), *Joseigaku Nenpō* 12, Nihon Joseigaku Kenkyūkai.

Go, Liza 1993 'Jūgun ianfu, karayuki, Japayuki: a Continuity in Commodification', *Health Alert*, 139, March 1993.

Grazai, Vittoria de 1992 *How Fascism Ruled Women: Italy, 1922–1945*, Berkeley and L.A., University of California Press.

Grossmann, Atina 1995 'A Question of Silence: The Rape of German Women by Occupation Soldiers', *October 72*, Spring 1995, MIT.

Habermas, Jürgen et al. 1987 *'Historikerstreit', Die Dokumentation der Kontroverse um die Einzigartigkeit der Nationalsozial-istischen Judenvernichtung*, Munich, Piper.

Hanasaki, Kōhei 1997 'Aikokushin wa akutō no saigo no kakuremino' (Patriotism is the final cloak concealing the villain), *Impaction 102*, April 1997, Tokyo, Impact Shuppankai.

Hata, Ikuhiko 1997 'Seiji no omocha ni sareru rekishi ninshiki: Rokōkyō, Nankin, nana san ichi (731), ianfu no kyojitsu o tou' (Historical awareness made into the toy of politics: the fabricated debate concerning the Marco Polo Bridge incident, Nanking, Unit 731 and the comfort women), *Shokun* September 1997, Tokyo, Bungeishunjusha.

Hein, Laura and Selden, Mark 2000 'Lessons of War, Global Power, and Social Change', in Laura and Selden (eds.) *Censoring History: Citizenship and Memory in Japan, Germany, and the United States*, New York and London, M.E. Sharpe.

Hikaku Kazokushi Gakkai (supervising editor) 1997 *Jendā to josei* (Women and gender), Tokyo, Waseda Daigaku Shuppanbu.

Hikosaka, Tei 1991 *Dansei shinwa* (The male myth), Tokyo, Komichi Shobō.

Himeoka, Toshiko 1993 *Kindai Doitsu no bosei shugi feminizumu* (The maternalist feminism of modern Germany), Tokyo, Keisō Shobō.

.... 1995 'Josei besshi to bosei raisan: Nachi no josei seisaku'

(The contempt for women, the glorification of women: Nazi women's policy) in Kanō, Mikiyo (ed.) 'Bosei fashizumu' (Maternal fascism), *New Feminism Review 6*, Tokyo, Gakuyō Shobō

Hiratsuka, Raichō, 1911 '*Genshi josei wa taiyo de atta: "Seitō" hakkan ni saishite*' (Once woman was the sun: introduction to 'Blue Stocking'), *Seitō*, Tokyo, Seitōsha.

.... 1917 'Hinin no kahi o ronzu' (Arguing about the pros or cons of contraception), reprinted in 1984 *Hiratsuka Raichō chosaku shū* (The collected works of Hiratsuka Raichō), Vol. 2, Tokyo, Ōtsuki Shoten.

.... 1920 'Shakai kaizō ni taisuru fuijn no shimei' (Women's mission concerning social reform), reprinted in 1984 in *Hiratsuka Raichō chosaku shū* (The collected works of Hiratsuka Raichō), Vol.3, Tokyo, Ōtsuki Shoten.

.... 1984 *Hiratsuka Raichō chosaku shū* (The collected works of Hiratus Raichō: the complete 8 volumes), Tokyo, Ōtsuki Shoten.

Hirayama, Chōji 1995 *Ie shakai to kojin shugi* (The household society and individualism), Tokyo, Nihon Kezai Shinbunsha.

Hirota, Masaki 1995 *Sensō no katarare kata* (Narratives of war). Paper presented at the symposium 'Rekishi to hyōshō' (History and representation) at the annual convention of the Japan Society of the History of Thought (Nihon Shisōshi Gakkai), October 22, 1995.

.... 1996 'Bunka kōryūshi no kadai to hōhō' (Issues and methodology in the history of cultural exchange), *Osaka Daigaku Bungakubu Kiyō* 36, OsakaUniversity.

Hobsbawm, E. and Ranger, T. 1983 *The Invention of Tradition*, Cambridge, Cambridge University Press.

Hori, Sachiko 1984 'Jugo nen sensō ka no joshi rōdō' (Women's labour during the 15-year war), *Rekishi Hyōron* 207: 37–2 March 1984.

Horiba, Kiyoko (ed.) 1991 '*Seitō' Josei Kaihō Ronshū* (Collected Essays for Women's Liberation in 'Blue Stocking'), Tokyo, Iwanami Shoten.

Ichikawa, Fusae 1940 'Taisei yokusan undō to fujin' (Imperial assistance movement and women), *Fujin tenbō*. Reprinted in Suzuki, Yūko 1986 *Feminizumu to sensō* (Feminism and war), Tokyo, Marujusha.

.... 1943a 'Shinpen zakki' (Essays on my everyday life), *Fujin Mondai kenkyūsho shohō* 6, October 30 1943. Reprinted in

Suzuki, Yūko 1986 *Feminizumu to sensō* (Feminism and war), Tokyo, Marujusha.

.... 1943b 'Senji fujin dokuhon' (A reader on women and war), in Suzuki, Yūko 1986 *Feminizumu to sensō* (Feminism and war), Tokyo, Marujusha.

.... 1974a *Ichikawa Fusae jiden: senzenhen* (The memoirs of Ichikawa Fusae: pre-war edition), Tokyo, Shinjuku Shobō.

.... 1974b *Ichikawa Fusae jiden: sengohen* (The memoirs of Ichikawa Fusae: post-war edition), Tokyo, Shinjuku Shobō.

.... 1976 *Nihon fujin mondai shiryō shūsei, Dai 2 kan, Seiji* (A Collection of documentation on Japanese women's issues, vol. 2, politics), Tokyo, Domesu Shuppan.

Ichikawa Fusae to iu Hito' Kankō Iinkai (ed.) 1982 *Ichikawa Fusae to iu hito: 100 nin no kaisō* (Ichikawa Fusae: the recollections of 100 people), Tokyo, Shinjuku Shobō.

Ikezawa, Natsuki 1997 'Bungei jihyō: rekishi to katarikuchi' (Monthly literary review: history and narrative) *Asahi Shinbun*, 26 August 1997.

Inoue, Kiyoshi 1948 *Nihon joseishi* (Japanese women's history), Tokyo, San Ichi Shobō.

Inoue, Teruko, Chizuko Ueno, Yumiko Ehara and Masako Amano (eds.) 1994 *Nihon no Feminizumu 1: Ribu to Feminizumu* (Japanese feminisms, vol. 1, women's liberation and feminism), Tokyo, Iwanami Shoten.

Irokawa, Daikichi 1997 'Jigyaku shikan to Nihon nashionarizumu 13: Irokawa Daikichi san ni kiku' (The masochistic view of history and Japanese nationalism 13: an interview with Irokawa Daikichi) vols. 1 and 2, *Tōitsu Nippō*, 12–13 September 1997.

Jang, Jing 1995 *Kindai Chūgoku to 'ren-ai' no hakken* (Modern China and the discovery of 'love'), Tokyo, Iwanami Shoten.

Kameyama, Michiko 1984a 'Sensō to kangofu' (War and nurses), *Rekishi Hyōron* 407, 37–2, March 1984.

.... 1984b 'Sensō to kango' (War and nursing), in the series *Kindai Nihon kangoshi II* (Modern Japanese nursing history vol. II), Tokyo, Domesu Shuppan.

Kankoku Teishintai Mondai Kyōgikai, Teishintai Kenkyūkai (ed.) 1993 *Shōgen: kyōsei renkō sareta Chōsenjin ianfu tachi* (The testimony of Korean comfort women who were forcibly recruited), Tokyo, Akashi Shoten. Translated by the Jūgun Ianfu Mondai Uriyoson Nettowaku.

Kano, Masanao, and Horiba, Kiyoko 1977 *Takamure Itsue*, Tokyo, Asahi Shinbunsha.

Kanō, Mikiyo 1979a 'Takamure Itsue to kōkoku shikan' (Takamure Itsue and the imperialist view of history), in Kawano, Nobuko et al. 1979 *Takamure Itsue ronshū* (The collected articles of Takamura Itsue), Tokyo, JCA Shuppan.

.... 1979b *Josei to tennōsei* (Women and the emperor system), Tokyo, Shisō no Kagakusha.

.... 1987 *Onnatachi no 'jūgo'* (Women and the 'home front'), Tokyo, Chikuma Shobō.

.... (ed.) 1990 *Jiga no kanata e* (Beyond the self), Tokyo, Shakai Hōronsha.

.... (ed.) 1995a 'Bosei fashizumu'(Maternal fascism), *New Feminism Review* 6, Tokyo, Gakuyō Shobō.

.... (ed.) 1995b *Komentaru sengo gojū nen 5: Sei to kazoku* (A commentary on the fifty years since the war, Vol. 5, Sex and the family), Tokyo, Shakai Hōronsha.

.... 1995c 'Kindai joseishi ni totte no kuni to jiyū' (The state and freedom in modern women's history), *Shisō no Kagaku* August 1995, Tokyo, Shiso no Kagakusha.

Kasahara Tokushi, et al. 1997 *Rekishi no jijitsu o dō nintei shi dō oshieru ka: Kenshō 731 butai , Nankin gyakusatsu jiken, 'Jūgun ianfu'* (How do we authorize and teach historical facts: The verification of Unit 731, the Nanking Massacre and the 'comfort women'), Tokyo, Kyōiku Shiryō Shuppankai.

Kasai, Hirotaka 1996 'Maruyama Masao no Nihon' (Maruyama Masao's Japan), in Sakai, Naoki, Brett de Barry and Iyotani, Toshio (eds.), *Nashonarithi no datsu kōchiku* (Deconstructing nationality), Tokyo, Kashiwa Shobō.

Katō, Norihiro 1997 *Haisengo ron* (On the post-war era), Tokyo, Kōdansha.

Katō, Yōko 1996 *Chōheisei to kindai Nihon 1868–1945* (The military conscription system and modern Japan 1868–1945), Tokyo, Yoshikawa Kōbundō.

Katzoff, Beth 1997 *War and Feminism: Yamakawa Kikue 1931–1945*. Paper presented at the panel 'Women and Nationalism', at the Annual Convention of the Association of Asian Studies, 14 March 1997, Chicago, U.S.A.

Kawada, Fumiko 1987 *Akarenga no ie: Chōsen kara kita jūgun ianfu* (The Redbrick house: comfort women from Korea), Tokyo, Chikuma Shobō.

Kawahata, Tomoko 1995 'Seiteki doreisei kara no kaihō o motomete' (In search of liberation from sexual slavery), in Ehara, Yumiko (ed.) *Feminizumu no shuchō 2: Sei no shōhinka* (Feminist advocacy 2: the commodification of sex) , Tokyo, Keisō Shobō.

Kerber, Linda 1998 *No Constitutional Rights to be Ladies: Women and the Obligations of Citizenship*, New York, Hill and Wang.

Kim, Chonmi 1994 *Suihei undōshi kenkyū: Minzoku sabetsu hihan* (A study of the leveler movement: a criticism of ethnic discrimination), Tokyo, Gendai Kikakutshitsu.

Kim, Yōnghi 1998 'Is Forgetting a Kindness?' Translated by Sarah Kovner, in *U.S.-Japan Women's Journal*, English supplement No.14, 1998, U.S.-Japan Women's Journal.

Kim-Gibson, Dai Sil 1997 *Japanese Military Supplies: The Korean 'Comfort Women'*. Paper presented at the panel 'The 'Comfort Women': Contexts and Sub-texts', at the annual convention of the American Historical Association, New York.

Kim, Il-myon 1976 *Tennō no guntai to Chōsenjin ianfu* (The imperial army and Korean comfort women), Tokyo, San Ichi Shobō.

Kim, Pu-ja and Yang, Ching-ja et al. 1995 *Motto shiritai 'Ianfu' mondai : Sei to minzoku no shiten kara* (Finding out more about the 'comfort women' problem: from the perspectives of sex and ethnicity), Tokyo, Akashi Shoten.

Kim, Pu-ja 1996 'Sekai Josei Kaigi hōkoku: 'ianfu' mondai o chūshin ni' (Report of the World Women's Conference focusing on the 'comfort women' problem), in Ajia Keizai Kenkyūsho (ed.) *Daisan sekai no hataraku josei* (Working women in the third world), Tokyo, Akashi Shoten.

Kurahashi, Masanao 1989 'Jūgun ianfu zenshi: Nichi-Ro sensō no baai' (The prehistory of the comfort women: the case of the Japanese-Russo War), *Rekishi Hyōron* 467, 42–2 March 1989.

Kōketsu, Atsushi 1981 *Sōryokusen taisei kenkyū* (A study of the total war regime), Tokyo, San Ichi Shobō.

Komagome, Takeshi 1997 'Jiyū shugi shikan wa watashitachi o jiyū ni suru no ka?' (Will the liberal view of history make us free?), *Sekai* April 1997, Tokyo, Iwanami Shoten.

Kondō, Kazuko 1995 'Onna to sensō: bosei / kazoku / kokka' (Women and war: motherhood, family and the state) in Okuda, Akiko (ed.) 1995 *Onna to otoko no jiku: Nihon joseishi saikō V, Semegiau onna to otoko: kindai* (Space and time of women and men: a reconsideration of Japanese women's history , vol. V,

Women and men in conflict: the modern period), Tokyo, Fujiwara Shoten.

Kōno, Nobuko et al., 1979 *Takamure Itsue ronshū* (The collected articles of Takamura Itsue), Tokyo, JCA Shuppan.

Koonz, Claudia 1987 *Mothers in the Fatherland*, New York, St. Martin's Press.

Kōuchi, Nobuko (ed.) 1984 *Shiryō bosei hogo ronsō* (Documentation on the motherhood protection debate), Tokyo, Domesu Shuppan.

Koyama, Shizuko 1991 *Ryōsaikenbo to iu kihan* (The norm of the good wife, wise mother), Tokyo, Keisō Shobō.

Kurahashi, Masanao 1994 *Jūgun ianfu mondai no rekishiteki kenkyū* (A historical study of the military comfort women), Tokyo, Kyōei Shobō.

Kurihara, Hiroshi 1994 *Takamure Itsue no kon-in joseishizō no kenkyū* (A study of Takamure Itsue's research of images of married women in history), Tokyo, Takashina Shoten.

.... 1997 'Takamure Itsue no joseishizō' (Tamamure Itsue's images of women's history), in Tabata, Yasuko, Chizuko Ueno, and Sanae Fukutō, (eds), Hikaku Kazokushi Gakkai (supervising editor) *Jendā to josei* (Women and gender), Tokyo, Waseda Daigaku Shuppanbu.

Kurihara, Yukio 1997 'Rekishi no saishin ni mukete: Watashi mo mata revijionisuto de aru' (Toward a revision of history: I too am a revisionist!), *Impaction* 102 April 1997, Tokyo, Impact Shuppankai.

Maeda, Akira 1997a 'Sabetsu to jinken: kihanteki shikō' (Discrimination and human rights: a normative approach), *Impaction* 102 April 1997, Tokyo, Impact Shuppankai.

.... 1997b 'Ueno Chizuko no "Kioku chigai no seijigaku": Nihongun "ianfu" mondai o dō miru ka?' (Ueno Chizuko's 'politics of misconceived memory': how should we view the military 'comfort women' issue?), *Masukomi Shimin* September 1997.

.... 1997c 'Tettei tsuikyū jiyūshugi shikan Kokuren ni okeru 'ianfu' tōgi to Nihon seifu' (The outright objections of the Liberal View of History group: discussions concerning the 'comfort women' by the United Nations and the Japanese government), *Shūkan Kinyōbi* 25 July 1997.

Maruoka, Hideko (ed.) 1976 'Nihon fujin mondai shiryō shūsei, dai 8 kan'(Collected documentation on Japanese women's issues, vol. 8) *Shichō* (Thoughts), No.1, Tokyo, Domesu Shuppan.

Maruyama, Masao 1946, 'Chō-kokkashugi no ronri to shinri' (The logic and psychology of ultra-nationalism), *Sekai*, May 1946, Tokyo, Iwanami Shoten. Reprinted in 1995 *Sekai shuyō ronbun sen 1946–1995* (The best selection of leading essays of the time in *Sekai*, 1946–1995), Tokyo, Iwanami Shoten.

Maruyama, Yukiko 1977, 1995 'Dansei raita no kaita 'jūgun ianfu' o kiru' (Criticising the 'military comfort women' written by male writers), in Kanō, Mikiyo (ed.) *Komentaru sengo 50 nen, vol. 5: Sei to kazoku* (A commentary on the 50 years since the war, vol. 5, Sex and the family), Tokyo, Shakai Hyōronsha.

McCormack, Gavan 2000 'The Japanese Movement to "Correct" History', in Hein, Laura and Mark Selden (eds) *Censoring History: Citizenship and Memory in Japan, Germany, and the United States*, New York and London, M.E. Sharpe.

McDougal, Gay 1998 *Contemporary Forms of Slavery, Systematic Rape, Sexual Slavery and Slave-like Practices During Armed Conflict, Final Report of the Special Rapporteur of the Commission of Human Rights*, Geneva, United Nations Commission on Human Rights.

Merry, Sally Engle 2001 'Women, Violence and the Human Rights System', in Agosín Marjorie (ed.) *Women, Gender and Human Rights*, New Brunswick, New Jersey and London, Rutgers University Press.

Midgley, Clare 1992 *Women Against Slavery: The British Campaigns, 1780–1870*, London and New York, Routledge.

Miyake, Yoshiko 1994 'Kindai Nihon joseishi no saisōzō no tame ni: Tekisuto no yomikae' (Towards a re-creation of modern women's history: re-interpretation of the texts), *Shakai no Hakken*, Kanagawa Daigaku Hyōron Sōsho 4, Kanagawa University.

Mizuta, Tamae 1997 'Nihon ni okeru feminizumu shisō no juyō' (Acceptence of feminists ideas in Japan), in Rekishigaku Kenkyūkai (ed.) *Kōza Sekaishi 7: 'Kindai' wa hito o dō kaete kita ka* (A series of world history 7: How has the modern period changed people?), Tokyo, Tokyo Daigaku Shuppankai.

Morgan, Robin (ed.) 1984 *Sisterhood is Global*, New York, Anchor Books.

Morisaki, Kazue 1965, 1992 *Daisan no sei* (The third sex), Tokyo, Kawade Shobō Shinsha.

Murai, Atsushi 1997 'Jiyūshugi shikan kenkyūkai no kyōshi tachi: Genba kyōshi e no kikitori chōsa kara' (Concerning the teachers of the Liberal History Research Group: drawing on an interview survey of classroom teachers), *Sekai* April 1997, Tokyo, Iwanami Shoten.

Murakami, Nobuhiko 1978 *Nihon no fujin monda* (Japanese women's issues), Tokyo, Iwanami Shoten.

Nagahara, Kazuko 1985 'Josei tōgō to bosei' (Women's unity and motherhood), in Wakita, Haruko (ed.) *Bosei o tou, ge* (Questioning Motherhood, vol. 2), Kyoto, Jinbun Shoin.

.... 1989 'Josei wa naze sensō ni kyōryoku shitaka?' (Why did women support the war?) in Fujiwara et al. (eds) *Nihon kindai no kyozō to jitsuzō* 3 (The fictitious and real images of modern Japan), Tokyo, Ōtsuki Shoten.

Nagahara, Kazuko and Yoneda, Sayoko 1996 *Zōhoban onna no Shōwa shi* (An expanded edition of Shōwa women's history), Tokyo, Yūhikaku.

Nakamura, Ikuo 1994 *Nihon no kami to ōken* (Japanese devinity and kingship), Kyoto, Hōzōkan.

Narita, Ryūichi 1995 'Haha no kuni no onnatachi : Oku Mumeo no senji to sengo' (The women of the mother land: Oku Mumeo pre- and post-war), in Yamanouchi, Yasushi, Victor Koschmann, and Ryūich Narita, (eds) *Sōryokusen to gendaika* (Total war and modernization), Tokyo, Kashiwa Shobō.

Nishikawa, Nagao 1992 *Kokkyō no koekata* (How to transcend national boundaries), Tokyo, Chikuma Shobō.

.... 1993 'Kokka ideorogi to shite no bunmei to bunka' (Civilization and culture as state ideologies), *Shisō* 827, May 1993, Tokyo, Iwanami Shoten.

Nishikawa, Nagao 1995 'Nihongata kokumin kokka no keisei' (The formation of the Japanese model of the nation-state), in Nishikawa, Nagao and Matsumiya Shūji (eds) *Bakumatsu/Meiji ki no kokumin kokka keisei to bunka henyō* (The formation of the nation-state and cultural transformation at the end of the Tokugawa Shogunate and in the Meiji period), Tokyo, Shin-yōsha.

Nishikawa, Yūko 1982a *Mori no ie no miko* (The shamaness of the house in the woods), Tokyo, Shinchōsha; reprinted in 1990 *Takamure Itsue*, Tokyo, Daisan Bunmeisha.

.... 1982b 'Sensō e no keisha to yokusan no fujin' (The predisposition of women towards war and their wartime collaboration), in Joseishi Sōgō Kenkyūkai (ed.) *Joseishi 5: Kindai* (Japanese women's history Vol. 5, The modern period), Tokyo, Tokyo Daigaku Shuppankai.

.... 1997 'Takamure Itsue no kindai kazoku ron' (Takamure Itsue's theory on the modern family), in Tabata, Yasuko, Chizuko Ueno, and Sanae Fukutō, (eds), Hikaku Kazokushi Gakkai (supervising editor) 1997 *Jendā to josei* (Women and gender), Tokyo, Waseda Daigaku Shuppanbu.

Nishino, Rumiko 1992 *Jūgun Ianfu: Moto heishi tachi no shōgen* (The testimony of former comfort women and soldiers), Tokyo, Akashi Shoten.

Nishio, Kazumi 1990 'Joseishi to iu shiza' (The perspective of women's history), *Rekishi Hyōron* 479, March 1990.

Nomura, Koya 1997 Sabetsu, doka, 'Okinawa-jin' (Discrimination, assimilation and the 'Okinawans'), *Bulletin of Sanyō Gakuin Junior College*, Vol. 28, December 1997.

Ogino, Miho 1993 'Nihon ni okeru joseishi kenkyū to feminizumu' (Women's studies and feminism in Japan), *Nihon no Kagakusha* 28(12).

Ōgoshi, Aiko and Takahashi, Tetsuya 1997 'Taidan jendā to sensō sekinin' (A dialogue about gender and war responsibility), *Gendai Shisō* 25(10) September 1997, Tokyo, Seidosha.

Oguma, Eiji 1995 *Tan-itsu minzoku shinwa no kigen* (The origins of the myth of a homogenous nation), Tokyo, Shin-yōsha. English translation by David Askew 2002 *A Genealogy of Japanese Self-images*, Melbourne, Trans Pacific Press.

Ogura, Chikako 1988 *Sekkusu shinwa kaitai shinsho* (A new book for dismantling the sex myth), Tokyo, Gakuyō Shobō.

Oku, Takenori 1995 'Kokumin kokka no naka no josei: Meiji ki o chūshin ni' (Women in the nation-state: focusing on the Meiji period) in Okuda, Akiko (ed.) *Onna to otoko no jiku: Nihon joseishi saiko V, Semegiau onna to otoko: Kindai* (The space and time of women and men: a reconsideration of Japanese women's history, vol. V, Women and men in conflict: modern period), Tokyo, Fujiwara Shoten.

Okuda, Akiko (ed.) 1995 *Onna to otoko no jiku: Nihon joseishi saiko V, Semegiau onna to otoko: Kindai* (The space and time of women and men: a reconsideration of Japanese women's history, vol. V, Women and men in conflict: modern period), Tokyo, Fujiwara Shoten.

Ōmori, Kahoru 1997 *Hiratsuka Raichō no hikari to kage* (The light and shade of Hiratsuka Raichō), Tokyo, Daiichi Shorin.

Ōtsuka, Eiji 1989 *Shōjo minzokugaku* (Folklore studies of girls), Tokyo, Kōbunsha.

Perrot, Michelle and Duby, George 1995 *A History of Women in the West,* Vol. 3, Cambridge, Harvard University Press.

Rayner, Richard 1997 'Women in the Warrior Culture', *New York Times Magazine,* 22 June.

Ryūkyū Shinpō 1997 'Kokumei kyohi no izoku mo: Kankoku shusshinsha no kokumei sagyō ni kakawaru Hong shi intabyū' (The bereaved families also reject the inscription of names: An interview with Mr. Hong involved with the engraving work) *Ryūkyū Shinpōsha* 23 June 1997.

.... 1997 'Hito: Kankoku Myong Ji Dai kyōju. Hong Jong Pil san' (People: Professor Hong Jong Phil of Korea's Myongji University), *Ryūkyū Shinpō,* 23 June 1997.

Sakai, Naoki, Brett de Barry and Toshio Iyotani (eds) 1996 *Nashonarithi no datsu kōchiku* (Deconstructing nationality), Tokyo, Kashiwa Shobō.

Sakurai, Yoshiko 1997 'Mitsuyaku gaikō no daishō : ianfu mondai wa naze kojireta ka' (Secret diplomacy for compensation: why is the comfort women problem so entangled?), *Bungei Shunjū* April 1997, Tokyo, Bungeishunjūsha.

Sand, Jordan 1999 'Introduction to Ueno Chizuko's "The Politics of Memory: Nation, Individual and Self"', *History and Memory,* 2(2).

Sander, Helke and Johr, Barbara 1995 *Befreier und Belfreite: Krieg, Vergwaltigungen, Kinder,* Munich, Antje Kemstman.

Scott, Joan Wallach 1996 *Only Paradoxes to Offer: French Feminism and the Rights of Man,* Cambridge, Harvard University Press.

.... 1999 *Gender and the Politics of History,* New York, Columbia University Press.

Senda, Kakō 1973 *Jūgun ianfu* (The comfort women), Tokyo, Futabasha, (reprinted in 1984 by Kōdansha Bunko).

.... 1997 'Jūgun ianfu no shinjitsu' (The truth about the 'comfort women'), *Ronza,* August 1997, Tokyo, Asahi Shinbunsha.

Sensō giseisha o kokoro ni kizamu kai (Official name, Taiheiyō Chiiki no sensō giseisha ni omoi o hase, kokoro ni kizamu shūkai jikkō iinkai) (ed.) 1997 *Watashi wa 'ianfu' de wa nai: Nihon no shinryaku to seidorei* (I am not a 'comfort woman': Japanese invasion and sexual slavery), Osaka, Tōhō Shuppan.

Sone, Hiromi 1990 'Baita kō: Kinsei no baishun' (Considering prostitutes: prostitution in the early modern age), in Joseishi Sōgō Kenkyūkai (ed.) *Nihon josei seikatsushi 3, Kinsei* (A history of Japanese women's lives in Japan, vol. 3, The modern period), Tokyo, Tokyo Daigaku Shuppankai.

.... 1998 'Baishun gainen o megutte' (On the concept of prostitution) Sakata, Yoshinori (ed.) *Gendai no Esupuri 366, Sei no shosō* (The contemporary Espirit 366, Diversity of sexuality), Tokyo, Shibundō.

Spivak, Gayatri Chakravorty 1999 *The Post-Colonial Critic*, London and New York, Routledge, Chapman and Hall.

Suzuki, Yūko 1986 *Feminizumu to sensō* (Feminism and war), Tokyo, Marujusha.

.... 1989a *Joseishi o hiraku 1: Haha to onna* (Creating women's history 1: women and mothers), Tokyo, Miraisha.

.... 1989b *Joseishi o hiraku 2: Yokusan to teikō* (Creating women's history 2: Collaboration and resistance), Tokyo, Miraisha.

.... 1991 *Chōsenjin jūgun ianfu* (Korean military comfort women), Tokyo, Iwanami Shoten (Iwanami Booklet).

.... 1993 *Jūgun ianfu mondai to sei bōryoku* (The comfort women issue and sexual violence), Tokyo, Miraisha.

.... 1996a *Joseishi o hiraku 3: Onna to sengo 50 nen* (Creating women's history 3: Women and the 50 years since the end of the war), Tokyo, Miraisha.

.... 1996b *Joseishi o hiraku 4: 'Ianfu' mondai to sengo sekinin* (Creating women's history 4: The 'comfort women' issue and post-war responsibility), Tokyo, Miraisha.

.... 1997a 'Nihongun "ianfu" (sei doreisei) mondai no shindankai to han "ianfu" kyanpen' , 2 volumes (A new stage of the Japanese military 'comfort women' (sexual slaves) problem and the anti-comfort women campaign, vols. 1 and 2), *Mirai* 365/366, February–March 1997.

.... 1997b *Sensō sekinin to jendā* (War responsibility and gender), Tokyo, Miraisha.

Tabata, Kaya 1995 'Shokuminchi no Chōsen de kurashita Nihon josei tachi' (Japanese women who lived in colonial Korea). Paper presented at the special session *Feminism and War* at the spring convention of the Women's Studies Association of Japan.

Tabata, Yasuko, Chizuko Ueno and Sanae Fukutō, (eds), Hikaku Kazokushi Gakkai (supervising editor) 1997 *Jendā to josei* (Women and gender), Tokyo, Waseda Daigaku Shuppanbu.

Tachi, Kaoru 1994 'Josei no sanseiken to jendā' (Women's right to vote and gender), in Hara, Hiroko (ed.) *Raiburari Sōkan kagaku 2: Jendā* (Library interdisciplinary social sciences vol. 2: gender), Tokyo, Shinseisha.

Takahashi, Tetsuya 1995 *Kioku no echika: sensō /tetsugaku/ Aushuwittsu* (The Ethics of Memory: War, Philosophy and Auschwitz), Tokyo, Iwanami Shoten.

.... 2001 'Nani ga chokuzen ni kesaretaka: NHK "Towareru senji seibōryoku" kaihen o kangaeru' (What was cut just before the broadcast?: A consideration of the alterations made to NHK's 'Questioning wartime sexual violence'), *Sekai*, 2001(5), Tokyo, Iwanami Shoten.

Takamure, Itsue 1938, 1966 *Bokeisei no kenkyū* (A study of matriarchy); reprinted in *Takamure Itsue zenshū* 1 (The collected works of Takamure Itsue, vol. 1), Tokyo, Rironsha.

.... 1966–70 *Takamure Itsue zenshū, Zen 10 kan* (The collected works of Takamure Itsue, complete 10 volumes), Tokyo, Rironsha.

Takeda, Seiji, Yoshinori Kobayashi and Daizaburō Hashizume 1997 *Seigi, Sensō, Kokka Ron* (On justice, war and the state), Tokyo, Komichi Shobō.

Tanaka, Hiroshi 1993 'Nihon no sengo sekinin to Ajia: Sengo hoshō to rekishi ninshiki' (Japan's post-war responsibility and Asia: Post-war compensation and historical awareness), in *Kōza kindai Nihon to shokuminchi 8: Ajia no reisen to datsu shokuminchi ka* (Series modern Japan and colonialism, vol. 8, The Asian cold-war and de-colonization), Tokyo, Iwanami Shoten.

Tanaka, Toshiyuki 1993 *Shirarezaru sensō hanzai* (Unknown war crimes), Tokyo, Ōtsuki Shoten.

.... 1996 'Naze Beigun wa jūgun ianfu mondai o mushi shita no ka', 2 volumes (Why did the American army ignore the military comfort women issue? Vols. 1 and 2), *Sekai* 627/628 November and December 1996, Tokyo, Iwanami Shoten.

Tateiwa, Shinya 1997 *Shiteki Shoyūron* (Private ownership theory), Tokyo, Keisō Shobō.

Tokyo Daigaku Kyōiku Gakubu Kyōikugaku Kenkyūshitsu Kitsuke '1209 Kirokushū Sakusei Chimu' 1997 *Kirokushu Nanumu no Ie kara wakamono tachi e: Kankoku moto 'Ianfu' no ima* (Memorial collection: From 'Nanumu House' to young people: former Korean 'comfort women' today). Tokyo, Dept. of Pedagogy, The University of Tokyo.

Tomiyama, Ichirō 1990 *Kindai Nihon shakai to 'Okinawajin'* (Modern Japanese society and the 'Okinawans'), Tokyo, Nihon Hyōronsha.

.... 1997 'Shohyō: Oguma Eiji cho "Tan-itsu minzoku shinwa no kigen"' (Book review : 'The Origins of myth of the homogenous society' by Eiji Oguma), *Nihonshi Kenkyū* 413.

Tonkin, Elizabeth 1992 *Narrating the Past: The Social Construction of Oral History*, Cambridge, Cambridge University Press.

Tonosaki, Mitsuhiro and Okabe, Masako (eds) 1979 *Yamakawa Kikue no kōseki* (The tracks of Yamakawa Kikue), Tokyo, Domesu Shuppan.

Tsukuru Kai Sandōnin Intabyu- 1997 'Hiki komogomo no sandōnin jijō' (The bittersweet circumstances of the supporters for the Orthodox History Textbook Group), *Ronza* May 1997, Tokyo, Asahi Shinbunsha.

Ueno, Chizuko 1985 *Shihonshugi to kaji rōdō* (Capitalism and domestic labour), Tokyo, Kaimeisha.

.... 1990 *Kafuchōsei to shihonsei* (Patriarchy and capitalism), Tokyo, Iwanami Shoten.

.... 1991 *90 nendai no Adamu to Ibu* (Adam and Eve of the 1990s), Tokyo, NHK Shuppan.

.... 1994a *Kindai kazoku no seiritsu to shūen* (The rise and fall of the modern family), Tokyo, Iwanami Shoten.

.... 1994b 'Nihon no ribu: sono shisō to haikei' (Japanese women's liberation movement: its ideas and background) in Inoue et al. (eds) *Nihon no feminizumu 1: Ribu to feminizumu* (Japanese feminism 1: women's liberation and feminism), Tokyo, Iwanami Shoten.

.... 1995a 'Rekishigaku to feminizumu: "joseishi" o koete' (History and feminism: transcending women's history), in the series *Iwanami kōza Nihon tsu-shi bekkan 1: Rekishi ishiki no genzai* (Iwanami lectures Japanese history special series 1: historical consciousness today), Tokyo, Iwanami Shoten.

.... 1995b 'Sai no seijigaku' (The politics of difference), in Ueno et al. (eds) *Iwanami koza gendai shakaigaku 11: Jendā no shakaigaku* (Series Contemporary sociology 11: sociology of gender), Tokyo, Iwanami Shoten.

.... (ed.) 1996 *Kitto kaerareru seisabetsu go: Watashitachi no gaidorain* (Sexist language that can be changed for sure: our guidelines), Tokyo, Sanseidō.

.... 1997a 'Kioku no seijigaku: kokumin, kojin, watashi'(The Politics of memory: the nation, the individual and I), *Impaction* 103, June 1976, Tokyo, Impact Shuppankai.

.... 1997b 'Hiratsuka Raichō', *Asahi Shinbun*, 5 December 1997.

.... 1997c *Feminists' Active Participation in Japan's Ultra-nationalism*. Paper presented at the panel 'Women and Nationalism', Annual Convention of the Association of Asian Studies, March 14, 1997, Chicago, U.S.A.

.... 1998a *Hatsujō sōchi* (Erotic apparatus), Tokyo, Chikuma Shobō.

.... 1998b 'Posuto reisen to 'Nihonban rekishi shūsei shugi' (The post-cold war Japanese version of historical revisionism), *Ronza* March 1998, Tokyo, Asahi Shinbunsha.

.... 1998c 'Josei heishi no kōchiku' (The Construction of female soldiers) in Ehara Yumiko (ed.) *Sei, bōryoku, neshon* (Sex, violence and the nation), Tokyo, Keisō Shobō.

.... 1999 'Eirei ninaru kenri o josei nimo? : jendā byōdō no wana' (Should women also be given the right to become 'the spirits of war dead'?: the trap of gender equality), *Doshisha Amerika Kenkyū*, No. 25, Center for American Studies, Doshisha University.

.... 1999b 'The Politics of Memory: Nation, Individual and Self', *History and Memory*, 2 (2). Translated and with an introduction by Jordan Sand.

.... 2003 'Jendāshi to rekishigaku no hōhō' (Gender history and the methodology of history) in Nihon no Sensō Sekinin Shiryō Senta (ed) *Nashonarizumu to 'ianfu' mondai* (Nationalism and the 'comfort women' issue), Tokyo, Aoki Shoten. First edition 1998.

Ueno, Chizuko, Miyuki Tanaka and Michiko Mae 1994 *Doitsu no mienai kabe: onna ga toinaosu tōitsu* (The invisible wall in Germany: women re-questioning unification), Tokyo, Iwanami Shoten.

Uesugi, Satoshi 1997 *Datsu gōmanizumu sengen* (The 'anti-gōmanism' declaration), Osaka, Tōhō Shuppan.

Ukai, Satoshi 1997 'Rekishi shūsei shugi: Yōroppa to Nihon' (Historical revisionism: Europe and Japan), *Impaction* 102, April 1997, Tokyo, Impact Shuppankai.

Wakakuwa, Midori 1995 *Sensō ga tsukuru joseizō: Dai 2 ji sekai taisen ka no Nihon josei do-in no shikakuteki puropaganda zō* (Images of women created by war: visual propaganda used in the mobilization of Japanese women during the Second World War), Tokyo, Chikuma Shobō.

.... 1997 '"Jendā shigaku" no shiten kara rekishi shūsei shugisha o hihan suru' (A critique of historical revisionism from the perspective of 'gender history'), *Shūkan Kinyōbi* 181, 1 August 1997.

Yamada, Meiko 1991 *Ianfu tachi no Taiheiyō Sensō* (The comfort women's Pacific War), Tokyo, Kōjinsha.

.... 1992 *Senryōgun Ianfu: Kokusaku baishun no onnatachi no higeki* (The comfort women of the occupation forces: the tragedy of the women used in the state's prostitution policy), Tokyo, Kōjinsha.

Yamakawa, Kikue 1918 *Bosei hogo to keizaiteki dokuritsu : Yosano, Hiratsuka 2 shi no ronsō* (Maternal protection and economic independence: the debate between Yosano and Hiratsuka). Reprinted in Kouchi, Nobuko (ed.), 1984 *Shiryō: Bosei hogo ronsō* (Documentation on the motherhood protection debate), Tokyo, Domesu Shuppan.

.... 1943, 1983 *Buke no josei* (A Woman from a Samurai Family), Tokyo, Iwanami Shoten.

.... 1974 *Oboegaki, Bakumatsu no Mitohan* (Notes on the Mito Domain at the end of the Tokugawa Shogunate). Reprinted in 1982, *Yamakawa Kikue shū* (The Collected Works of Yamakawa Kikue), Tokyo, Iwanami Shoten.

.... 1979 'Watashi no undōshi' (My personal history of activism), in Toyama, Mitsuyiro and Okabe, Masako (ed.) 1979 *Yamakawa Kikue no kōseki* (The tracks of Yamakawa Kikue), Tokyo, Domesu Shuppan.

Yamanouchi, Yasushi 1996a *Sisutemu shakai no gendaiteki isō* (The contemporary phase of the system society), Tokyo, Iwanami Shoten.

Yamanouchi, Yasushi, interviewed by Ryūichi Narita, and Hirokazu Ōuchi 1996b 'Intabyu-: Sōryokusen, kokumin kokka , sisutemu shakai' (An interview on the total war, the nation-state and the system society), *Gendai Shisō* 24–7 June 1996.

Yamanouchi, Yasushi, Victor Koschmann, and Ryūich Narita, (eds) 1995 *Sōryokusen to gendaika* (Total war and modernization), Tokyo, Kashiwa Shobō.

Yamashita, Chieko 1985 *Maboroshi no tō: Hausukipa Kumazawa Mitsuko no baai* (The phantom tower: the case of housekeeper Kumazawa Mitsuko), Tokyo, BOC Shuppan.

Yamashita, Etsuko 1988 *Takamure Itsue: 'Haha' no arukeoroji* (Takamure Itsue: Archeology of the 'mother'), Tokyo, Kawade Shobō Shinsha.

Yamashita, Yong-e 1994 'Ianfu mondai no ninshiki o megutte' (Concerning the awareness of the comfort women issue), *Kikan Akurosu* (journal of the citizen's group Kenpō o ikasu Shimin no Kai), November 1994.

.... 1996 'Kankoku joseigaku to minzoku: Nihongun "ianfu" mondai o meguru "minzoku" giron o chūshin ni' (Nationalism in Korean women's studies: addressing the nationalist discourses surrounding the 'comfort women' issue), *Joseigaku* 4, The Japanese Society of Women's Studies.

.... 1998 Nationalism in Korean Women's Studies: Addressing the Nationalist Discourses Surrounding the "Comfort Women" Issue', *U.S.–Japan Women's Journal*, English supplement , No.15, 1998, The U.S.-Japan Women's Center.

Yamataka, Shigeri 1943 *Dai 4 kai chuo kyoryoku kaigiroku* (Fourth meeting of the central cooperation committee: conference report). Reprinted in Suzuki, Yūko 1986 *Feminizumu to sensō* (Feminism and war), Tokyo, Marujusha.

Yamazaki, Hiromi 1995 'Minkan bokin wa "jūgun ianfu" o 2 do korosu' (The civic fundraising will kill the 'military comfort women' twice), *Shūkan Kinyōbi* 30 June 1995.

Yamazaki, Masakazu 1990 *Nihon bunka to kojin shugi* (Japanese culture and individualism), Tokyo, Chūō Kōronsha.

Yasukawa, Junosuke 1996 'Jidai o koeru koto no mutsukashisa: Sensō sekinin ron to no kakawari de' (The difficulty of transcending the epoch: in relation to the issue of war responsibility), *Gakushikai Kaihō* 811 1996-II.

Yi, Hyo Jei, Yun Jong Ok, Chi Eun Hui and Pak Won Sun 1995 'Shin Tōa Sekai kyōdō kikaku Nihongun "ianfu" mondai o dou kangaeru ka? Nikkan chishikijin ōfuku shokan, henshin: yahari kikin no teian wa ukeirerarenai' (Joint project by Shin Tōa and Sekai, Exchange letters between Japanese and Korean intellectuals: how should we understand the Japanese military 'comfort women' issue? Reply: Having considered the matter, we cannot accept the fund proposal.) *Sekai* November 1995, Tokyo, Iwanami Shoten.

Yoneda, Sayoko 1996 'Hiratsuka Raichō no senso sekinin ron josetsu' (An introduction to the debate over Hiratsuka Raichō's war responsibility), *Rekishi Hyōron* April 1996.

.... 2002 *Hiratsuka Raichō: Kindai Nihon no demokurashi to jendā* (Hiratsuka Raichō: Democracy and gender in modern Japan), Tokyo, Yoshikawakōbunkan.

Yonemoto, Shōhei 1989 *Iden kanri shakai: Nachisu to kin mirai* (Genetic management society: Nazism and the near future), Tokyo, Kōbundō.

Yosano, Akiko, 1918a 'Nendo Jizō' (Self-portrait of clay: Review of women's issues), *Taiyō*, 24(7), June 1918. Reprinted in Kouchi, Nobuko (ed.) 1984 *Shiryō bosei hogo ronsō* (Documentation on the motherhood protection debate), Tokyo, Domesu Shuppan.

.... 1918b 'Hiratsuka, Yamakawa, Yamada , 3 joshi ni kotau' (In response to the three women, Ms. Hiratsuka, Ms. Yamakawa, and Ms.Yamada), *Taiyō*, 24(13), November 1918. Reprinted in Kouchi, Nobuko (ed.) 1984 *Shiryō bosei hogo ronsō* (Documentation on the motherhood protection debate), Tokyo, Domesu Shuppan.

.... 1919 'Gyakufu Kōseki' (Traces against the window), *Taiyō*, 25(2), February 1918. Reprinted as 'To Mr. Sakai Kosen', in Kouchi, Nobuko (ed.) 1984 *Shiryō bosei hogo ronsō* (Documentation on the motherhood protection debate), Tokyo, Domesu Shuppan.

Yoshida, Seiji 1977 *Chōsenjin ianfu to Nihonjin* (The Korean comfort women and the Japanese), Tokyo, Shin Jinbutsu Ōraisha.

Yoshimi, Shūko (ed.) 1977 *Nihon fashizumu to josei* (Japanese fascism and women), Tokyo, Gōdō Shuppan.

Yoshimi, Shunya 1996 'Media tennōsei no shatei' (The scope of the media emperor system) in *Riarithi Toranjitto* (Reality Transit), Tokyo, Kinokuniya Shoten.

Yoshimi, Yoshiaki (ed.) 1992 *Jūgun ianfu shiryōshū* (A collection of documents concerning the military comfort women), Tokyo, Ōtsuki Shoten.

.... 1995 *Jūgun ianfu* (The comfort women), Tokyo, Iwanami Shoten. English translation by Suzanne O'Brien 1995 *Comfort Women*, New York and Chichester, Columbia University Press.

.... 1996 '"Jūgun ianfu" mondai no kaiketsu no tame ni' (Towards a solution to the 'comfort women' issue), *Sekai* September 1996, Tokyo, Iwanami Shoten.

.... 1997 'Kōsho ron ni hanron suru: Nihongun "ianfu" mondai no honshitsu to wa' (A counter-argument to the theory of the state licensed prostitutes: what is the nature of the Japanese military 'comfort women' problem?), special issue: 'Rekishi shiryō o dou yomu ka?' (How should we read historical documents?), *Sekai* March 1997, Tokyo, Iwanami Shoten.

.... 2003 '"Jūgun ianfu" mondai to rekishizō: Ueno Chizuko-shi ni kotaeru' (The 'comfort women' problem and historical awareness: a reply to Ueno Chizuko), in Nihon no sensō sekinin shiryō senta (ed) *Nashonarizumu to 'Ianfu mondai'* (Nationalism and the 'comfort women' issue), Tokyo, Aoki Shoten. First edition 1998.

Yoshimi, Yoshiaki and Hayashi, Hiroshi (eds) 1995 *Kyōdō kenkyū: Nihongun ianfu* (Joint research concerning the Japanese military comfort women), Tokyo, Ōtsuki Shoten.

Yun, Jong-ok 1997, 'Kokumin kikin wa nani o rikai shite inai ka' (What is it that the Asian Women's Fund fails to understand?), *Sekai* November 1997, Tokyo, Iwanami Shoten.

.... 1992 *Chōsenjin josei ga mita 'ianfu mondai'* (The 'comfort women' issue as seen by Korean women), Tokyo, San-ichi Shobō.

Zenkoku Josei Nyūsu 1997 'Rekishi no jijitsu o sunao ni mitome yo' (Let's accept historical facts without hesitation) *Zenkoku Josei Nyūsu* 20 January 1997.

Index

historical revisionism, xxiii,
xxviii, xxx, 3–5, 98, 105,
109, 112, 114, 117, 119,
122, 125, 179, 213
historical subject dispute, 138
Historikerstreit, xviii, xxx, 97
history of the women of
greater Japan, the (Dai-
Nippon Joseishi), 54, 207
Hitler, Adolf, 110
Hobsbawm, Eric, 6
Holy Mother and Child, 20
Holocaust, 97–8
home front, xxii, 16, 38, 44,
47, 149, 219
Horiba, Kiyoko, 30, 34, 53
House of Peers, 18, 188
House of Representatives, 18,
188, 221
House of Sharing (Nanumu),
130, 141, 195, 217
Housewives' Federation
(Shufu Rengōkai), 46
human rights (jinken), x, xi,
xii, xiv, xviii, 12–3, 72–3,
87–8, 90, 93–4, 99, 120–
1, 145–6, 164, 194, 202,
209, 211
Hussein, Saddam, 51, 177,
220

ianjo (comfort station), 211
Ibsen, Henrik, 203
Ichikawa Fusae Memorial
Hall, 23, 207
Ichikawa, Fusae, 16, 22–24,
28, 31, 38, 40–1, 45, 52–
4, 190, 192, 206–7
Ichioku sōzange, 151, 181,
220, 226
Ie (household), 200

Ienaga, Saburō, 114
Ikeda, Keiko, 185
Ikegami, Yoshihiko, 186
imagined community, 10, 14,
58, 62, 111, 138, 218
Impaction, 186
Impakushon, 112
imperial declaration of
surrender, 53
imperial feminism, 145, 174,
217
Imperial Headquarters, 152,
190, 220
Imperial Rule Assistance
System, 30, 56
Imperial Rule Assistance
Association, the (Taisei
Yokusankai), 16, 40–1,
190
imperial subject, 14, 81, 100,
202
imperial view of history, 25,
31
Imperial Way, 189
Inoue, Kiyoshi, 54, 207, 209,
219–20
Institute for Population
Problems (Jinkō mondai
kenkyūsho), 190
integration model, 17, 19,
23, 28, 43, 60–1, 63–4,
202
integrationist (strategy), 22–
3, 49–50, 60
International Court of Justice,
157
International Criminal Court,
223
International Labour
Organisation Treaty
No.29, 90, 120

violence against women in
armed conflict, 87–8
Violence Against Women in
War Network
International (VAWW-
NET International), 195
Volunteer Military Service
Law (Giyūheieki Hō), 17,
192, 202

Wada, Haruki, 185
Wakakuwa, Midori, 15, 17–8,
20–1, 46, 59, 135, 168,
175, 214, 224
Wakita, Haruko, 185
Walker, Alice, 218
war cheerleaders, 59, 135, 175
war crimes, xiii, xxi, xxiv,
xxv, 86, 88–9, 96, 98,
116, 134–6, 146, 152–3,
163, 174–7, 195, 197–8,
211, 223
War of Independence, 162, 166
war responsibility, viii, ix,
xx, xxi, xxv, 15, 22–3,
38–41, 59, 115, 134–6,
139, 149, 151–2, 185,
197, 204, 220
war criminals, 135, 151, 193,
220
Watanabe, Kōzō, 185
Weber, 104
Weimar Republic, 43
welfare state, 26, 166, 201–2,
207
Wives of Heroes Society
(Yūshi tsuma no kai), 47
Wollstonecraft, Mary, 27, 34
Women Volunteer Corps
(Teishintai), xiv, xxiii,
18, 70, 101, 209

Women's Civil Rights Act, 188
women's history, xix, xxi,
xxii, xxviii, xxix, xxx, 4,
14–5, 22–5, 31–2, 38, 50,
52, 54–5, 59–61, 100,
113, 123, 125, 130–5,
149, 162, 174, 185, 202,
204–5, 207, 211, 217–20
Women's Patriotic
Association (Aikoku
Fujinkai), 17, 36, 40, 191
Women's Suffrage League
(Fusen Kakutoku Dōmei),
22, 190, 192
women's suffrage movement,
23, 28, 36, 41, 52, 202,
204, 206
women's rights, xi, xii, 24,
34, 94, 173
Women's Association for
National Defence (Kokubō
Fujinkai), 16–7, 40, 47,
96, 189, 191
Women's Civil Rights Act
(Fujin kōminken hō), 188
Women's Defence
Association, 38
women's human rights, xii,
88, 90, 94
Women's International War
Crimes Tribunal, xiii,
175–6, 195
Women's Total Action
Central Rally (Fujin
sōkekki taikai), 191
Women's Voluntary Labour
Ordinance (Joshi
teishinkinrō rei), 191
Working Group on
Contemporary Forms of
Slavery, 194, 211